BALMAIN BENNY

IRONBARK PRESS

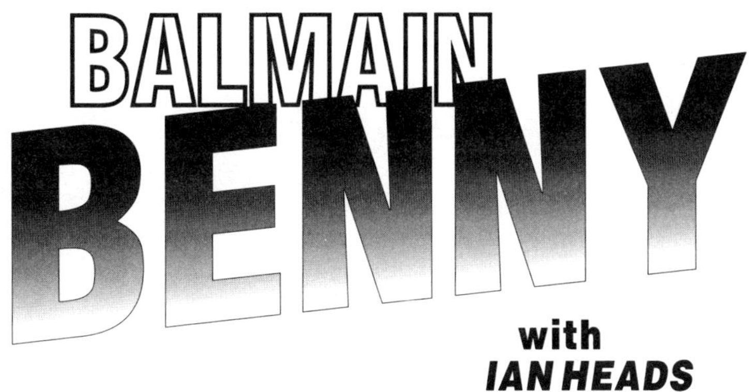

with
IAN HEADS

The stormy league career of
BEN ELIAS
Foreword by JIMMY BARNES

IRONBARK
PRESS

Published in 1993 by Ironbark Press
Level 1, 175 Alison Road, Randwick NSW 2031
Reprinted 1993

National Library of Australia
Cataloguing-in-Publication:

Elias, Benny.
Balmain Benny
ISBN 1 875471 33 2.
1. Elias, Benny. 2. Rugby League football players - New South Wales - Biography. I. Title.
796.338

Editor: Geoff Armstrong
Production: Geoff Armstrong
Design and finished art: Lynne Segal and Craig Cranko
Cover design: Jayem Productions
Front cover photography: John Elliott

Printed by McPhersons Print Group, Mulgrave, Victoria.

CONTENTS

ACKNOWLEDGEMENTS

Thanks to Ian Heads, who is a tireless worker, and to the rest of the crew at Ironbark Press.

Thanks also to my Testimonial Committee, who helped make my important year so special and successful: Keith Barnes, Graeme Goldberg, David Fookes, Stephen Elias, John Martin, Warren Carey, Alan Jones and Mark Richards.

Special thanks to Jimmy Barnes, a great example of achievement, and a mate.

And also: Mum and Dad, Ray Hadley, Peter Sterling, Wayne Pearce, Steve Roach, Ray Segar, Brian Doyle, John Singleton, Dawn Fraser, Kelly Crawford-Elias, Jon Harker, Robyn and Terry Crawford, David Lazarus, John Kerr, Kate Munt and Jane Scott.

PHOTOGRAPHS

Many thanks to Norm Tasker, managing editor of *Rugby League Week*, for the generous access to the magazine's photo files. Thanks also to the photo sales departments at News Limited and the John Fairfax Group Pty Ltd, to John Booth and Chris Karas at *The Weekly Times*, to Andrew Varley and Sportsphoto Agency for material from the 1990 Kangaroo tour, and to Ern McQuillan for his assistance.

Ian Heads began writing on rugby league in 1963, as a cadet with the Sydney *Daily Telegraph*. He was chief league writer with the *Daily Telegraph* and *Sunday Telegraph* between 1969 and 1980, and for six years from 1981, was managing-editor of *Rugby League Week*. In recent years, Heads has written a number of books on the sport, including the acclaimed *True Blue: The Story of the NSW Rugby League, The Kangaroos: The Saga of Rugby League's Great Tours*, and the histories of the South Sydney and St George clubs. He was also the author of the best-selling league biographies, *Sterlo: The Story of a Champion* and *Local Hero: The Wayne Pearce Story*, and with Jack Gibson produced two books, *Played Strong, Done Fine* and *Winning Starts on Monday*.

This book is dedicated to my best friend - my wife Kelly - who brings so much joy to my hectic life. And to my parents who have always been there for me.

FOREWORD

By Jimmy Barnes

BENNY ELIAS DROPPED into my place by helicopter one day in 1991 and we've been mates ever since.

It was State of Origin time. Benny was captain of the Blues and I was booked in as part of the promotional build-up to the Sydney game. I sang in the rain at the Sydney Football Stadium before the match that year, and stayed to cheer on the Blues as they brought off a famous victory. A few days before the event someone had figured it would be a good idea to get Benny and me together for some publicity shots.

That's how it was that Benny came calling that May morning, bearing gifts of a NSW jersey and a football autographed by the team. These were promptly snaffled by my son Jackie, who became an instant Benny and Balmain fan - and has been ever since. That night, Jackie slept in the football jumper, with the autographed football tucked alongside.

I have for a long time been a fan of rugby league and have great respect for the men who play it. I have been lucky enough to get the chance to meet some of these champions, which was great after admiring them for so long. Benny is definitely one of the best.

I consider him a giant on and off the field. He plays the game with great spirit, and carries that spirit past the sideline, out to the people.

Since becoming a friend of his, I have seen him time and time again make the effort to talk to the people who have cheered him on to greatness. Even when rushed off his feet with commitments, he will stop to sign an autograph or pose for a photo with one of his many fans.

Rugby league is a tough game, probably one of the toughest in the world, and men like Benny play the game with so much courage that it amazes me. People say that the music business is hard, but I would rather sing in front of hundreds of thousands than try to stop some of the guys I've seen Benny tackle.

I had always liked what I saw of Benny, and it was a great pleasure to meet him that day in '91. I have got to know him well in the time since and my admiration for him has strengthened. Added to the qualities I had seen from afar, I gradually became aware of the other Elias attributes - the sense of humour that sparkles in him, the concern and interest in children, the deep sense of loyalty and commitment to the job at hand - whatever it happens to be - and to those he regards as his friends. In May 1991, the task was to go out and win the SFS Origin match. That night will stay long in my memory - and especially the ice-cool Michael O'Connor goal from touch which got Benny's Blues home, 14-12.

I am delighted that Ben Elias has told his story in *Balmain Benny*. It is a tale which can provide inspiration for anyone, of any age, who sets out to be a success. A genuine working-class man from deep within the heart of a loving family, Benny never had it easy. What he has achieved in his life he has worked for. Nothing has come on a silver platter. Yet in 12 seasons in first grade football he has achieved mightily at every level - all the way to the very top as a proud member of the Australian team.

The game won't soon forget him. Almost single-handedly he has changed the way that rugby league hookers play. He's brought new skills to the position. Ducking, dodging, weaving, dummying, kicking with astute judgement ... he was, and is, a constant menace to any team he faces. That other hookers now play the way he does is the greatest compliment of all to his standing in the game.

I wish him well for whatever lies ahead for him in rugby league ... and life. Benny is rising 30 as this book goes to press, but it seems to me that he has worked harder and harder at his game in recent seasons, and has lost nothing at all as a supreme exponent of the sport of rugby league.

As far as I'm concerned, both he and the game he plays are ... simply the best.

INTRODUCTION

By Ian Heads

BENNY ELIAS' CAREER in rugby league has been littered with obstacles. Time and again he has been rocked by events which have overtaken his life - on and off the field. Serious illness and injury, a sexual assault charge, a character-destroying whispering campaign against him, bitter feuds with other players, the loss of the captaincy of both his club and state when his career was in full bloom, a shock suspension in 1993. Somehow Elias has survived each jolt - while all the time resolutely building one of the outstanding careers of modern football. "I have learned over the years to draw strength from adversity," he says.

He has been called a football genius, and the most talented hooker ever to play the game. Identified as a budding superstar by the Balmain club when he was barely a teenager, he has played his entire career with the Tigers, as did another "local hero", Wayne Pearce, before him. At times he has knocked back huge offers from other clubs, as in 1989 when the English club, Wigan, offered him a king's ransom to become their hooker.

In a football sense Benny Elias has been a revolutionary. For most of the years of the life of rugby league the game's hookers were of a particular breed - tough, dogged men who were there to win the ball in the scrums, and not too much else. In earlier seasons many of them lacked mobility and general-play skills. In the changing game of the 1980s and '90s, Elias, with his extraordinary bag of tricks, was the front-runner in shaping the role of the new rugby league hooker.

Introduction

He could weave and dart and dummy, kick field goals and general-play touch-finders with pinpoint accuracy. He could win you a game - and at Balmain, and later for NSW and Australia, he often did.

The 1948 Kangaroo hooker, Frank Johnson, said to him one day: "I have seen all the great hooker-forwards. You are the most complete. No-one had all your skills".

Elias represents the new Aussie footballer in another sense, too. Born in Tripoli, Lebanon in 1963, one of seven children in the loving family of Norm and Barbara Elias, he has been at the vanguard of the multi-cultural revolution in Australian rugby league. Great players such as Tom Raudonikis and George Peponis before him, and many more since, have introduced the game to new people from countless different backgrounds, and thus widened its horizons.

Balmain Benny tells the story of Benny Elias' chequered path to the top in his sport - from battling childhood days in Sydney's western suburbs to fame and fortune as one of Australia's most renowned sporting identities.

It is a controversial and honest book - at times painfully so. Elias' motivation, in part, for writing it was to express for the first time the agony and despair he lived through in 1987. Early in that year he was charged with sexual assault, resulting from a visit to the north-west NSW town of Armidale in January. Six months later the charge against him was dismissed by magistrate Neil Stackpool in Parramatta Court. But, as Elias makes clear, the finding gave him only partial respite. The whispers and the rumours remained, surfacing again viciously when he was on tour as vice-captain of the 1990 Kangaroos.

Said Elias: "I wanted people to know what it is like to face a charge of which you are innocent ... the absolute helplessness and frustration you feel as your name is bandied about. It was the worst time of my life."

At those and other difficult periods of his life, Elias has

shown the grit of another Balmain champion - the incomparable Dawn Fraser. During her own career, in which she negotiated many hurdles on her way to swimming immortality, Dawn said: "At times I've been tempted to quit; but I've always figured that to make a decision like that, just because you're down, is to surrender to the forces that got you down."

So it has been with Benny Elias.

Balmain Benny is more than anything a celebration of spirit, will and talent triumphing in one of the world's toughest sports. People always told Benny he was too small to play rugby league - all the way from early school days up to the landmark occasion on which he first became a Test player in 1985.

He *was* small for a top-grade league player. Elias stood 170cm (5ft 7in) tall and weighed 71 kilos (11st 3lbs) when he first came to grade football in 1982. He gradually built up his weight to a chunky 84 kilos (13st 3lbs), but even at that had to live with the fact of giving away considerable beef to virtually every opponent he faced.

Despite this handicap he carved out a brilliant career which seemed sure to have a considerable period of fruitful time left in it as this book went to press. Turning 30 in November, 1993, Elias has declared that he will review his football future at the end of the '94 season with Balmain.

A remarkable tale of success gained, and almost gained, unfolds in the pages of *Balmain Benny*. There are full and revealing insights into Elias' two successful Kangaroo tours, into his remarkable State of Origin experiences, into Balmain's triumphs and near-misses of the 1980s, and sharp observations of Balmain's seasons of unfulfilled promise in the 1990s. Elias profiles in full and sometimes prickly detail the coaches of his experience - including Jack Gibson, Frank Stanton, Warren Ryan, Tim Sheens and Alan Jones - and talks as never before of his "blood feuds" with Mario Fenech and Steve Walters.

Introduction

He throws new light on the stinging disappointments of grand finals lost by Balmain in 1988 and '89. Elias contends that but for an injury to a key man (Ellery Hanley) in one and a much discussed coaching decision in the other, the Tigers would have won both games.

The story of Ben Elias could fairly be sub-titled "My Controversial Career". Drama and controversy seem to have pursued him almost from the day he stepped into Balmain first grade as a teenager, back in 1982. At times the pressures have almost worn him down and he reveals how in 1987 he nearly threw in the towel and went to England to complete his career.

But the strong and redoubtable spirit of his parents flows through Benny Elias. Norm and Barbara Elias came to Australia in the 1950s with nothing - and through sheer hard work and determination built full and fruitful lives, and a fine Aussie family. Following their lead, Benny has jumped his own hurdles to become one of the best and most famous rugby league players of modern times.

This is his story.

Ian Heads
July 1993

"Our greatest joy is not in never falling,
but in rising after every fall ..."

1

A Living Nightmare

ON A JANUARY morning in 1987, five years along the track of a rugby league career which had given me great pleasure and not too much pain, I was on the NSW South Coast, having just completed work on a Cancer Foundation fund-raising project. Life couldn't have been better. I was an established Australian player, not long back from a sensational Kangaroo tour on which I had had the supreme honour of captaining my country. On this fateful day, together with a bunch of Balmain pals - Junior Pearce, Blocker Roach, David Brooks and Kerry Hemsley - I was aboard a splendid boat, 10 kilometres off the city of Wollongong, fishing for marlin. Fortunately for the fish we were catching nothing more than the sun and the breeze.

The call that signalled the nightmare that was to overtake my life came mid-morning, crackling across the two-way radio.

"You must come in. There's an urgent message for Benny Elias from his father ... you must come in!"

I thought the worst. Something dreadful must have happened in the family. The trip back in through the gentle swell that morning was the slowest and most disturbing I had ever taken, or probably will ever take, in my life.

Back on dry land the message was a brief one. "Look mate, you've got to ring your parents straight away," said the bloke who had called us back to shore.

It was my father Norman who answered my call to home. "Do you know anything about this?" he asked. "About this girl claiming that you sexually assaulted her?"

"This is ludicrous ... what are you talking about?" I answered.

"It's serious," dad said. "We've had the detectives over here this morning and they want to question you. Joe (my brother) is on his way down there now to pick you up."

And so it began, a living nightmare that was to haunt my every waking moment in the months ahead, driving me and my family to the limits of despair.

The events moved swiftly when I got back to Sydney. I rang the police at Chatswood Station, on Sydney's north shore, and a detective told me: "Mate, we want you to come in and answer some questions about the claims made by this lady." Christ! I thought, it was serious alright.

So, I went, and there began a demeaning process: the questions ... skin tests, hair tests, fingernail tests. And then the declaration from the policeman involved: "Look mate, we're going to have to charge you, because it's our duty as public servants to look after citizens. It's got to be up to the court to decide whether you're guilty or not."

As he was talking I was thinking: 'You've got to be joking ... this can't be happening ... I'm surely dreaming all of this.'

It was no dream. The next day, in the company of my legal representatives, I was charged with one count of sexual assault, over an incident alleged to have happened in the north-west NSW town of Armidale, a couple of days before. I had been in Armidale as a member of the coaching staff at the excellent camp staged there for young elite players each year. Steve Martin, ex-Manly and Balmain star, 1978 Kangaroo and later successful coach, was charged separately, on two counts, around the same time.

On this horrible day I was the biggest news in town. “League Star On Sex Charges” screamed the billboards.

I will now jump ahead in my re-telling of this painful story, and tell you that the charges against me (and Steve Martin) were dismissed by magistrate Neil Stackpool in Parramatta Court on June 23. The magistrate’s hearing of submissions and his decision to dismiss the charges followed earlier closed committal hearings in Armidale (two days) and Tamworth (one day). My case had been handled by one of the country’s finest barristers, Mr Chester Porter QC. I raced from the court that day to ring my parents with the good news. I felt like the weight of the world had been lifted from my shoulders.

I am bound by legal constraints from telling the full story of the worst five months of my life, because, unfortunately, the hearing that cleared my name was held in closed court - at the request of the 22-year-old woman who made the allegations. Prosecutor Sergeant Ian Burkinshaw made that application on her behalf. From my point of view, in no way did I want the court closed. I was NOT guilty ... NOT guilty and I wanted to world to know that through making publicly available the evidence that emerged. Because the hearing was in a closed court, I will never be able to do that. It is a significant point to make however that if there had been *any* doubt at all about my innocence the matter would have proceeded to the next stage - a trial.

I was cleared through the strict and correct processes of the law, yet I soon became aware of rumours circulating which whispered that “deals” had been done. Those rumours were garbage, but typical of the sort of slimy innuendo that I had to contend with. There were no deals - just plain justice.

Because the evidence was not made available to the public, and cannot be made available, I will live with an unfair stain for as long as my life lasts. There will always be people who make snide remarks, who mutter behind their hands that no matter what the court's finding they *know* that Benny Elias was guilty. I have no choice but to live with that for the rest of my days, and I can tell you, it cuts deep.

At the time I was charged I wanted to go to the media and shout my story to the world. It was immensely frustrating. I needed to tell my story, but my attorneys were advising me that it had to be: "No comment." Nothing has changed now. I am still bound not to tell the real story of what happened. I only wish I could.

To get across to ordinary people the pain of what I perceive as a supreme injustice - my feeling of absolute helplessness and hopelessness - was one of my prime reasons for writing this book. I would like readers to put themselves in my place, to try and get some sort of idea of what it was like in those horrific months between January and June, 1987. Consider yourself wrongfully charged with a serious crime, and imagine what it would be like trying to live a normal day-to-day life as you waited for the trial that might clear you, *knowing* you were innocent, but still unsure and fearful of what might occur.

Because I am what might be termed "high-profile", as an international sportsman in a popular code, I became fair game. The fact of the charges against me was recorded in type sizes generally reserved for major disasters. I was the lead item on radio and television news. It seemed to me that in the eyes of many people I was judged, convicted and hanged right then. Yet I had absolutely no comeback. None. I would have wished the court hearing to be on national television the next day, to set it right. But, of course, it doesn't work that way.

So my name was dragged into the gutter, and terrible pain inflicted on my parents and family. In those long months my life continued as if in some sort of ghastly dream. If you ask me about Balmain's season in 1987, and my contribution to it, I can tell you barely anything. It was as if I was in some sort of trance-state. I continued training, playing, living ... and I continued waking at 3 o'clock every morning with my mind asking me was it worth going on. At those times I would say to myself: 'Mate, you know what the truth is. You know that you're innocent. You've got to make life go on the best it can.'

And I would remember wise words offered to me by my father: "Son, these things are meant to test you," he would say. "God gives tests to everybody through their lives." The despair and frustration of that time go a lot deeper than the sort of words I can now find to explain them.

Sydney being Sydney, the rumours began straight away. It seemed everyone knew a policeman involved in the case ... everyone had seen transcripts of the reports. Clubs and pubs buzzed with the *real* story of Benny Elias in Armidale. Sometimes those rumours would reach my ears and I would ring my legal people seeking re-assurance - and get it in their calm confidence that justice would ultimately be done.

Going to the football became a test of will each week. I was fair game for a twisted few among the spectators - the imbeciles who would shout their taunts. On the field I copped plenty too. The sledging was hostile and regular, all of it based on the charges I faced.

Cruel jokes did the rounds, and some of them inevitably reached my ears. One of them, published in a newspaper later, was: "Have you heard about St George wanting to sign up Ben Elias? They think he could be a new Raper." I had no choice but to grin, through gritted teeth, and bear it.

My spirits sunk so low that I seriously considered leaving Balmain, leaving Sydney, and going to England to play out the years left in my career once the mess was settled. For the first and only time in my life I even lost my zest for rugby league. There was no drive in me. I no longer looked forward to going to training, or to matches. I looked forward to nothing. I stopped watching the football on Saturday and

Sunday nights. Even the shining light of rugby league had gone out in me.

If there was an upside of such a time it lay in the support I received. Keith Barnes, the boss of Balmain, was magnificent. I was Development Officer at the club at that time and I made a decision to resign in the interest of the club. Keith wouldn't let me. He counselled me to stay strong. "I know the true story, your close friends know the story, your family knows the story," he said to me. "The others don't matter."

The Tigers' coach, Billy Anderson, the players and the staff at Balmain stuck solid around me, and I appreciated that. On the night of the day I was cleared they greeted me at Leichhardt Oval with a rousing burst of applause which sent tingles up my spine. NSW Rugby League general manager John Quayle was terrific too, and so was Ken Arthurson (NSWRL chairman). The support of such people, of those close to me and most of all of my loving family, helped get me through. It was a time in my life when I got to know who my true friends were.

There was outside support - from people I knew vaguely, or didn't know at all. Telegrams, and bundles of letters and telephone calls. I appreciated every one of them, and took strength from them.

The dismissing of the charges was a monumental relief, yet even that example of justice being done could never go close to repairing the damage that had been wrought. Sometimes I think the rumours will never stop, that I'll get them for the rest of my life. The sad thing is that our world consists of more than enough people who thrive on the discomfort and dragging down of others. Those sort of people would rather believe that Benny Elias was guilty of the charges. Those sort of people are shit to me. It was their kind, no doubt, who started the sickening rumours that emerged to plague me again in 1990, a wicked smear campaign that had no foundation whatsoever. I will talk more of that later.

Mud sticks, and I have to live with that. The fact of human nature is that people love a bit of scandal ... they love to believe the worst. It's exactly why the gossip magazines sell so well, pandering to that aspect of human character. People don't want to know about Michael Jackson doing vast amounts of work to help under-privileged kids. They'd rather read about him being in hospital, getting his cheekbones done.

I am well aware that I am not in any way unique in experiencing the Australian syndrome of a high-profile person being accused of something - and then being subjected to a media feeding frenzy, and the grinding of the rumour mills. The finding of innocence, as in my case, is almost incidental - dismissed in a few paragraphs in the papers. By then the damage has long since been done. In the pubs and clubs a much more succulent conclusion over a few beers is that you are guilty. People remember the headlines ... "Elias On Sex Charge" ... they don't want a story with a happy ending.

The other side of the coin in cases such as mine is the reality that the person who laid the charges - charges which were dismissed by a respected magistrate - remained anonymous throughout. Her privacy and anonymity were protected; my name was trumpeted loud for all to hear.

I will never completely get over the events of 1987. What happened ate away at me like a cancer, and killed my confidence. At any gathering of people I felt as if I was under special scrutiny, some sort of oddity. It took a long, long time before I gradually got back to something like normal living.

A few days after the charges had been dismissed a small party of us dined at Harpoon Harry's Restaurant in Sydney. I would not call it a celebration. My main emotion was relief. I knew deep down in my heart that the events of 1987 had undermined my life, and that the repair could never be complete.

If there is any plus factor in the whole painful business it was that at the end of it I was a stronger, more resilient person. The experience toughened me up. As I lived through that time I gained strength from the thought that no matter what, life *had* to go on. It was on some of those black early mornings, as I lay awake thinking of my dilemma, that I came to realise that the messages, and the manner of my upbringing in the Elias family in early, struggling years, was the deep-down strength, the well-spring that could get me through ...

2

Tripoli to Tigertown

I HAVE NO memory of the place where I was born - the city of Tripoli in Lebanon, 72km NNE along the Mediterranean coast from the capital, Beirut. I know of my birthplace only what I have read: that it is an ancient city, founded hundreds of years B.C.; that it is an exporter of citrus fruits, cotton and tobacco; and that it has a large oil refinery at which ends a pipeline that snakes all the way from Iraq. There is a large community of people from Tripoli in Sydney and they claim me as one of their own - even though I was only in the city a very short time. I am unique among the seven children of Norman and Barbara Elias - in that the other six were born in Australia.

Mum and dad had come to Australia in the 1950s - dad in 1950, and mum in 1955. They married here and decided that Australia was to be their future, but the draw of the homeland has always remained strong. In 1963, when my mother was pregnant with me, they rounded up the four kids who comprised the Elias family at that stage, and flew to Lebanon for a holiday. Their stay turned out to be longer than they had planned, and so it was that Chaiben Paul

Elias (that's me!) was born in a hospital in Tripoli, on November 15, 1963.

The name Chaiben is after my grandfather, my Dad's father. My father was the third-born son, and so was I - and apparently soon after I was born my grandfather visited me in the hospital in Tripoli and declared: "This boy is going to be named after me." Dad's old man was pretty smart, a real businessman. My father tells me that the first time my grandfather saw me he said: "That's my son." My dad can still look at photos and see a remarkable resemblance between his father and me.

As soon as I was born my father contacted the Australian authorities to register my birth. There were no facilities for that in Tripoli, and he had to register the birth in Athens, Greece. Dad was determined that his new son was going to be an Aussie.

I am in the middle of the scrum of Elias kids, fitting in after Leo, Rhonda, Tony and Lynette and before Joe and Ella. I was only a few months old when mum and dad brought the family home to Australia in 1964. Australia was a land of opportunity, and my folks came from working-class families. They were looking for a better life - at a time when Australia was welcoming migrants to help build the future.

They arrived with nothing much more than a strong work ethic and plenty of hope, and set up home initially in the Sydney suburb of West Ryde and then in a basic rented cottage in nearby Meadowbank, which we shared with dad's brother Herbie and his family. There were four or five kids to a bedroom.

My strongest memory from childhood is of my mother and father working enormously hard. I recall dad having three jobs at once. We had a shop at Kings Cross, and later one at Ryde - a milkbar/fruit shop - which mum would look after while wrestling with the task of bringing up a large flock of kids. Dad worked as a labourer during the daytime, helped in the shop when he could, then headed out to do a taxi run at night.

The house at Meadowbank was about as ordinary as a house can be, smack bang in the middle of an industrial estate. It was noisy and crowded, but a happy place - a very temporary home as my parents saved furiously to scrape up enough to get our own place.

When I was about seven that goal was achieved, and we shifted to a cottage in Falconer Street, West Ryde, which was to be my home for the next 20 years or so. It was an ordinary Australian suburban cottage, but on a big block of land - and with a sizeable backyard. It could be said, I suppose, that it was right there in that backyard that my football career began.

There was never any shortage of kids around and I can recall scrambling about in the backyard in never-ending games, kicking a ball. More organised football games were played on an open paddock known as Anzac Park, 50 metres up the road. We shared that territory with a couple of horses which grazed there. On afternoons, when school was done, a motley crew of kids would play football ... rugby league, calling fulltime only when evening had closed in.

It was on Anzac Park that I scored my first "try". Probably I threw my first dummy there too. My Mum was not a fan of my brothers Leo, Tony and me playing rugby league. She admits candidly, even today: "I didn't want them to play." I was well aware of the feelings of my parents and tried to hide my footballing pursuits from them. One day I came home with a swollen eye after taking a direct hit from a football, but there was no way I was going to tell my mother what had happened. "It's nothing Mum," I answered when she posed the obvious question.

My dad tells a long-forgotten story which reflects my passion for the game even when I was a tiny tot. One day he came home early, and saw me playing football, all by myself in the park. I was still wearing my school uniform.

Dad tells what happened next:

He used to count the minutes before he knocked off school so he could get down the park to play football. On this day I thought it was him I saw, and I stopped the car to make sure. As soon as he spotted me he dived into the long grass. I yelled at him to come out. "What on earth are you doing, still in your uniform?" I asked. He answered: "Dad, I was just looking for something I've lost in the grass." He would not even take the time to change out of his school uniform. That's how much he loved his football.

He knew that we weren't in favour of football. So he got a job selling newspapers and he saved his money for those things we didn't know about - footballs, jumpers, football boots. He would hide them from us.

Balmain, the mighty Tigers, were always my team, and especially so after the great party that my Uncle Ken threw on the day they played Souths in the 1969 grand final. Uncle Ken fired up the barbecue and invited over all the relations, declaring: "If the Tigers win the game, I'll jump off the roof". When 3/1 outsiders Balmain won 11-2, Ken Elias leapt spectacularly from the second-storey roof of his house. I'll never forget it.

It was because of Uncle Ken's love of the Tigers that I became a Balmain fan. I was quickly hooked, hanging off every word of Frank Hyde's gravelly-voiced radio call of matches - and especially games that involved the Tigers. Frank made it sound so exciting, and so did television's Rex Mossop on Seven's *Big League* on a Sunday night. I knew I was just going to have to find out what this game was all about.

For a long time my love affair with the major world of rugby league, and the Tigers was from afar - fed only by radio and television. Very early idols included Arthur Beetson and Kangaroo fullback/utility back Allan McMahon. For a time Mum used to call me "Benny McMahon". "McMahon," she'd say, "come in here".

Not until I was a teenager, 15 in fact, did I start going regularly to Leichhardt to cheer for Balmain. I remember the year well, 1978 - the season in which the brilliant Aboriginal winger Larry Corowa joined Balmain. Larry was an early Benny Elias hero, although the blond-haired halfback, Greg Cox, who left Balmain at the end of 1977, had long been my No. 1 man.

It's probably not as well known - but like Junior Pearce I did an apprenticeship in the "outer" at Leichhardt. Junior was a hot dog seller, but drinks were my caper. I would patrol the ground with a tray hooked around my neck flogging soft drinks - stumbling around the place because I was always watching the football, and not where I was going. I sold drinks for four or five seasons there for a bloke named Freddy. I still don't know his surname. I was there on the Amco Cup Final night that the ace English forward, Brian Lockwood, and lock Neil Pringle worked the old magic-pass trick, and Balmain won the Cup. I'll never forget that; I jumped for sheer joy, and the bloody drinks went everywhere. I made $35 that night - more money than I had ever had in my life.

I had a terrific childhood in the midst of a large and wonderfully close family. There were nine of us coming and going at Falconer Street; you knew that whenever you fell over there would always be someone on hand to pick you up. The preparation of lunches was like a production line for mum who would hack through four loaves of bread, and slice off great piles of ham and corned beef.

Dad's hard work paid off when he branched into property, investing the money he had earned through sheer hard yakka into the purchase of another cottage. It was a great time to be buying property in Sydney, and dad soon became involved in a big way - eventually managing properties for other people. At one stage he and mum had almost 100 properties on their books. In the school holidays there would always be some work for the kids - and I'd be out cleaning, and cutting grass to earn some extra bucks.

Mum and dad were not interested in football in the early days - although that sure changed later on. At least with a football-mad kid like me there was one consolation - they would always know where to find me. Any afternoon I'd be up the park kicking a ball around. When I was about 10 they bought Tony and me a Balmain jersey each. I can remember how proud we both were when we had our picture taken that day, down at the nearby Lane Cove National Park. But my parents were reluctant fans. They had heard how rough and dangerous this Aussie winter game was - and they weren't too keen for their boys to get involved.

Discipline was a part of life in our noisy and crowded house. Dad had a big strap and if any of us did something seriously wrong we'd cop it across the legs. When dad said "jump" ... we jumped. His discipline, though, was of a very fair kind. After any punishment he'd always explain why it had been necessary. The last thrashing I got was one day after I'd hit my little sister. "You're such a big man!" he shouted ... and gave me the world's biggest hiding. It was a tough task, trying to bring up seven kids, and mum and dad did it phenomenally well.

My family will always be one of the biggest things in my life. I just hope I can pass on the closeness that we all share to the next generation - to my own family. I consider myself very lucky to have been brought up in such a family - in which the Lebanese way was intermingled with the happy-go-lucky Australian way. The members of the Elias clan were always tremendously close, and I know a lot of my Australian friends envied what we had. They'd say: "Oh, we only see our family once a year - at Christmas." My own football commitments notwithstanding, we try to get together *every* week - with all the kids, and at the last count that included around 13 nieces and nephews.

My father says: "If there is ever any one week when the family gathering doesn't happen then there has to have been a very good reason. This is the way we were brought up, always hoping that the next generation will adopt a similar approach. It's a beautiful thing - to keep the family together. You don't realise the importance of it until D-day, when you're really pushed down. That's when you find the family support comes through."

No-one has benefited more than me from the support of the Elias family over the years ...

3

Hooked on League

IT WAS NOT easy being a migrant kid trying to make your way through an Aussie school 20 years ago. My first school was St Michael's, Meadowbank, and deep-rooted attitudes of racism and prejudice there made life very difficult at times. I'd like a dollar for every time I was called a "wog" or for every fight that I had because of my birthplace.

Along with the other ethnic kids at the school I was an outsider, isolated from what the others were doing - from what the *Australians* were doing. It reached the stage where people were being so aggressive and so unfair to us that we banded together and formed our own clan of Lebanese, Greeks and Italian kids. It was like a little private club, and I was voted the leader. It was my responsibility to try and look after the younger members in the club - and I can tell you we had some wimpy little kids! Fighting became part of my early school life.

It was at St Michael's that I first pulled on a jersey to play a *real* game of rugby league. The jersey was dark blue with a light blue V, and the team was the under-sevens. I had just turned six, a scrawny little thing. But, boy - was I keen to play the game! I was a halfback then, knee-high to a corner post, and my first game with the under-sevens was played at an oval at Rydalmere, about five kilometres west of Meadowbank. Later on, our little team of all nations won a knockout comp at Holy Cross, Ryde - my first experience of winning anything special in football - and at the end-of-year presentation night, I won the best-and-fairest award for the season. I was hooked on league.

I played three seasons in the two-blues of St Michael's, and won the best-and-fairest award in each of them. Then the school ran out of football teams. By fifth class I had turned my gaze on Holy Cross College at Ryde. I knew they were an especially strong football school, and that was more than enough reason for me to want to go there. I had a problem, though. My brothers, Leo and Tony, had gone to Marist Brothers, Eastwood, and dad was adamant that I would go there too.

Persistent kids have a way of getting their wishes, as all parents know. My mum now and then tells the story of how I tricked her, to prevent me going to Eastwood:

I told Ben that when the time came he would have to get a form from St Michael's which I would fill in. Then he could go to Eastwood. But when the forms were handed out, Ben hid his. I asked him about it - and he said he had no form. By the time I went to Eastwood to organise things, it was too late. Ben hid the form from me because he wanted to go to Holy Cross.

I chipped away at dad - and the fact I had a cousin going to Holy Cross helped the case. Eventually I was allowed to sit for an entrance examination to the school. I was rapt when dad broke the news: "Okay, you've passed the test, and the school has accepted you.

"You can go to Holy Cross."

And so my life changed ... because of football. Each morning I'd catch the 505 bus up the hill to Top Ryde, a bus which became known as the "Lebanese Express" because of the number of Lebanese kids who caught it. Then the 500 to Holy Cross. All the while, with my parents thinking "academic", I was thinking "football".

Academically I got into 5B, football-wise I made it to the "A" team. My parents were happy, and so was I. The Holy Cross Under-11 "A's" were coached by Brother Columban, with some expert assistance from a former Balmain player, Harry Raven, who had a son in the side - Stephen, also a halfback. It was later that I realised how much of a stalwart Harry Raven had been with the Tigers, staying seven seasons to play 113 first grade games.

It was Harry Raven who made me a hooker. At training one day before the season started he called me out, and said: "Look son, you and Stephen can't both be halfbacks. What I want you to do is go to hooker. You don't have to change your game ... you can still play your normal game." It didn't worry me one bit; as long as I was in the top side, I was happy.

Having made the change, Harry went out of his way to help me. Guiding me in my new role as a dummy-half, he taught me a little trick which was to bring me many tries in the years ahead. It was (and is) such a simple thing - to look one way from dummy-half, then wheel a full 360 degrees and head in the other direction. I can still hear the call of Harry Raven shouting from the sideline: "Wheel Benny ... wheel!"

From that time onwards, with just two exceptions (160 minutes of first grade football), I have been a rugby league hooker. The year I made the profound change that was to create a new path in my life in football was 1974.

I had immense luck with the influences on my early football life. After a time Harry Raven stepped away from his coaching association with the team - and in stepped an ex-first grade hooker, John O'Brien, and a former first grade and Kangaroo lock forward, Kevin Smyth. With Brother Columban they provided a fantastic wealth of football lore and knowledge for the kids who first got together in that Holy Cross under-11s team. That coaching unit was with us for years, and we went through unbeaten, season after season - all the way from the under-11s to the Under-16s.

Being an old hooker himself, John O'Brien took me under his wing. He provided a lot of time, and a lot of support. He taught me the tricks of the trade - about scrummaging, dummy-half play, positional play. He schooled me too in the dirty tricks department. "You've got to know these things," he explained. "The certainty of any match is that the other hooker is going to be out to get on top of you. You need to have some tricks up your sleeve." The tricks from the O'Brien manual of hooking included such things as packing in with a loose arm, grabbing the other hooker by the hair ... and then pulling your head out of the scrum with a loud "Owww!" ... while bringing up your knee on your opponent. "These are just safety measures ... just precautions," he would say. "You need to know them."

John O'Brien insisted I take pride in my role as a hooker. He taught me to always make it a head-to-head, one-on-one thing with my rival in the No. 12 (as it was then) jumper. From the coaches of those growing years I received the important message that to get it right in football you had to focus on your own backyard, to get your own game right.

It was one of the best messages I learned - concentrate on getting your own act together, work hard on your own involvement ... and you have a chance.

For six magic years in the weekend competition we were undefeated. For five years not a point was scored against us! Thriving under the guidance we were getting, I developed as a footballer, and there was a growing need at home to find places for the trophies that came my way.

There are many things that stick in my memory from those years - especially the messages that coaches Smyth and O'Brien drummed into the team. Fundamentally, they taught us the truth that football was exactly like life. Like life the game of football provides its ups and down, its disappointments and its joys. To succeed at football you had to work hard - just as you do at life. If you took a kick in the teeth, well, you just had to pick yourself up and keep going.

When I was about 16, I remember one of them telling us: "There's only one thing better in life than winning a first grade premiership ... and that's making love." 'Oh yeah?' thought the young footballing Elias. 'I know what I'd rather do'. It was sometime a little further down the track, when my interests broadened to include both football *and* females, that I started thinking that maybe they weren't so far off the mark.

Despite the football successes, all was far from rosy at school. I started at Holy Cross in class 5B, made it through to 6B, but the following year receiving notification that I was to be demoted to 7C. That year a letter arrived with my report card. "Ben's commitment to his studies has suffered because of his interest in football," read the letter. "His emphasis is much more on football than on his education. To try and help him we have decided that next year he will be demoted to the C class."

At home this was not good news. At this stage all my dad cared about was my *academic* performance at school ... my results. I wasn't pleased either - in fact I was devastated. All my football friends were in the A and B classes, and now I was going to be the dummy in the C class.

One evening, soon after that letter had been absorbed in the Elias household, my dad pulled me aside from the others. "Look son," he said. "I have made a decision to take football away from you. Until your results improve at school you are not allowed to play sport."

I was shattered. All my pleadings were in vain. "There is nothing I can do ... it's for the best," said dad. "The decision is made and now it's up to you." I cried for hours that night. Deep inside it felt as though my world had fallen apart.

At school the next day I took the news to the head coach, Brother Columban. "Oh, my," he said. "Well, we *need* you; we have to have you in the side." He pondered for a minute. "Is there any chance I could come over and have a talk with your father?"

And so it came about that Norman Elias and Brother Columban of Holy Cross College sat for five hours one autumn afternoon and discussed football, life and a variety of other things. I was only briefly allowed in the room and I recall them talking of how Ireland was at war, and how Lebanon was at war. That may be so, I thought. But what about me playing football?

Brother Columban must have been very persuasive that day in the cause of rugby league. My Dad tells it this way: "He absolutely convinced me that what I had heard about rugby league was not altogether true. I told him that I wanted to see my children well-educated - that I knew that sporting lives were only short-lived. He assured me that my son would be specially looked after, that he would lose nothing in his education."

It was about 9.30pm when my father called me back into the lounge room. "Son," he said. "I'm giving you one more chance. Brother Columban is going to oversee your education. If you don't show any improvement in your studies over the next six months you will be demoted, and there will be no more football."

I was humble in victory. Inside I was screaming:

Beauty!!!!!!!

The carrot that had been dangled in front of me did the trick. I managed a better balance of studies and football (although there was never a doubt as to which one held sway). From 7C I was promoted the next year to 8B, then 9A and 10A. In my School Certificate year, I earned Grade ones in Maths and English. Brother Columban had taught me important lessons about managing my time better, and about the importance of a balanced approach to the various obligations I had at school.

It was football, though, that still consumed my life. I was playing twice a week with the school team, on Thursdays and Sundays, and after I had broken into the Balmain junior representative teams - SG Ball (under-15s) and then Jersey Flegg (under-17s) - I would play representative football on Saturdays. There were training obligations on top of that, and extra commitments too - such as playing for the combined Metropolitan Catholic Colleges team. And if I had a spare moment I'd be down at Anzac Park, playing a pick-up game with some mates.

I wasn't the only footballer in the family. My older brothers, Leo and Tony, were both very good players who represented Balmain at junior level. However their lives headed in different directions, and for vastly different reasons both gave football away. Leo, the oldest, decided he wanted to party. He was a fanatical disco man. Tony headed along a quieter track, graduating with honours in economics at the University of NSW.

I suppose I had elements of both of them in me. Like Leo, I didn't mind a party. And the messages from Tony were a bonus for me as my football career unfolded, whether I consciously realised it or not. Tony wasn't an outstanding student; he was no natural. His degree was gained through tremendous hard work. I'd wake at 3 or 4 o'clock some mornings and elsewhere in the house a light would still be on. Tony would be studying. At just about the same time brother Leo would be getting home from the disco ...

When I look back I realise that I probably had a sense very early that the game of rugby league was going to provide the great window of opportunity in the life of Benny Elias. I was happy to go out and play the game to the best of my ability, and enjoy myself. But it became evident very early that the Balmain club - *my* club - had pinpointed me as someone they wanted to have around in the future, and that they were expecting big things of me.

Things were happening at breakneck speed in my life. In 1978, when I was in Year 9, John O'Brien came and told me he wanted me to play in the Holy Cross Amco Shield team. This was a big deal - the Amco Shield was the televised schools' competition which was the forerunner to today's Commonwealth Bank Cup. In no way did I think I was ready for that. I was just a 15-year-old kid, and they were asking me to play against these blokes two and three years older than me. O'Brien re-assured me: "You're ready," he said. "You're good enough to play against these blokes."

I was as scared as hell, and I'll never forget that first, rainy day out in Sydney's western suburbs. We played Blacktown High, one of the really hot school outfits, on their home ground. A bunch of my mates wagged school and Murray Butt, who had his P-plates, drove them out there to give us a cheer. We ended up winning 6-3, and I scored a try.

One moment in the game will always stick in my mind. Blacktown High had this special move and John O'Brien had studied it carefully, and timed it. It was a run-around from a tap play and at a certain point the ball always reached their big front-rower. We practised and practised at training and O'Brien had it worked out like clockwork that our own big front-rower, Ariocha Casa, would arrive right on time and put their big bloke out of business. "I want you to kamikaze him, put your shoulder right into him," the coach demanded of Ariocha.

And that was exactly the way it worked out. Ariocha creamed the Blacktown star with one of the sweetest-timed hits you would ever see, and knocked him out of the game. Wow! I thought. How professional is that! The things that you practice at training don't often work so well - but this was a gem in my early career.

We went on to considerable success in the Shield, playing Ashcroft High in the final the following year (1979) under lights at Leichhardt - a grand, razzle-dazzle occasion at which we had the entire school behind us as a cheer squad, plus a band. We were beaten by a good side ... but we were proud to have made it that far. That final was the first of three we would make in a row, though only once, in 1981 against Fairfield Patrician Brothers, did we win the competition. For me it was both a productive and lucrative experience. In 1980 and '81 I won tertiary education scholarships, valued in total at $7000. It was a pleasure to go to school during that time ... it really was. It was also hard to keep my feet on the ground. I remember Graham McNeice, then of Channel 10 in Sydney, coming to school to do an interview with me. Here I was, 16 or 17, and with my head on television. Soon after, a story about me, written by Julia Sheppard, appeared on the back page of the Sydney *Sun*. And a bloke who was to later become a great mate and mentor, John Brennan, uttered this colourful line while calling one Amco Shield game on television: "If the good Lord made the world in six days then he must have made this kid (me!) on his day off." I could probably be excused if I was tending to be just a little starry-eyed.

In 1979 I had the supreme thrill of making it into the Australian Schoolboys team to tour England and France. Billy Noke (later a first grade player with Saints, Brisbane, Souths and Wests) and myself were the real Joeys in the side, at 15. I celebrated my 16th birthday on tour. Coached by Alex Kolomeitz and Ray Montgomery, it turned out to be a tremendous outfit, and featured 17 players who went on to successful first grade careers, including Andrew Farrar, Mal Cochrane, Neil Hunt, Tony Rampling and David Brooks.

We went through unbeaten, and I played in all the Tests, getting my chance when Tony Rampling suffered a broken leg early on. At that point, Mal Cochrane, the first-choice hooker, switched to prop - and I came into the team. We were away for eight weeks or so, and it was a fabulous time, and one that whetted my appetite for the Kangaroo experience.

In the French town of Carcassonne, dominated by its

ancient walled "citee", I tasted alcohol for the first time. It was New Year's Eve, 1979, and there was no way I was going to be left behind by the 17 and 18-year-olds in the team. I recall having a couple of glasses of beer and feeling pretty seedy ... and all the while trying to appear very much in control and grown-up.

In my latter years at Holy Cross I plugged away under the watchful eye of Brother Columban, completing the job by getting my Higher School Certificate in 1981. My plan was to go on and do physiotherapy, but I missed out by just three marks on the course I wanted. Instead I went to the University of Western Sydney to do a Bachelor of Business course. But I never did get my degree. When football finally overwhelmed my life, as it had always threatened to do, I still had three subjects to finish. The thing that stuffed me up was the computer. I'm just hopeless with computers - I failed the computer course three times and ultimately I lost the will to go to uni because of it.

It was in 1981, my last year at school, that I signed my first contract with Balmain - a two-year agreement, with an option for a further year if things worked out. The then Balmain secretary, Keith Gittoes, signed me over a dinner he hosted for mum, dad and me at Balmain Leagues Club, with the deal being that I would start my grade career with the Tigers in 1982. The club paid me $2000 and I spent the next few weeks pinching myself. Was this really happening to *me*?

I think dad was more amazed at the amount of money than I was. Up until then he hadn't taken much interest in rugby league; for the first time he realised there was perhaps a chance for me to succeed in a *business* sense at the sport I loved.

With my new-found wealth I bought a car, a Datsun 1600, purchased from brother Tony. A bunch of us would pile into it and head to Maroubra beach or to Coogee. If the friendships of life are among its very best treasures - then

I've been very lucky. I had a great bunch of pals - then, now, and for life - and on regular holiday trips away to a place called Chittaway Point on the central coast, north of Sydney, there was the starting of lifelong friendships with blokes such as Andrew Cox, Murray Butt, Glen Besgrove, Darren Horrigan, Glen Gould and Mark Donovan. We grew up together on those trips - a bunch of normal, rowdy teenagers, having a beer or two, taking a puff of a cigarette and thinking we were tough. We played the pinnies in the local pub, and walked the streets of the nearby town of The Entrance.

It was on these trips that I started noticing the other half of humanity, too - the female half. Seeing as how ours was a boys-only, sports-mad school, football had always had a distinct edge on females, even if the occasional strictly-supervised dances with our sister school Woolwich had been fun.

But into the 1980s I discovered women. It wasn't long before the disappointment of a broken puppy-love affair was to play temporary havoc with both my football career, and my life.

4

Teenage Blues

ON A NIGHT in late May, 1983, my career, and life, briefly touched rock bottom. My problems were twofold. I was brooding over my first serious girlfriend, who had announced that our relationship was finished; compounding my low state, I was suffering the aftershock of a heavy knock I had taken in a match the day before. By that time, my career with Balmain was nicely established, and the world should have been rosy. But I had fallen for a girl who decided that I was not the one for her, and I was hurting.

That night I was at home on my own with an ever-worsening headache - the result of a high tackle in a match against Parramatta - and compounding my low physical state, I was allowing worry about the broken romance to eat away at me. By about 10 o'clock, my head was pounding, and I was doing it tough. Present and past worries surfaced in my mind as I lay there trying to get to sleep. In my unhappy condition, I especially thought of my dad, and the battle he had had to recover from injuries suffered in a bad car accident which had almost ended his life. That time had been one of the worst I had ever experienced.

The accident had happened back in 1981, around the time that I had made that year's Australian Schoolboys side. The trials had been at Tweed Heads and I had flown back home, as happy as it was possible to be. As soon as I walked through the door I knew something was wrong.

"Mate, we've had some real bad news," said my brother Tony. "Dad's been in a car accident." They had towed the car back to our garage, and it looked like the Sydney Harbour Bridge had fallen on it.

"Where's dad?" I asked.

"You can't see him," they told me. "He's in intensive care in Westmead Hospital, and he's real bad."

It was a couple of days before my father came out of the coma. He had a broken arm, a broken leg and serious head injuries. He was a mess - and it took him a long, long time to recover.

By the time my folks came home on that night of my own distress, the effects of the delayed concussion had really flattened me. Alarmed at my condition they immediately called an ambulance - and I was rushed to Ryde Hospital, where I was to spend the next four days recovering. Officials at the Balmain club revealed the news to the press.

My life was a real mess at the time. I hadn't handled things at all well since my girlfriend had told me emphatically that it was over. I was a victim of the "growing up" syndrome, of the experience of teenage romance that most people go through - brief, sweet affairs that flourish then die, leaving some hurt behind.

For a brief period of my life just about everything went down the gurgler. I was on the grog, and my studies were out the window. I thought things couldn't get any worse in life. It was the toughest thing I had faced so far, and I wasn't handling it.

One night after a drinking session I went around to my girlfriend's place, drunk, to try and patch things up. She showed excellent judgement - and wouldn't let me in. I was making plenty of noise, and a nuisance of myself and she rang Maroubra Police Station. So the coppers came over, and took me back to the station. They put me in a cell, and one of the policemen came in and played cards with me, and talked. I told him the whole story, and he listened and, basically, counselled me.

"Mate, it's happened to me," he said ... "and it's not worth it." We talked for a long time, and he made plenty of sense. Finally, he drove me home. But I was soon back in the doldrums again.

Late in my stay in hospital the girl at the heart of my problem visited me. It was a short, sharp visit. When she realised I was okay, she made it very clear that it was over between us, and wheeled around and was gone. I never saw her again. I thought she had been cruel that day - but, of course, she had just been fair dinkum. When they discharged me from hospital I was down in the dumps, and after a week or so I was still moping around at home, going nowhere.

It was then that my father did something that changed my life. One morning he asked me: "Son, can I have next Sunday morning with you?"

"Well ... sure ... why?" I answered.

"I just want to spend some time with you," he said.

On that Sunday he drove me to a hospital. I'm not sure which one it was. But I remember the ward number ... ward seven. It was a long room full of young people, about 20 of them. They were all in wheelchairs or laying flat on their beds, immobile.

"Dad, what are we doing?" I said to him.

"Just have a look at these people," he answered quietly.

We passed through with no further conversation and at the end he said to me: "Son, any one of those kids in there would swap places with you. They would do anything to change their lives. You must wake up to yourself ... you are throwing your life away."

That was all he said to me - and we climbed back into the car.

For the rest of that day, and long into the night, I thought about that ward, and those tragic young people. There were kids there who hadn't been able to feed themselves from the day they were born. Some of them couldn't walk, couldn't talk, couldn't see. Some of them had never seen the sun.

It was at that moment that I started to get better. I thought to myself - what the hell are you moping around for? You have plenty of blessings to count ... get out there and get on with your life.

It was one of the great lessons, one of the true turning points of my life. I'll never forget what my dad did for me at that time, and I remind him of that now and then.

Balmain club supported me loyally during the period of my distress, and hospitalisation. A Phil Rothfield story in the *Daily Telegraph* gave the official club version under the headline: "Elias Sidelined After Blackout". The story read:

Balmain's young hooker Benny Elias has been ordered to take a month's rest from football after collapsing at home and being rushed to hospital.

Elia blacked out after the Tigers' match against Parramatta and was kept in hospital for four days last week.

Doctors have diagnosed problems with his nervous system as a sequel to several heavy knocks in the match against the Eels.

The brilliant young rake said last night he fell unconscious on the Monday after the game and came to in hospital the following morning.

"I woke up in Ryde hospital on Tuesday morning and I didn't know what was happening," Elias said.

"All I can remember is that I had a bad headache on the Monday and next thing I woke up in hospital.

"My mother told me I was rushed to hospital in an ambulance with the siren blaring and everything."

Balmain coach Frank Stanton commented: "He seemed quite normal after the game and we were surprised when he didn't come to training on the Tuesday night."

Rothfield's story was near-enough to right, except that he was not privy to the very personal information about my teenage romance problems.

I guess all of us carry a bruise or a scar from an early romance which didn't work out the way we wanted it to. Mine was probably no worse or no better than your own. But, boy, it hurt!

I was young and immature, and I really fell for her. I must have been a real pain. But at the time I couldn't accept the rebuff at all. I started drinking heavily, neglected my football and was dropped from first grade to reserves. I failed a semester at uni, and at home I must have been a shit to live with. The tough guy footballer was a total marshmallow at that time, and it took my father to snap me out of it.

She was my first true girlfriend, although I had had earlier crushes. There was a girl from down the road at West Ryde who was a couple of years older than me. The Older Woman Syndrome. We even went as far as holding hands. I used to ride my pushbike down past her place and do wheelies out the front to impress her. And we would go ice-skating. It was there, on the ice rink, that we first held hands, and that was really something. In three or four years of this fragile teenage romance we would have held hands all of ... four times. And I kissed her once.

Then I met a girl from our sister school, Woolwich, and we were something like boyfriend-girlfriend for a time. Like me, she was from a migrant background, and we went out for a couple of years. Even though we were only 16 or 17, we used to talk about the future, and about marriage and life and what it all meant, as young people do. She was my sweetheart, my friend in that awkward growing-up time.

The masterly lesson provided by my father when I was at such a low ebb came late in 1983, with a disappointing football season behind me. I made up my mind that I would start all over again in 1984, and I left '83 chastened, bruised ... but wiser. As summer came on I set about doing the work that would rebuild my football career the next season. I was over the bumpy period, and by then my life was healing nicely.

5

Making the Grade

I HAVE ALWAYS been too small to play football. When I was at Holy Cross it was common opinion that I wasn't big enough to play in the first XIII. Kevin Smyth and John O'Brien asked me the $64 question one day: "Do *you* think you're too small?" I told them I wasn't. When I was playing in the Balmain junior representative teams the popular theory was that I was a good player, but certainly too small for grade. When I got to grade, I was too small to make it in Firsts. When I got to first grade, I was too small to represent. Only when I finally played for Australia was the theory buried for good.

Ian Walsh, a champion hooker for St George and Australia in the 1960s, put it into words in a notorious column he wrote in the *Daily Telegraph* in 1985. This is what he said:

When it comes to talking hookers, Elias to me looks like a doll you'd expect to see some supporter carrying at a match in Balmain colours. He's too small. I would shudder for his safety if Elias ever found himself in an international match. Throwing Elias into a Test team would make the Romans feeding Christians to the lions seem a charitable act in comparison.

When I came to grade football with Balmain in 1982 I weighed 71 kilos (11st 3lb). I had stopped growing (upwards) and was 170cm (5ft 7in) tall. As I write this book I am still 170cm, but considerably heavier, at my right playing weight of 84 kilos (13st 3lb). The build-up came through natural growth and plenty of weight work in the years since 1982.

I joined Balmain at the same year that Frank Stanton arrived at the club. The Tigers were at a low ebb, wooden-spooners in 1981 - but with real hopes for better times ahead now that they had signed the incumbent Australian coach.

I was a starry-eyed 17-year-old fresh off the hill at Leichhardt, suddenly pitched into the same squad as my heroes, such as Larry Corowa. It was pretty daunting. I remember Garry Jack, who had joined the Tigers that year from Western Suburbs, coming up to me and saying: "You're that little superstar from the schoolboys, aren't you? Mate, you play some good football." I had already met Junior Pearce, and I knew Steve "Blocker" Roach. Steve had spent some time with the Balmain Police team in the juniors, and I had played against him.

Because I was a contracted player, I was part of the pre-season "elite" squad, in the midst of all the Balmain stars. I had never trained so hard in my life. We started on November 1, 1981, and boy, did we train. I became intimately acquainted with the hills at Cooper Park, in Bellevue Hill in Sydney's eastern suburbs - and anyone who has worked those monsters will know how tough they are.

For the first time in my life I started making sacrifices. Training was often at the crack of dawn on weekends, so I was giving up the Friday and Saturday nights out with my mates. There were parties left, right and centre, but I was saying no. I had reached a crossroads in my life - and I knew which path I wanted to take.

I first pulled on the Balmain jersey, as a graded player, in a pre-season lower-grade trial game against Parramatta, played at Nelson Bay on the mid-north coast. The jersey wasn't really new to me as I had worn it in the SG Ball and Jersey Flegg teams. But it was very special all the same. I remember George Stone, who is now club president, talking about the Balmain jersey one day. "It's a wonderful thing to wear the black and gold," said George. "When you put the jersey on, the badge is over your heart. Wear it with pride. You have earned it, and no-one can take it away from you." George had tears in his eyes as he spoke.

My career in premiership football with the Balmain Tigers began on Sunday, February 28, 1982 - in reserve grade. Laurie Freier had joined the club as reserves coach that year. One day he grabbed me at training and said: "Mate, you're coming with me."

We played Cronulla at Endeavour (later Caltex) Field, and the wind blew as it always seems to down there. We won the game in a tight one, 12-10, and I scored a try, in the left-hand corner down the Botany Bay end - from the old dummy trick. They hadn't woken to my little speciality at that stage ... but they soon did. The coach seemed happy. He came up to me after the game and said: "Keep doing what you did today and you'll be in my side every time."

I was on top of the world. But football can ankle tap you pretty quickly, as I found out a few short weeks later. I had bought a new car, a Gemini, and had driven up to the Central Coast on a training day. Unfortunately the car broke down. I was late for training - and Laurie dropped me. It was before a match against Canberra and I remember flying down to the national capital, feeling pretty gloomy and thinking: 'I'm never going to let that happen again.'

That's the beautiful thing about league - it teaches you any number of good lessons. It has certainly taught me the importance of discipline in my life. Discipline doesn't come naturally, it's not inherited. You must be taught it. If you're going to have a chance of succeeding in football or life you have to learn about discipline, about punctuality, about respect. Rugby league has taught me all these things. As it turned out I had a big game in Thirds in Canberra, scoring a couple of tries in a 20-12 win which kept the team at the top of the competition. It was a performance good enough to pitchfork me straight back into reserve grade.

On April 21, 1982, I played my first first grade game with Balmain - a KB Cup match against Brisbane at Lang Park. Our regular hooker and club captain, Neil Whittaker, was a late withdrawal because of injury, and I received the call on the morning of the game. It was all a bit of a blur, arriving at that level so soon - but I remember that our five-eighth, Gary Bridge, had a blinder, and we won 13-10.

"Schoolboy Elias Makes Grade In Balmain Win" read the headline in the *Daily Mirror* next day.

"He handled the rise with no great difficulty," reported the *Mirror's* writer, Paul Malone.

My quote to the press (was it my first press conference?) was a diplomatic one: "I won the scrums 10-6 and the coach and players were happy with me, so therefore, I'm happy".

No problems there.

Opposing us that night was a bloke I was going to see plenty of in the seasons ahead - Wally Lewis.

Frank Stanton blooded me quietly in first grade in that exciting year. When I look back I am deeply appreciative of the skilful way he *gradually* introduced me to the big time. He'd throw me on here and there with 10 minutes to go, just to give me a taste.

The first time was a match against St George, one of the hot sides of that time. We were getting a flogging, and Frank gave me the last 10 minutes. Shit! It was like being in another world. The Saints were going at 100mph, really belting us. Their side included international forwards such as Craig Young and "Rocket" Reddy. Suddenly I was out in the middle of it, and thinking all the while ... I'm not sure I can handle this. It frightened me, really frightened me. God, I'm not ready for *this*, I thought.

I was not really competing for the first grade spot that first year; I was up against the club captain and incumbent, Neil Whittaker, a very respected, very good player. My occasional chances came when Neil was missing through injury - and the first of them, my first full premiership game, was against the Illawarra Steelers at Wollongong Showground. The date was May 23, 1982, and the final score 17-16 to Illawarra. We scored four tries (including one to B. Elias) to three, but the goalkicking skills of their highly-respected fullback, John Dorahy, got the Steelers home.

In July I played in two first grade games which will stand out like sore thumbs in my career - no matter if I play on for a hundred years. Laurie Freier for several weeks had been urging Stanton to give me a go in first grade, whether at hooker or elsewhere. The regular halfback, Steve Martin, had been out injured for a few weeks, and when his replacement, Greg Lane, dropped out of the match against Souths to be played at Redfern Oval on Sunday, July 4, Frank slotted me in. Halfback!!! I hadn't played there since the under-9s.

It was one of those magic days when everything went right. The *Daily Mirror* of July 5 reported the story this way, under a very large headline which read "Brilliant Benny!":

The little genius took us back at Redfern Oval yesterday to the good ol' days of Raper, Gasnier, Beetson and co. as he led Balmain to a remarkable 35-16 win over South Sydney.

Benny Elias has it all and he showed the lot to the 6596 patrons as he bewildered the locals in one of the best 80-minute displays in recent years.

The reluctant 18-year-old - he didn't want to play grade this year because of the abolition of the Under-23s -

completely annihilated the Rabbitohs.

You name it - the kid can do it; tackle (he made 29), line kick from both general play and penalties ... and those hands!

His timing of the pass would have done Arthur Beetson proud and he continually broke the Souths defensive line with clever short and long passes to his runners.

Rugby League Week the following Thursday reported:

Elias hadn't played halfback since his primary school days. But on Sunday he played there magnificently, setting up play after play with his cleverness around the ruck. He scored two key tries to shoot Balmain to the lead, and backed up his attacking brilliance by making 29 tackles.

There was a special thrill after this match when the *Daily Mirror's* judge gave me eight points in the Dally M awards. "A super display," he wrote.

The Dally M judge was none other than Clive Churchill - rugby league's "Little Master". I never met the man, but I cherish the rating he gave me that day.

The plaudits continued on the following Thursday, when I featured on the colour front page of *Rugby League Week* - labelled a "genius". Alongside me was Manly's teenage halfback, Phil Blake, also the subject of glowing praise. Blakey and I were good mates, and it just happened on that day that we were having a round of golf together at Balgowlah. We saw the paper ... looked at each other and said ... shiiit!

My half of that front-page story was one for the scrapbook, and was duly cut and pasted in the Elias household. Headlined "Elias A Genius!' it read:

Benny Elias' magnificent game against Souths last Sunday confirmed the Balmain 18-year-old as a new super talent of League.

"He's a bloody genius," declared Keith Barnes, high priest of the Tigers.

"He's as good an all-round player as I have ever seen at

that age. He's got tons of confidence, he can read a game, he's got all the skills. Basically he's got the lot.

"... His skills are amazing," said Barnes. "Apart from everything else he is an outstanding goalkicker and line-kicker."

Barnes and Tigers coach Frank Stanton agree that Elias' future lies as a hooker.

"His potential is undoubted," said Stanton. "He now has to work on his physical capacity - and embark on a strength and weight program.

"And he must be able to handle all the 'wraps' that will come his way, without letting the praise affect him."

At that time Phil Blake was the most exciting thing on two feet in rugby league. I rate him and Scott Gale - a good mate of mine for years, and Balmain's halfback in the mid-1980s - as two of the really outstanding natural talents of the modern game.

As is generally the way, the game of rugby league did not let me rest on my laurels for too long. Balmain backed me up at half the following week, against Wests at Lidcombe Oval - a game in which I faced one of my boyhood idols, Greg Cox. Greg was a Holy Cross boy, although a few years ahead of me. I had played my school football with his younger brother Andrew. Greg had been my hero when he was Balmain's halfback - a good-looking, self-assured, stylish player who had a great-looking girlfriend, could kick goals, and do just about everything well. I really admired him. As a matter of fact, when I was a kid I idolised the bloke. We used to go the same church - St Theresa's at Denistone - and I'd sit upstairs and star-gaze at him. But, as I was to find out, it's not easy being matched head-to-head with your boyhood idol.

Greg's career had gone into decline somewhat since he left the Tigers - to join Cronulla, and then Wests. But on that day we played Wests in 1982 he had obviously made up his mind that he was going to put this little upstart right on his backside. And didn't he do it! Cox and the Magpies' young five-eighth, Terry Lamb, just gave it to me, gave me a real shellacking. It was the 150th encounter between the two clubs, but it was no vintage Balmain display - and Wests beat us 14-8. Coach Stanton sort of gulped and said: "Mate, I think we'll put you back in reserve grade for a few more weeks."

So back I went, to link again with Laurie Freier. It was the right place for me at the time, and Laurie was the right bloke. I rank him as probably the most knowledgeable league man I've come across. Laurie's problem has always been that he can be abrasive in dealing with people. But as a coach he was a thorough and shrewd professional and he taught me plenty. He showed tremendous faith in me that year - and at one stage took the team's captaincy away from the veteran, Neil "Bing" Pringle, and gave it to me.

Under Freier's firm hand that year we went on to win the reserve grade premiership for Balmain - beating Easts 17-12 in the grand final. We were the underdogs right through that finals series, but we were a well-coached team, and a team on a mission.

Centre Wayne Miranda produced the tackle of his life to save us in the grand final. Two minutes from the end Miranda knocked the Roosters' Russel Gartner into touch right on the corner post with a fabulous tackle. I had the thrill of scoring a grand final try after chasing a Pringle kick-through.

When we won the title before that huge crowd of over 52,000 at the Sydney Cricket Ground, it was the biggest thing that had ever happened to me. Yet I had the sense straight away that the public wasn't all *that* interested. It's a stiff lesson to take in - to have played your guts out, and to have won ... then to realise that people are not all that impressed or interested anyway. That's the way it is in the Sydney premiership; the early grades are merely warm-ups for the Big Event. But Balmain club gave us a blazer each, and I'm proud of mine, and still have it tucked safely away.

My first year as a grade footballer was a terrific mix of the joys and disappointments that make up what football is all about. I tasted first grade, I shared in the winning of a premiership, and I learned heaps about the need for personal discipline, and team responsibility.

I consider myself fortunate to have had someone such as Frank Stanton as a guiding hand in my early years at the club. I think the world of Frank - he's such a solid, honest, professional guy. He came into that club in '82 with a really tough job on his hands - to try and pick a real rag-tag bunch off the bottom. He went about it in his steady, serious way, and at the end of the '82 season he weeded out a large group of players that he didn't believe would contribute to the sort of club he was trying to build. Frank didn't win a comp in his time at Leichhardt, but he sure did make us competitive. He made us believe in each other - and he fostered a mateship, a closeness on which the club's successes later in the 1980s were built. He stressed unity as the most important thing - that we were all together, and had to be prepared to lay our bodies on the line ... all working towards the same goal. I think Frank was a great coach - and his record at all levels confirms that.

Towards the end of 1982 someone even suggested that I (and Phil Blake) should be taken on the Kangaroo tour. That was never on - but there was quite a celebration anyway on the night that Wayne Pearce was named in the side. We were all in the leagues club when the news came through, and something extraordinary happened: Junior drank a glass of champagne! We were all over the moon for him, delighted that he had made the side. I thought to myself - I'm going to try and get there one day. At what was then a battling club, Junior had provided hope for us all.

Wayne was a great and positive influence on the way I prepare to play football. I admire him enormously. I have never before or since seen anyone who maximised their energies and skills to the extent that Junior did through his career. My diet changed because of him, my work with the weights got smarter and more specific, my training improved. He was the total package and his messages rubbed off on all of us.

Things were perfectly in place for me to have an excellent second season, in 1983. But as I revealed in Chapter 4, my personal life reared up and got in the way. Everything was as rosy as it could have been at the start of that year of promise. Late in '82, Balmain had hit me with a new contract which I was delighted to sign. Keith Gittoes said to me one day: "Mate, what we're going to do - we're going to rip up that first contract, double your money for next year, and give you even more the following year. We see a lot of future in you, and we plan to look after you."

I was rapt in that - and things were looking much better for the club as Frank Stanton's methods began to bite. We had a lively and very young pack of forwards, and early in '83 *RLW* featured a photo of the six of us on the front page - Junior, Blocker, Kerry Hemsley, Tony Keevil, Kevin Hardwick and me - under the screaming headline: "Balmainia!"

At that stage of the season we had won four in a row and were starting to rebuild hope in the district after the rock-bottom events of season 1981. The *RLW* story read:

Balmainia! It's the epidemic that promises to lift rugby league out of its doldrums in 1983.

Faced with flagging crowds and a jumbled start to the season, the League desperately needs a boost.

The "Balmain Babes", built on a foundation of the youngest forward pack ever to represent a Sydney first grade side, are starting to look like just the required tonic.

They're fresh, fit and fearless, and, amazingly in the toughest body contact sport in the world, average just 21 years 7 months of age.

Tigertots!

Keith Barnes at the time called us "potentially the most exciting Balmain side for 25 years" - and things were looking fine.

Sadly, after a start of such promise, I ran right off the rails, and it turned out to be a patchy year for me. I was dropped at one stage (I ended up playing 16 of a possible 26 matches), and finished up pretty disappointed with the way I handled things. But at least I learned some stern lessons.

We young Tigers crashed after our early month of victories, and lost six of our next seven premiership games. But we re-grouped and began a long and sustained charge towards the semi-finals.

In the second round of that long premiership campaign (26 matches in the competition proper), the Firsts won 10 of 13 games, including a magnificent 22-20 win over the reigning premiers, Parramatta, at Leichhardt in late August. David Brooks' last-minute pressure goal got us home that day against a team laced with legends - Sterling, Kenny, Grothe, Cronin, Price and so on.

I was in Seconds at the time, unable to push out Neil Whittaker. A last-round win over Norths (16-12) set up an epic semi-final confrontation with St George.

In a match that ran 100 minutes, after the former Canterbury winger, Steve Gearin, had pushed it into extra time with a 78th-minute penalty goal for 14-all, St George scraped home 17-14 with another Gearin goal (98th minute) and a Michael O'Connor field goal 60 seconds later. I came on late in the game - my first experience of the pressures of a first grade semi-final.

It was not a good day for the club. Earlier, the reserve grade's season had ended in frustrating circumstances against Canterbury. A goalkick by our five-eighth, Gary Mara, hit one upright, and then the other before rebounding into the field of play ... and we went down 6-4.

For Balmain it had been a season of great promise,

ultimately unfulfilled. We were building steadily towards better things, and in the streets of the old suburbs which comprise the Tiger district there was a growing sense of good times ahead.

1984, the third year of Frank Stanton's reign, was another year that ended in frustrating circumstances. Our season came down to the winning of a late-August match against St George at home. Victory on that day would have had us in the semi-finals. But we blew cold in the first half, despite a stiff wind at our backs - and at half time we were down 20-nil, with Michael O'Connor tearing us to shreds. Frank Stanton gave us a right royal blast at halftime and the second half produced a near-famous comeback in which we failed by just four points to peg back the Saints. We missed the semis by two points.

I played 16 first grade games that year and my form was pretty sound. I felt I was settling in well to the demands of top-level football.

First grade rugby league is a learning experience and I had some real confidence-building days that year in matches in which everything seemed to "click". After a match against Canberra at Leichhardt which we won 39-12, the Raiders (later Australian) coach, Don Furner, commented: "Elias destroyed us."

After that game, *Rugby League Week's* Neil Cadigan wrote perceptively of my somewhat chequered progress since leaving high school:

It was ironic that a schoolboy Test preceded one of Ben Elias' most spectacular performances at Leichhardt last Saturday.

Elias would have thought back to 1980 as he watched the Australian lads give their English opposition a hiding before he went into the Balmain dressing-room to ready himself for a desperate battle with Canberra.

For the flamboyant little Tigers hooker was a whiz as a schoolboy, starring in the Test series in England in 1980 and being rated as the most sensational young forward from the metropolitan area in years.

But as the complimentary comments flowed last Saturday about the youngsters "going all the way when they graduated from schoolboy level", little Benny was testimony that it's not quite so easy.

With his former Australian Schoolboys team-mate, Mal Cochrane from Manly, Elias has taken longer than his schoolmates to make it in the "Big League".

But his effort in destroying the Raiders, equal to his great performance when brought up by Frank Stanton eight weeks ago, showed that Elias' career is now into top gear - with representative honours ahead.

That earlier performance referred to by Cadigan, in a mid-June match against Manly, had brought glowing praise from two champion hookers. Mike Stephenson, the multi-talented former Great Britain and Penrith player, wrote in the Sydney *Sun*:

Young Balmain hooker Benny Elias grew up on Saturday.

He finally shook off his "schoolboy star" tag and steered Balmain back on the premiership trail ... in a match that left more-fancied Manly devastated 15-4.

Elias played like a veteran to take control of the Brookvale Oval game. Elias came of age, turning the corner to the road to success.

His four scrum wins against the head and three rakebacks at play-the-balls were a bonus to his fine distribution and line kicks from general play.

I particularly valued some praise I received from the recently-retired Max Krilich after that win over the Sea Eagles. I admired him more than any other hooker of that time. Max, a Manly man to the soles of his boots, walked over to me in the dressing-room after the game and just said: "Well played Ben - you killed 'em".

Max Krilich was the most innovative of the hooking

breed at a time when the game was changing, and the old hard-headed hookers, whose strengths were limited mainly to toughness and scrum skills, were dying out. I admired Max for his stickability, too. He had persisted for years in the shadow of the legendary Freddie Jones at Manly and then finally broken through to carve his own outstanding career at the top level. He probably helped my case a bit too, because he was a hooker who could do a bit extra with the ball. He would run from dummy-half; he could kick the ball. Most of the other hookers around were of the head-down, bum-up style.

I'm sure that my somewhat radical approach went against me in the early days. I was basically a halfback playing hooker, and at that time it was unheard of for a hooker to kick from dummy-half, or chip-kick over the top. At the start, when I was duelling for representative spots, I was matched against hookers of the older style, such as Penrith's Royce Simmons and the Queenslander, Greg Conescu.

Hookers had played the same way for 70 years or so, and rugby league is traditionally pretty conservative and slow to change. Max Krilich did something towards breaking the hooker's mould, and I have no doubt he helped my cause.

In the late '70s there was a bloke at Balmain who was also perhaps a little ahead of his time in the hooking department. Noel Maybury finished up breaking an arm on three different occasions - and that would be enough to make anyone give the game away. But when he was hale and hearty he was a hooker of special skills, a genuine ball-player who could slip a pass or make some territory with a well-timed run. His was a career of abundant promise - but an unlucky one.

In that 1984 match against Manly I won four scrums against the feed. Scrums were still scrums then, and I had learned the trade well, starting with the lessons given by John O'Brien. There weren't too many tricks he hadn't taught me, and at Balmain we competed strongly in the scrums, always aware of the value of pinching a couple against the feed. We did a lot of scrummaging practice at the time, and Neil Whittaker and I would swap techniques - and tricks.

The days of competitive scrums are now gone and, setting aside a small sense of regret, I applaud the change. As the game moved into the '90s, scrums became not much more than a pause in play, with the forwards dragged in together, and the team feeding the ball winning it 99 times out of 100. I think the change is good from the spectators' point of view, and I have no doubt that it reduces the chance of scrum injury, particularly from collapsed scrums that resulted from forward packs straining and struggling the way they used to.

From the hooker's point of view, the skill factor is gone from scrums, and that's something of a shame - but to me the advantages of the change far outweigh the disadvantages. Skill is pretty much limited now to the halfback putting the ball in properly - "properly" in this context meaning in a way that guarantees that his team gets the ball back. If you get one against the feed today, it probably just means that the other mob have accidentally kicked it through.

Scrummaging practice is now non-existent. In former days we used to get scrum experts to come in and advise us, and we'd pack down against a scrummaging machine. Those days are long gone - and the hooker of today is a much sleeker, slicker, quicker model than his counterpart from years gone by. Better looking, too.

6

The Origin Experience

THE FIRST TIME I played State of Origin football I was frightened like you could not believe. I had never experienced anything like it. I was not much more than a kid, still wet behind the ears, but I had made the side for the opening match of the 1985 series (at Brisbane's Lang Park), beating such players as Royce Simmons, Mario Fenech and Mal Cochrane - and I was rapt! It was not until I got to Brisbane, to our base at the Parkroyal Hotel across from the Botanical Gardens, that it really hit me as to what I had walked into.

You could smell the hate for NSW in the streets of Brisbane in the days leading up to the game. Luckily I had a solid phalanx of Tigers around me to help get me through ... Junior, Blocker and "Jimmy" Jack. And then on the night - the fireworks, the cannons booming, the smoke everywhere - and inevitably that Lang Park ROOAAR! I was terrified.

The final half-hour countdown to the match had been extraordinary. Barely a word had been spoken within the NSW team. We had lapsed into an intense silence in the wake of a magnificent and inspiring piece of leadership by our captain and halfback, Steve Mortimer.

The story is a well-known one - of "Turvey" demanding that our driver stop the bus as we neared Lang Park. Around us on both sides, all we could see was a wave of humanity, people streaming towards the ground.

Mortimer marshalled the entire team down the back of the bus and gestured towards the throngs outside. "Look at these bastards," he said. "They hate us - they're here to see us get beaten. Well, we're gonna disappoint them. NSW has never won a series, but tonight is the turning point" ... And on he went, our captain - with enormous passion and emotion. He reminded us that we were carrying the expectations of an entire state. He talked about our families. "We're playing for our lives up here," he said. When he finished, it was as if each one us retreated into our own personal cocoon. There was barely another word spoken until kick-off ... just this intense silence as each of us pictured within ourselves what we had to do. We were going to die for each other if we had to.

State of Origin football can be a very intimidating experience, and especially the first time at a place like Lang Park. The atmosphere crushes down on you, and the primitive roar from 30,000 throats nearly knocks you over. I have grown to love the experience over the years, but on that first night I was just a scared kid when I ran out. But it's a funny thing about football - once you get under way, once you make a tackle, or touch the ball, you're okay. And so it was that first time.

We went out there on a wet and hostile night, and killed 'em. Our star centre and goalkicker, Michael O'Connor, had one of the magic games of his career, and scored all 18 points. It was his debut game, too. We won 18-2.

We had the lead only 4-2 after a rugged first half in which every tackle jolted. The turning point came 14 minutes into the second half, after we had soaked up a period of Maroon

Sportsphoto Agency

Right: The Elias family in 1964. That's me, the best part of a year old, on my dad's right arm.

Below: One of the earliest photos of Benny Elias, footballer, in the colours of St Michael's, Meadowbank. I'm the footballer sixth from left, with the socks not quite pulled up as far as they should be.

Weekly Times

Above: A memory that remains one of the most treasured of my league career — man of the match in Holy Cross College's triumph in the final of the 1981 Commonwealth Bank Cup. My little team-mate is Eddie Basile.

Below: I had the good fortune to play my schoolboy league when the sponsorship of junior football by big business was really emerging.

RLW

RLW

Above: The 1979-80 Australian Schoolboys celebrate Christmas in France.

Left: This photo appeared on the front page of Rugby League Week *the week after I had made a big impression playing halfback against Souths in 1982, my first season of premiership football.*

Weekly Times

RLW

RLW

Top: Six young Tigers who made up the Balmain first grade pack during the early rounds of the 1983 season. Left to right: Kerry Hemsley, Kevin Hardwick, Wayne Pearce, Ben Elias, Steve Roach and Tony Keevil.

Above: Darting away from dummy-half against Penrith in 1982.

Right: With Frank Stanton, a superb coach and great influence during my first five seasons at Balmain.

My first taste of State of Origin football came at a rain-soaked Lang Park in 1985. The experience was a daunting one, but I survived and we won the match comfortably, 18-2.

RLW

The man most responsible for NSW's series win in 1985 was our captain, Steve Mortimer.

Left: I look on while Steve (left) wrestles with Queensland centre (and later Australian captain), Mal Meninga, at Lang Park.

Below: With Steve after we clinched the series at the SCG.

RLW

Weekly Times

Left: After winning selection for the 1985 Australian tour of New Zealand, the first time I was chosen in an Australian side, I wasted no time getting this photo taken at Leichhardt Oval.

Below: The Tigers celebrate winning the National Panasonic Cup in 1987. Left to right: David Brooks, Michael Marketo, John Owens, Mick Neil (obscured), Ben Elias, Stephen Humphreys, Scott Gale, Wayne Pearce (obscured), Paul Sironen (obscured), Russel Gartner, Garry Jack, Ross Conlon, Paul Clarke.

RLW

RLW

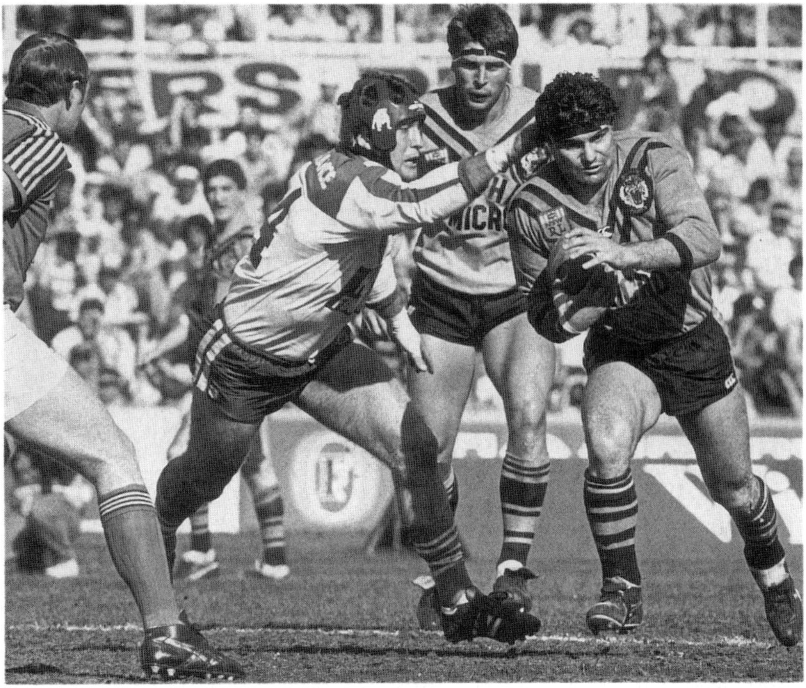

Above and below: Escaping the clutches of Canterbury's Peter Kelly during the early stages of the dramatic major preliminary semi-final in 1985.

RLW

RLW

Above: The 1986 Kangaroos, pictured at their medical before the tour. At Back: (left to right) Les Kiss, Gary Belcher, Noel Cleal, Steve Roach, Martin Bella, Phil Daley, Paul Sironen, Les Davidson, Chris Mortimer. Middle: Des Hasler, Dale Shearer, Bob Lindner, Don Furner (coach), Greg Dowling, Wally Lewis (captain), Paul Langmack, Terry Lamb, Brett Kenny (behind Lamb), Garry Jack, Bryan Niebling, Gene Miles, Paul Dunn, Eric Grothe (who was ruled out). In front: Ben Elias, Peter Sterling, Michael O'Connor, Steve Folkes, Royce Simmons.

RLW

Right: With our tough prop, Kerry Hemsley (left), and second-rower David Brooks, after our come-from-behind defeat of Manly in the 1986 minor preliminary semi-final.

Below: Balmain legend, and long-serving Chief Executive, Keith Barnes.

Balmain Leagues Club

All pics RLW

Above: Trying to avoid the player with whom I had my longest and most bitter football feud — Mario Fenech of Souths (and later Norths). My troubles with Fenech date back to our first meeting, in a reserve grade match in 1982, but today the animosity I once felt has gone, and I respect the man for his skill, his durability and his enormous competitiveness.

Bottom left: Sent to the sin bin with Mark Bugden of Canterbury.

Bottom right: Evading an attempted tackle by Queensland hooker Greg Conescu.

RLW

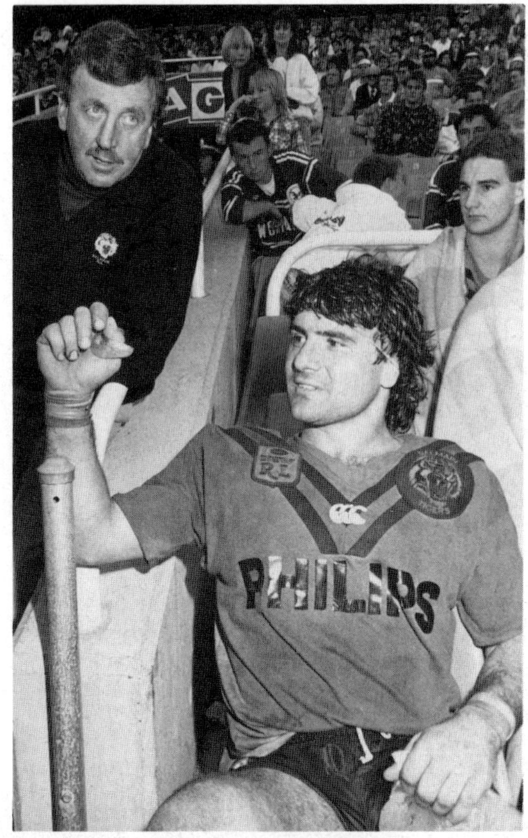

Left: With controversial coach Warren Ryan, after he'd given me an early mark near the end of our win over Manly in the 1988 minor preliminary semi-final.

Below: The worst part about playing for City in the annual Origin match against Country was packing down against my Balmain team-mate Steve Roach. I much preferred playing with the guy! Here Blocker has brought me down in the 1990 match. The other players near the action are Country captain Dean Lance (no. 13), City's Paul Sironen (at back) and Country hooker Steve Carter.

News Ltd

Three of the many great players to wear the Balmain jumper during my career.

Left: The fantastic Great Britain captain, Ellery Hanley, who had such an extraordinary impact during his stay at Leichhardt in 1988.

Below left: Garry Schofield, who gave the Tigers backline an enormous amount of class between 1985 and 1987.

Below: Big "Sirro" — Paul Sironen — a powerful mainstay for so long in the Balmain, NSW and Australian packs.

All pics RLW

News Ltd

With Wayne "Junior" Pearce, a great Tiger, great influence, great captain, great player and great bloke.

All pics RLW

Above: Balmain players celebrate Scott Gale's key try in the last-round defeat of Brisbane in 1988. Left to right: Ross Conlon, Gale, Garry Jack, Ellery Hanley, Bruce McGuire, Ben Elias and Paul Sironen.

Right: Backing up Blocker Roach during our play-off defeat of Penrith in 1988.

Below: Ducking away from Kiwi halfback Clayton Friend during the 1988 World Cup final.

Quentin Jones

With Balmain's (and rugby league's) greatest fan, the remarkable Laurie Nicholls, after the Tigers' 14-6 triumph over Canberra in the minor semi-final of 1988.

attack. From a quick play-the-ball I got a pass away to Wayne Pearce, then on to Brett Kenny and Chris Mortimer. "Snoz" O'Connor linked up and hared away, racing diagonally for the corner. Queensland fullback Colin Scott came at him, but O'Connor brushed through the high tackle, and went over for the try.

The former leading referee, Greg Hartley, wrote in the *Sun-Herald* that the Blues - and especially me - should have been counting our blessings over the surprise appointment of experienced Sydney referee Kevin Roberts to the match, ahead of the North Queenslander, Barry Gomersall. Hartley observed that Gomersall's "stand back and let 'em punch it out style" could have spelled trouble for me, for it was obvious the Maroons' front row of Dave Brown, Greg Conescu and Greg Dowling would be paying particular attention to me, the rookie, in my first game. I was certainly happy to have a strong referee such as Roberts there in preference to Gomersall, of whom I shall write more later.

Turvey Mortimer was dead right. That match was the turning point after five years of Queensland domination. When we came home to Sydney for the second game there was a new spirit in the air, and an expectation that things would now be different.

The second match, again in wet conditions, was a fabulous contest at the Sydney Cricket Ground. We got away to a dream start and led 12-nil - and I scored a try! What I remember most about that was Noel "Crusher" Cleal almost squeezing the life out of me in celebration. The Maroons fought back, and the contest wasn't decided until the final minutes, when Brett Kenny found a half-gap near the line and dived through it.

Queensland journalist Barry Dick called the match "one of the classic rugby league encounters of modern times" and it probably was, full of drama and knife-edge excitement as Queensland clawed their way back to lead us 14-12, 16 minutes into the second half, before our winning surge for 21-14.

On fulltime Steve Mortimer sunk on his knees to the turf, tears running down his face. He and coach Terry Fearnley had turned out to be an inspired partnership and the credit for breaking the Origin drought lies very much with them. We were a happy camp. There was nothing complicated - we were just totally focused on what we had to do, and bound close together by a special spirit.

The balance between Mortimer as captain and Fearnley as coach was just about perfect. Terry is a reserved sort of bloke, but with an analytical mind, and a sharp perception about football. When it was time for the emotional stuff, he was shrewd enough to fade back and let Turvey step onto centre stage. I think we were as well prepared for that series as any football team I have ever been associated with. I still have my first Origin jumper - No. 12, with "Elias" on the back - and it's one of my most precious possessions.

The drama of that game didn't end on the football field. In the dressing-room afterwards, Turvey called us all down to one end and announced emotionally that he was retiring from representative football - that this had been his last game. "This is the greatest moment of my life," he told pressmen soon afterwards. "I can't better it." We were happy and sad, all at the one time.

I have often wondered how different the New Zealand tour that followed this second Origin match would have turned out if Turvey Mortimer had gone away as vice-captain. Junior Pearce was pitchforked belatedly into the extremely tough job of trying to be a buffer between the Australian and Queensland captain, Wally Lewis, and the Australian and NSW coach, Terry Fearnley. Turvey, a more experienced captain at that level and with a pretty fair working relationship with Lewis after their shared experiences of the 1982 Kangaroo tour (when they went away as the top halfback pairing but didn't get to start a Test), may have been a better middleman on that difficult assignment.

It was quite a year, '85, a roller-coaster year in which

there were plenty more ups than downs. I even surpassed the personal goals I had set, when I made that Australian team that went to New Zealand. I'll talk more of that tour in the following chapter. There was lavish praise for me in the press. Respected league journalist Alan Clarkson described me as a "rugby league adventurer" and wrote: "He is one of the new school of players who will take the game into the next decade."

And to make the State of Origin team - in the season that NSW won for the first time - was one of the great thrills of my life.

Adding to the glitter was a supremely exciting Balmain year, in which we gave the premiership a hefty rattle before stumbling in the semi-finals and had the bonus of winning the mid-week National Panasonic Cup.

The demands on the representative players were extraordinary at that time. With Junior, Blocker and Jimmy Jack, I was playing Origin football for NSW on Tuesday nights - then coming back to play the mid-week game for Balmain the next night, followed by the premiership match at the weekend. I'm not quite sure how we survived, but being young sure was a help! I doubt I'd handle it these days. I know the challenge bound Junior, Blocker, Jimmy and me tremendously close.

Five days after the first Origin game, I took a real pasting in a match against Souths. They targeted me, without doubt, and I blew up to the media guys after the game. "I like playing a good hard game but when they put in stuff like that, I hate it, I really resent it," I told them. "Mario (Fenech) apparently reckons he has the physique to play Test football and I haven't. He thinks I'm not tough enough. I thought you were supposed to be humble when you talked about opponents. You don't big mouth unless you're like Muhammad Ali - and he's nothing like that. Mario is a good footballer, there's no doubt. But maybe he's too busy proving how tough he is and not how good he is. I enjoy playing rugby league but when they gouge your eyes and pull your hair, I can't understand it ... I really can't."

All the sledging and treatment we received that day only served to fire us up more - and we won 24-12 at Redfern, a most satisfying result.

Rugby League Week's Neil Cadigan reported:

South Sydney's plans to "out-muscle" the overworked Balmain Tigers, and to test the mettle of NSW hooker Ben Elias, backfired at Redfern Oval last Sunday ...

The more attention they gave to little Elias seemed to do nothing more than inspire prop Steve Roach and the other Tiger forwards.

The more attention and sledging Elias received, the hotter became the blood of the Balmain forwards, and the more energy reserves they seemed to find.

Cadigan wrote of me being a "target" in the match, and the *Mirror* got some strong quotes from Mrs Barbara Elias, my mum.

"I am very worried for Benny," said my mother. "While I watch him play I am worried from start to finish. He is such a gentle boy."

I'm sure the media have relished the "feud" between Mario and me over the years. It has certainly provided some column inches in the papers. I'll talk more about it in depth later on.

Season 1985 was the one in which Frank Stanton received his rewards for the hard work and expertise he had injected into Balmain. With fairer luck it could have brought him a premiership to add to the two he had won at Manly in 1976 and 1978. Frank was the backbone of everything good that happened at Balmain in the mid-1980s. He taught us a lot about togetherness, about giving and taking, about mateship. Funny thing about Frank - I didn't realise until he had gone how much I thought of him, how great an influence he had been on all of us - and on the club.

At least we won the National Panasonic Cup for him,

beating Cronulla in the '85 Cup Final at Leichhardt in a game in which we were akin to a 1200 metres horse tackling a 1600 metres race ... and running out of puff after setting up a big lead. Smack in the middle of the representative season, the game was a test of both body and will for our key men. We led 14-nil and hung on to win 14-12 after the Sharks came with a great charge in the final quarter. The media called it "a night to remember".

We had some spectacular wins, such as the 50-10 pasting of Wests at Leichhardt one day, and featured in some truly epic battles such as the top-of-the-ladder tussle with St George at Leichhardt in which they beat us 17-15 in a game which went right down to the wire. Saints coach Roy Masters called it "one of the most amazing matches I have ever seen."

"It had everything," said Masters. "And the tactics were intriguing; it was like a game of chess."

The premiership turned out to be a frustrating story of missed opportunity after a season of abundant promise. We led the table, or were close to it, nearly all the way and entered the semis full of hope - although deep down I'm sure we had been rocked by a shattering loss to Parramatta a couple of weeks before the semi-finals. They really took us apart on a Belmore Sports Ground dustbowl, 40-8, in their last appearance on their temporary home ground (they returned to the ultra-modern Parramatta Stadium in 1986). A loss like that does you no good whatsoever. We steadied with a last-round win against Souths at Leichhardt (30-12), a match in which Mario Fenech was rated as having the better of me in our now inevitable "head-to-head" clash, and entered the semis believing we were in with a real chance.

But in the major semi, on September 9, it all went horribly wrong. Ill-fortune in an epic match against Canterbury cheated us of a win we should have had. In the 23rd minute of the second half, Wayne Pearce reeled away from a tackle clutching his face. Bleeding from the right eye, he left the field, bound for hospital with a severe eye injury for the second time in his career. It was the end of Junior's season. We knew it was serious the moment he turned to leave the field. Our skipper was the sort of bloke who would never leave a game unless something was drastically wrong.

This cruel and unrelentingly hard match ran for 100 minutes, moving into extra time after Ross Conlon had kicked a 79th-minute goal for us to level it up 8-all.

The moment that none of we Tigers will ever forget came four minutes into the extra time period. Our English import, Garry Schofield, dummied to kick, passed to winger Stephen Humphreys, and then doubled around to take a return pass and dive over. Somehow Mick Stone, a scrupulously honest and well-respected referee, made a huge blunder. Mick whistled it back, ruling that the Schofield pass to Humphreys was forward, to our total disbelief. We all thought the pass was okay, as did Frank Stanton, who was sitting near the sideline, almost directly in line with where the crucial play took place.

We battled and battled for the minutes that remained, but Lady Luck had done a bunk on us that day. In the 99th minute, Canterbury centre Andrew Farrar burst down the right to score the try that won the game. After the game I called that try "the worst moment of my life".

With Junior gone, Gary Bridge was made captain for the next week, our showdown with Parramatta in the knockout semi. We went in to the game more in hope than confidence. Without doubt the 100-minute war against Canterbury had drained us, mentally and physically. On an SCG gluepot Parramatta came out and did *exactly* what they had done to us three weeks before. This time it was 32-4. Our season had ended. Parramatta played football of a remarkable quality that day, tearing us to shreds through their brilliant backline after we had clung to them, 4-10, at halftime. The ground that day was a muddy mess; the previous week against Canterbury it had been like concrete.

It was Canterbury who went on to win the premiership, and we were left lamenting what might have been. I drove Garry Schofield to the airport the day after the Parramatta match and put him on the plane home. Scoey had planned to stay on in Australia for a time, but he was so disappointed with the way the season had ended that he decided to go home. Gee, he was a good player - one of a number of Englishmen we had at Balmain in the 1980s ... and certainly one of the best.

I'd rate him alongside the amazing Canterbury five-eighth, Terry Lamb, as the best "backer-upper" I've ever seen on a football paddock. Schofield was one of those blokes who could sniff out a scoring chance from a mile away. He brought with him a classy touch of English attacking football at its best. The Sydney game was in its defence-orientated mould at that time, largely through the influence of that very hard, very successful Canterbury side, and Scoey brought in something different. He was a difficult bloke to lock down in any match. He created uncertainty in the defence because of his ability to produce something unexpected, from virtually anywhere on the field.

We had a string of Poms at Balmain over the seasons, and all of them contributed something positive, in varying degrees, to the cause - Schofield, Lee Crooks, Daryl Powell, Andy Currier, Tony Myler, Shaun Edwards, and the undoubted dux of the class, Ellery Hanley, of whom I'll say a good deal more a little further down the track.

Then, as now, the game needed its characters, and character - and the English imports provided some of that quality. But not all the characters were English. As far as personality players go, I reckon Balmain in the '80s had a real special one in our big prop, Kerry "Buckets" Hemsley. I can still recall my first glimpse of him roaring into

Leichhardt on his first night in Tigertown, aboard the big Harley Davidson that became his trademark, with his long hair flowing behind him. He was wearing standard gear of T-shirt and jeans. Hemsley revved the bike right up to the dressing-room door and just left it there as if he owned the place. The certainty was that no-one was going to ask him to move it. Big Buckets was a tough guy, who could be called genuinely larger than life. He never bothered with the weights - he was just naturally strong. His approach to life was tackled exclusively via the fast lane, and if you happened to get caught partying with Hemsley, well, you knew you were going to party hard.

He was also a very strong and uncompromising player who was extremely loyal to the Tigers. He got to 100 first grade games, and he was proud of that - real damned proud. He was something completely different, a bloke of strong opinions and high intelligence. I consider myself extremely fortunate to have had a couple of front-rowers such as Buckets and Blocker Roach alongside in the trenches. Their comforting presence gave a little hooker a nice sense of security.

Buckets Hemsley was never anything less than direct. I can still picture him lifting Jimmy Jack by the throat in a famous moment on our end-of-season trip in Hawaii in 1985. We had been at the bar for a while drinking all sorts of fancy cocktails, but when it came to Jimmy's turn to shout he came back with a small carafe of house wine, and four glasses. Hemsley promptly picked him up bodily and declared: "You go back to the bar and buy fancy drinks like everyone else." Wisely, Jimmy did.

I won my first Dally M trophy, the hooker of the year, in '85, a valued memento of a highly productive season. But even in the midst of that end-of-season let-down in Hawaii, I was thinking ahead to 1986. After all, '86 was a Kangaroo tour year, and you don't get too many shots at those. By November we were into serious training, and I was concentrating on two specific areas of improvement - speed and strength. Hooked firmly by the spell of big-time representative football, I needed no motivating ...

7

The Truth About New Zealand

A GREAT DEAL has been said and written about the Australian team's visit to New Zealand in 1985. The tour is now pretty much part of Australian rugby league folklore - although it is not a particularly happy story. But for all the disputes and disharmony, it is a tour that for one special reason I'll always remember. For it was on that campaign that I became an Australian player (at senior level) for the first time.

I heard the news of my selection over a car radio in Sydney, the night after we had won the second State of Origin match, to clinch the series. I was with a bunch of mates and, after my name was read out, I just said: "Turn around - I'm going home." When I got there, nobody believed me. No-one had expected they would take two hookers and, after all, Queensland's Greg Conescu was the established Test hooker at that time. "Fair dinkum," I said. "They're taking two hookers - and I'm the second one." It finally sunk in, and then it was party time ...

Programmed slap bang in the middle of an absolutely *fierce* Origin series, the tour can be judged today as a serious administrative bungle. Officials must have expected a miracle if they thought the players could forget about interstate rivalry once they landed in New Zealand. Well, it didn't happen, and coach Terry Fearnley was the luckless man in the middle.

I was a greenhorn kid as far as touring went, but it was apparent to me right from the start that there was a clear division between the NSW and Queensland players, and a breach between the Queenslanders and the coach. After all, Fearnley had just masterminded the first-ever NSW Origin series win over Queensland. The Maroon players were unlikely to be falling over themselves to be his best mate.

The ARL handed Terry a mission impossible and I doubt he received the official support that he could have done with. In particular the inflammatory remarks made by the Queensland Rugby League boss, Ron McAuliffe, late in the tour, after Fearnley had *dared* to drop four Queensland players for the Third Test, were destructive in the extreme. They were also disloyal, as McAuliffe was also an ARL heavy, and his loyalty and support should have been with the coach. All he did was stir up controversy in a classic piece of jingoism.

From the start it seemed to me that this Australian "team" was in reality made up of a NSW segment ... and a Queensland segment, with a coach caught in the middle.

It was NSW and Queensland. It was Wally Lewis, Queensland, captain and Wayne Pearce, NSW, vice-captain. At times the atmosphere was very, very uncomfortable.

There was still an Origin game to go, and the animosity from that series bubbled beneath the surface. I think that on the Queensland side of the fence there were some sour grapes because they had already lost the prize, 2-0. The New Zealand campaign was one of a number of tours that

I have been on over the years, and it remains the most disappointing of the lot. Tours in the green and gold should be about harmony and closeness and camaraderie.

This one was short-changed in all areas.

Yet, we won the series, clinching it in the last gasp of the Second Test through the sheer brilliance of fullback Garry Jack and winger John Ribot. Australia thus led 2-0, just as NSW led 2-0 in the Origin series. If you're talking success you couldn't do much better than that. But the Australian team had not been overly impressive, and Fearnley, as coach - and it must be said with the support of managers David Barnhill (NSW) and John Garrahy (Queensland) - had every right to pick the team he wanted for the Third Test. For doing that - for sticking to what he believed was the right path in the circumstances - he was crucified.

On his return home, the coach was to say: "To me, selecting a team to represent Australia and to give us a chance to win was more important than pleasing a rather outspoken individual (McAuliffe). It's a funny thing. I thought I was picking a team of *Australians* to represent Australia against a very strong New Zealand team."

Fearnley was to call the furore that erupted over the selection decisions on the New Zealand tour "the most ridiculous, small-minded and bitter note in the history of representative rugby league in Australia."

A lot of undermining went on during that tour. The coach did his best to bind it all together. But he was up against a very dominant personality in Wally Lewis. Wally had his Queensland comrade, Fatty Vautin, in his shadow - the pair of them old heads - and the pair were certainly not on the same wavelength as the coach. I think Wally felt threatened by Fearnley's obvious close link with the vice-captain, Wayne Pearce. The unease and animosity that was already present - thanks to the timing of the campaign - fed on that perception.

The captain and the coach were on vastly different

courses. I think Fearnley did his best to bring about a change in that situation, while Wally more or less just did what he wanted to do. I recall a training session at which we were doing some fairly hard physical work one morning - and Wally simply decided he wouldn't do it. He declared: "I'm not doing this". And he didn't - which wasn't particularly helpful. As the tour went on, things didn't improve. At different times Wally was late for training and left early from training. It was patently obvious to all of us that our captain and our coach didn't get on.

As far as I'm concerned there was never the slightest hint of Fearnley playing favourites. He was never less than fair and honest - always doing what he thought was right. Whether it *was* right is not for me to judge. I'm sure he felt totally isolated in that final week before the Third Test. He had been chosen to do a job over there and it seemed that the support he needed from the people who picked him was sadly missing.

I'll say this about Terry Fearnley - I was honoured to be part of his team. I thought he was a terrific person, and a very good coach. When he brought home a winning team from that series he deserved praise. But all he copped was criticism - to the extent that the sourness of the whole experience drove him right out of the game. That was rugby league's loss.

I don't recall any outward animosity among the players - despite the tendency for the tour to split socially into state-based groups. We were there to do a job, and we were mature enough and professional enough to do that. But it seemed to be just that - doing a job - without the closeness that the State of Origin experience or later Kangaroo tours generated.

For me it was a disappointment, and a puzzle. I was so, so proud to be an Australian player. I thought to myself: This is the pinnacle ... yet I knew that the feeling of being part of that team was nowhere near what it had been with the NSW Blues. It was not a tour to enjoy, and at the end of it I was happy to be going home.

Amid the raging controversy surrounding the dropping of the four Queenslanders (Greg Conescu, Chris Close, Mark Murray and Greg Dowling), I won my first Test jumper. I was proud to have it - but the Test of which I had dreamed for so long turned out to be a jolting experience. After the dropping of the Queenslanders - effectively upping the tension levels in the camp - our preparation was poor. In football, if you don't prepare right, you don't get it right ... and we didn't. The Test was a shocker - a real shocker, with the Kiwis belting us 18-nil. Five-eighth Olsen Filipaina had one of those days when he ran riot, their lock, Hugh McGahan, played magnificent football while half-back Clayton Friend scored two tries and was named man of the match. The game was a kick in the teeth for all of us. It was a fine New Zealand side and they just did everything right that day - to the delight of the mob at Auckland's Carlaw Park. They smashed us.

We had the Trans-Tasman Cup, but after that Third Test disaster we had our heads down and tails between our legs when he limped back into Sydney. The season had gone sour for a time, and things didn't get any better when Queensland stuck it to us in the third Origin match.

Gee, there was some hate in that game. The Queenslanders went out onto Lang Park as if they had a whole cartload of scores to settle. They came at us like maniacs ... I mean, they really went berserk. We knew it was going to be tough, but I don't think we were in any way ready for the depth of feeling that surfaced on that night.

The lowpoint came in an infamous moment in which Dowling, one of the four left out of the final Test in New Zealand, veered towards the touchline to give Terry Fearnley a mouthful of abuse after Queensland had scored in the second half. It was totally uncalled for - right out of order - and I think Dowling lost plenty of respect with a lot of players by doing what he did.

Queensland won the game comprehensively, 20-6, building the foundation in a first half in which the penalty count was 8-1 in their favour. Barry Gomersall refereed the match, and gained notoriety for his attitude to a wild brawl which erupted after the second scrum of the match. Although both touch judges raced on to the field, Gomersall chose to ignore the fracas, allowing play to proceed as we forwards battled it out. It was fairly typical of his quirky style of refereeing, a "bush" tactic which was incomprehensible in a showpiece such as State of Origin football.

I took a real belting, prompting something of an outburst when I talked to the Sydney *Sun's* Jenny Cooke:

"I took a bit of a bashing and for a while I thought: 'fair enough'. But there came a time when I thought: 'That's it, I'm not going to take it any more', so I retaliated - and that's not really my go."

Cooke wrote:

The next morning he could hardly move, his face covered with cuts, scratches, bumps and bruises.

"I like playing rugby league as it is - but when players do things like this that are not called for, it is degrading the code," says a young man obviously hurt more by the damage to the game he loves than the damage to his face.

This season Elias has been many things for Balmain: motivator, organiser - but above all, target.

The Queensland win brought a crowing such as you would not believe in the Brisbane press. Some of it was pathetic. Take the *Courier-Mail* match report, for example:

Queensland extracted sweet revenge from New South Wales and Australian rugby league coach Terry Fearnley when they sent the Blues packing to the tune of 20-6 in the third State of Origin match at Lang Park last night.

The comprehensive nature of last night's victory would not compensate for losing the 1985 series 1-2, but it would have given the four Queenslanders axed by Fearnley before the Third Test in Auckland a couple of short weeks ago plenty of satisfaction.

Christ!! Can you believe that? The match was "revenge" because an Australian coach had chosen the team that he believed was the right one for a Test match? Unbelievable! Talk about jingoism, bias and paranoia. Queensland is surely the home of all of them.

Veteran columnist Lawrie Kavanagh picked up the theme in an infamous "open letter" to Fearnley. He wrote:

Instead of being all for one and one for all, your sword play with just one particular section of the team split the touring party right down the middle ...

I don't think I have seen an Australian coach give so much unwitting help to another team as you did with the selection shambles. You took the sword to four scapegoat Queenslanders for that overall poor Australian performance in the Second Test.

And so ended a bitter-sweet representative year. Rugby league was a game on the move by the end of 1985, but I have no doubt it was chastened and knocked off stride by the unhappy New Zealand experience, and the sour State of Origin game that followed.

Never again did the ARL dabble with the folly of dispatching an Aussie side on an international mission midway through an Origin series. Furthermore, they decided that in future the Australian coach would not be in charge of either State of Origin side. Terry Fearnley turned his back forever on any official involvement in rugby league, and the door was opened for the genial Canberra Raiders mentor, Don Furner, to step into the top job as Australian coach.

8

The Unbeatables

I'LL REMEMBER 1986 for a lot of things. I'll remember it as the year I was in a Kombi van that rolled five times on a country road near Tamworth, in northern NSW, ripping my back open in the process; I still carry the scars. I'll remember it for the morning I woke with a headache so bad I thought my head would fall off my shoulders. A few hours later I was diagnosed as having viral meningitis. But most of all I'll remember 1986 for the fact that it was the year of my first Kangaroo tour.

What a sensational experience that was - to tour with Wally Lewis's "Unbeatables" (on the trail of the 1982 "Invincibles") - and to captain my country along the way.

I was 22 (I turned 23 on tour), still a young fella, and this triumphant campaign through England and France opened my eyes to a lot of things. I toured with a great football team which steam-rolled all opposition, winning 20 out of 20 games to match the achievements of Max Krilich's famous side of 1982.

The tour also provided my first experience of drug-taking in football. Six high-profile team-mates were occasional users of a popular social drug throughout the 10-week campaign. Obviously I can't (and would never) name them. We were part of a great sporting experience that year; what some of the other players chose to do with their money, and their time off the paddock was their business, not mine. But I was shocked - it really opened my eyes. Maybe I was naive, too. If drug-taking was rampant in everyday society - and it was - why wouldn't a team of 28 well-paid footballers reflect that reality to at least some degree? I suppose I just innocently presumed that someone involved in a high-level sport which required exceptional levels of fitness wouldn't be adding an illegal and expensive foreign substance to his system.

It was perhaps the first and only time that drug-taking was a fact of life on a Kangaroo tour. At the time of earlier tours the taking of social drugs was not so strongly entrenched in society. The letdown "drug" of Kangaroo tours had always been alcohol - and I'll admit to having my share of that as we celebrated the victories along the way in '86. By the next tour, 1990, the League had moved to slam shut the gate on illegal drug-taking. Random testing for drugs, backed by penalties strong enough to threaten a player's career, meant that, after an early blitz by the League, there were just no players who were going to take the odds about dabbling in drugs. To do so was to risk a career. But that came later, and in '86 things were freer and easier.

For me, it was a year that started horribly - and finished on the highest possible note. In January '86, I went to the annual country music festival in Tamworth with some mates. On a road just outside of town one afternoon, a car veered across towards our Kombi. We tipped, and then rolled five or six times. The first thing I recall is waking up in Tamworth Base Hospital being stitched up. I'd been knocked out in the accident.

I was amazingly lucky. My side of the van was just about squashed flat, but I wasn't strapped in. I was thrown out through the front window, and that's how I got badly cut.

They reckon that bad things come in threes, and that's

certainly the way it was for me in 1986. It wasn't long after the car accident that the second "leg" arrived. I was diagnosed as having meningitis. At the time I had a little bachelor's pad out the back of the family home. We had played a trial match in Ballina, on the NSW far-north coast, and I was uncomfortable, feeling "off" on the flight home. The next day I was struck down with a crushing headache; I took some Panadol and went to my room and lay down. It got worse and worse. I staggered outside and was nearly blinded by the light. I had an intercom in my room and I called my mother: "Mum, would you come to my room ... quick please."

Within a short time I was in the intensive care ward at Balmain Hospital. I felt like I was paralysed. They kept me there a week or so, and I gradually improved. But the virus had really flattened me, stripping off seven or eight kilos in weight, and Frank Stanton told me to forget football, take my time, and get well.

I finally got back onto the paddock, only to be crash-tackled by the inevitable third stroke of ill-fortune. I suffered a broken hand, in a National Panasonic Cup match against Canberra at Leichhardt, just as the rep games were coming around, and opened the door for Penrith's Royce Simmons. If anyone had to get hold of my NSW jumper, I was glad it was Royce. We're good mates - we've always shared a mutual respect. He's a great character Royce, a real good country bloke. He grabbed my spot in the Blues team, and made the very most of it as NSW brought off the first clean-sweep of a State of Origin series. Royce's fabulous performance in the first game, in which he was knocked rotten but came back to take the man-of-the-match award, ensured he was going to be the front-running hooker all year. When they picked the Test team to play New Zealand, he was a certainty.

In June, I was the subject of some ugly headlines when I was charged with biting Canterbury's tough prop, Peter

Kelly. We had whipped the Bulldogs, 28-nil at Parramatta Stadium, in a spiteful match in which the opposing hooker, Mark Bugden, and I had both spent 10 minutes in the sin bin. I have no idea whether Kelly was bitten or not, but the one thing I did know was that if he had been bitten - it wasn't by me.

The allegation was dismissed by the NSWRL Judiciary after Kelly had gone round in circles to some extent and finally came round to admitting that it might not have been me after all. I was represented at the hearing by a barrister, Steve Stanton, and a solicitor, Michael Conn. My relief was immense when the Judiciary chairman, John Riordan, declared: "The committee firmly believes that Kelly was bitten. But we find that the onus of proof has not been discharged and that there is no case to answer."

I could have done without the whole thing. The headlines created caused anguish for my parents, and that's what hurt me most.

My father's comments in the *Sun-Herald* at the time give a clear enough picture of what it did to them:

I felt sick in the stomach. It's a slur on Ben's character and good name to call him a biter. Ever since he was a seven-year-old he's been so much in love with the game. I've watched him all that time and I know what he will do and won't do on a football field. And I know he doesn't bite.

On the subject of foul play, there are three things that I deplore in the game - spitting, eye-gouging and biting. Those things have never been part of my game. Until the events of a certain afternoon in May, 1993, when I locked horns with a touch judge at Leichhardt, I had never been sent from the field, and can honestly say that I cannot recall one instance on the field - I'm talking about foul play, not mistakes or wrong options - when I thought to myself: "Shit, I shouldn't have done that!" I'm not an angel, but throughout my career my aim has been to play it hard, and to play it fair.

One way and another it had been a chequered first half of the year, and I copped some flak from *Rugby League Week's* mystery columnist "Sherlock". He (or she) wrote:

Recent events suggest that he (Elias) might be letting the pressure get to him. He has been complaining that a certain radio man has it in for him. He has been complaining that the press doesn't give him a fair go. He's been hopelessly preoccupied with the deeds of Mal Cochrane or Mario Fenech or Royce Simmons. In short he's worrying about everything except the one thing he should be worrying about - his *game. Come on Benny, relax! Stop worrying about all the side issues and pitch your concentration into the man who needs it - Benny Elias.*

When I read it now I think - hmmm, that was pretty fair advice. The radio man in question incidentally was 2KY's Ron Casey, who had seriously questioned Balmain's claims to be any sort of genuine premiership contenders - and done it in his usual forthright way.

"He's got to be joking - this is the best Balmain side I've played in," I had retorted in the press. "Casey simply likes sending people up, and as far as Balmain goes, he hasn't had a good thing to say for a while."

For a time that season I felt like a player under siege, to the extent that I decided to boycott the media. "I won't pick up a paper, watch sports shows on television or listen to the radio," I told the *Sun-Herald's* Ken Laws. "Every time I do I read, or hear, how badly I'm going. They're really giving it to me; I'm copping more off the field than I am on the paddock."

With Royce Simmons having slipped right under my guard in the matter of the no. 1 rep hooker's job, the task at hand was to make every post a winner at Balmain. And that we did in another excellent and highly competitive year, despite the occasional hiccup such as the day Western Suburbs flogged us 36-6 at Leichhardt. "Toothless Tigers!" roared the headlines the next day.

We lost our skipper, Junior Pearce, for the season when he wrecked a knee in the Third Test against the Kiwis at Lang Park. I took over as skipper, and we kept the momentum of 1985 going strongly to make it to the semi-finals. "We've had him in mind for a while as a future leader," said Frank Stanton, commenting on my elevation to the captaincy. "His maturity is showing through and we feel he can handle the job competently."

In a thrilling month of football we won four sudden-death matches in a row - Souths (final round 38-20), Norths (play-off for fifth 14-7), Manly (preliminary semi-final 29-22) and Souths (minor semi-final 36-11). After the Norths game, which finally got us into the semi-finals, some officials tried to bring champagne into the dressing room. We told them to piss it off. We had a long way to go - we weren't ready for champagne yet.

Our knockout semi-final win over Manly was one of Balmain's great days. The Sea Eagles had a team laced with internationals, and after just 16 minutes they had us down 12-nil and on the canvas. But, digging deep, we climbed back up and beat them, 29-22. *Rugby League Week* reported:

Balmain's rebound to win 29-22, and stay alive in the race for the title, will remain one of the great stories of the 1986 finals series - whatever else happens.

I was immensely satisfied with my own performance, and glowed with pride when Frank Stanton commented to the press that it had been "Elias' best all-round game." I scored a try and kicked a field goal, and relished every minute of that day at the Sydney Cricket Ground.

It was a tough and thrilling game. After being rocked by Manly's early onslaught we took charge. Scott Gale scored a try under the posts, Paul Sironen powered over for a second and then I scored after a simple wrap-around move. At 21-12 referee Kevin Roberts sent off Manly ace Cliff Lyons on a kneeing charge. With 13 playing 12 it should have been comfortable, but Manly pushed us all the way to the wire, getting to 25-22 after their fullback, Marty Gurr, scored a try nine minutes from the end. We didn't manage to close it all down until the 77th minute, when David Brooks charged over.

The following Saturday we faced the arch-enemy, Souths. The two old clubs have been deadly rivals ever since 1909, when Souths won the premiership on a forfeit - a day on which Balmain chose not to play the final as a protest at it being scheduled as a curtain-raiser to a "Wallabies v Kangaroos" game. At Balmain the theory has always been that Souths did the dirty that day after originally agreeing that they would also boycott the match. It was a long time ago, and the truth or otherwise of that belief is lost in the mists of antiquity, but I can vouch for the fact that Balmain-Souths games always have an extra edge to them.

This one sure did. *Rugby League Week* began their game report this way:

The scene was set before a ball was kicked. Mario Fenech, snarling, and Benny Elias, smiling, sledged furiously as Balmain and Souths took up their positions at the SCG last Saturday. It was a prelude to violent action - and to one of the most sensational semi-finals of modern times. The story is imprinted forever in the headlines. A semi-final, delicately poised at 8-all, was won and lost when referee Kevin Roberts peered deep into a scrum and in a moment of high drama, waved Rabbitoh skipper Fenech from the field, signalling ... 'gouging'.

It was a furious and controversial game and we romped home in the end, 36-11 - with Souths collapsing after Mario's send-off. Referee Roberts was the man in the eye of the storm. His send-off of Fenech was a brave and hugely contentious decision.

Late in the game referee Roberts incurred the full fury of the Souths camp when he failed to take action against Blocker Roach after what appeared to be a head butt in a tackle on the Rabbitohs' second-rower, Phil Gould. Blocker and Kerry Hemsley were towers of strength for us that day, stamping their authority on the game the way that dominant front-rowers should.

NSW Rugby League general manager John Quayle subsequently cited Block to appear before the Judiciary Committee the following Monday night. In his typically straight-down-the-middle manner, Blocker pleaded guilty to the charge, with his legal representative arguing for the Judiciary to consider a fine, a severe caution, or even a bond rather than suspend him.

But the Judiciary, headed by Richard Conti QC, took a hard line and suspended Roach. We would have to shape up for the final without him.

Gary Lester's view of the match in the *Sun* made interesting reading:

Souths' obsession with Balmain hooker Benny Elias in Saturday's dramatic minor semi-final at the SCG may have cost them their grand final dream ...

Souths had Elias in their sights from the time they ran onto the field.

One Souths player "mouthed" Elias before the game started and Balmain coach Frank Stanton believed Elias had been singled out from the first minute.

"When are they going to stop intimidating this kid?" Stanton said.

It had been a traumatic and testing day for me as Balmain captain, but I was as proud as punch ... and sore in every bone and muscle in my body. Souths were a very tough outfit indeed, with a fierce will to win that has never wavered at that club. My memories of the game are clouded as I "lost" virtually all the first half after taking a couple of heavy knocks. I didn't wake up until I was under the shower at halftime, but I know I copped a belting, as the match reports confirmed (one paper suggested I had been ambushed by a bunch of angry Rabbits). I was kayoed for the first time in only the fourth minute of play, and that set the scene. At least three times I was knocked down off the ball. In the dressing-room at halftime I was as sick as a dog, and coach Stanton asked me: "Can you go on?" I just nodded - there was no way I wasn't going to finish *that* game.

The match was continually physical. You weren't just tackled you were *hammered* every time you received the ball, and sometimes when you didn't. It was that sort of game. Ultimately we had the last laugh by sticking doggedly to our pre-match agenda of playing football, and forgetting the other stuff.

It was certainly one of my most satisfying matches. *Rugby League Week* rated Souths' hard man Les Davidson and myself as the men of the match. "Elias really came of age," declared *RLW* . "He took six scrums against the feed, some of them against a disrupted Souths pack, and provided courage that inspired his team to victory."

The victory celebrations were sweet that night, but short. We wanted to win the comp, and to do that we had to get past our nemesis of 1985, Canterbury, in the preliminary final.

On the same Monday night that Blocker was suspended, Mario Fenech was found guilty of a charge of "attacking the face of an opponent" and suspended for four matches. As it turned out, Mario served his sentence in England, with the Bradford Northern club.

Judiciary chairman Richard Conti announced the verdict after a marathon three-and-a-half hour hearing. The guilty finding was on a charge that differed from the one levelled by referee Roberts - "gouging the eyes of an opposing player".

Roberts told the hearing that he did not have the slightest doubt that Fenech had gouged me. He gave evidence that he looked into the scrum and saw Fenech's hand moving in an upward motion on my face.

It was a controversial ending to a highly controversial

match.

As has been often and accurately observed, a win only lasts a week - no matter how good it might have been. Within eight days our season was over. Canterbury had got the better of us again - and beat us 28-16. The pressure of the previous month had worn us down a notch, and the Bulldogs made the most of it. The clinching moment came when Steve Mortimer scorched through for one of *those* tries - his 71st for Canterbury - midway through the second half. We came back with late tries by Garry Jack and Garry Schofield, but the game was long gone by then.

My own season ended 16 minutes before fulltime. I had suffered a neck injury the previous week against Souths, and was in increasing pain as the Canterbury match developed, particularly in the scrums. Finally Stanton called me off, and sent utility forward John Owens into the fray. At the time the score was 22-4 and the contest was over. It had been a Balmain season of thrills and excitement - but again we had stumbled, with our goal tantalisingly in sight.

The Kangaroo tour dream sustained me through the next long and drawn-out week. I knew that Royce Simmons had one of the hooking spots sewn up, and all I could do now was to sit and hope that I could beat Greg Conescu to the other. I was in Balmain Leagues Club when the news came through - via the public address - with the team read out in alphabetical order. I had made it! My feeling at that moment is impossible to put into words ... it was relief, joy, anticipation and many other emotions all rolled into one. A supreme thrill of my life. To win selection on a Kangaroo tour is the pinnacle of achievement in rugby league. Benny Elias, the kid from Tripoli, Lebanon, who was too small to play football, had made it.

Selection for the tour, though, and the getting ready, was tinged with the disappointment I felt for my Balmain captain, Wayne Pearce. As is now a fact of rugby league history, Pearce was ruled out of the tour after "failing" a fitness test at Redfern Oval.

That remains surely one of the cruellest decisions ever made in the game of rugby league. Through late winter and into the spring of 1986, I had watched Junior Pearce work a miracle in fighting his way back to fitness. According to initial press reports the serious knee operation he underwent in the first week of August was to keep him out of football for 12 months. But Junior and his doctor, Merv Cross, saw it differently.

"How hard are you prepared to work?" the doctor asked Junior.

"I'll do anything to get it right," the Balmain captain replied.

And so began the most single-minded rehabilitation program that any Australian sportsman or woman has ever undergone. Pearce held in his mind the goal of making the '86 Kangaroo tour - against all the odds. With that dream firmly fixed he worked 10 ... sometimes 12 hours a day on his rehabilitation. "I pushed through barriers of pain I had never experienced before," Pearce recalled later in his 1990 autobiography, *Local Hero*. "Getting fit for the tour became my obsession."

I was well aware of Junior's fightback program, and urged him on. On crunch day, I was at Redfern Oval when he went through his fateful test ...

I doubt that any player in Australian sporting history has ever been given a more searching medical examination. Two hard men from Souths, Les Davidson and David Boyle, were there to help out as Bill Monaghan, the Australian Rugby League medico, and other ARL officials looked on.

Davidson and Boyle ran at Junior for almost half-an-hour, and he picked them up and dumped them, again and again. Then they tackled him. He did it all without a problem. His sprints were good, and his long stuff too.

Finally he had to do a 100-metre sprint across the

corrugated surface of Redfern to finish it off. I can see it now ... the fateful moment as his foot caught a pothole, or a bump. He stumbled slightly, then steadied and headed on without trouble. I knew he was a bit leg-sore after a long road run the previous day, and the stumble was nothing at all.

I left Redfern then, happy in the knowledge that Junior had achieved his goal, that he had beaten all the odds and proved his fitness for the tour.

It was on the car radio that I heard the news an hour or so later that he had been ruled out. I couldn't believe it. I'd seen the trial - I mean, the bloke was okay. Gee, I felt for him. I knew what he had been through, and knew how much it meant to him to make the tour. You don't get many shots at a Kangaroo tour in a football career and Junior had seen his last chance (as it turned out) whisked away from him. It was bloody cruel. He had been passed fit by one of the best orthopaedic specialists in the country in Merv Cross - and yet they had still ruled him out. On what I saw at Redfern that day as a footballer-layman, Wayne Pearce was as good as gold to tour.

A few days later the chosen Kangaroo tourists underwent a medical to judge our fitness to tour. We faced nothing like the test that had confronted Wayne Pearce. For us it was just the normal rep team "medical", conducted inside one of the dressing rooms at the Sydney Cricket Ground. Not for us any of the strenuous running, tackling, dodging that Junior had been put through.

Two players who had been in real trouble with injuries for weeks were cleared without problems to tour. Canterbury's Steve Folkes, who had been battling a serious groin injury, had not played a full match since being injured in the Third Test of 1986 against New Zealand. Manly's Dale Shearer had had a troubled path through the second round of the Winfield Cup, dragging a groin injury and other problems. Both were checked, and cleared to make the trip.

Folkes subsequently played six games of 20 on tour and Shearer 13.

Meanwhile the man who should have been the tour vice-captain, Wayne Pearce, stayed home. It was the toughest call of all in my years in rugby league.

Wayne's omission aside, the tour was everything I could have hoped for - except that I couldn't steal the No. 9 Test jersey away from my room-mate. Royce Simmons and I were "roomies" throughout the tour, separated by a line drawn down the middle of our pad at The Dragonara Hotel in Leeds, competing fiercely all the way for the prize of the Test jumper - but good and close mates all the same. We made a pledge that we would support each other, no matter how things turned out on tour.

I reckon I would have had to turn into the axe murderer to get the Test jumper away from Royce in 1986. He hung onto it with bull-terrier tenacity, and I understood that. I became the leaders of the Seconds - of "F Troop", as it became known within the team - and in that capacity had the honour of captaining Australia no less than seven times on tour. Coach Don Furner had a policy of virtually playing two separate teams - the top side, and the midweek team.

For my first game as captain there was an even greater thrill, when my mum, dad and my uncle Mowad flew over from Lebanon to watch me lead out the green and golds, against Hull Kingston Rovers. My parents were holidaying in Lebanon at the time, and had an extremely difficult time rushing from there to the north of England to see me lead the team out. But they made it, we won the game 46-10, and I scored two tries.

The tour was a fabulous experience, although the French leg was a huge anti-climax. The harmony in the Aussie team was extraordinary - there was none of the tension that had existed in New Zealand the previous year. We were a large and happy family, all heading in the same direction. I was just grateful to be there alongside so many brilliant players.

The management style was easy-going, via Furner and managers John Fleming and Gordon Treichel, and the mateship that was established was something that none of us will forget in our lifetimes. Peter Sterling was a key figure on that tour - a tremendous organiser who was always working something out, games and parties and outings. Wally, the skipper, wasn't interested in that role, so Sterlo, the official team vice-captain, took it over.

The tour once again linked the football careers of Elias B. and Fenech M. Suspended after his send-off in the semi-finals, Mario had joined Bradford Northern to serve out his suspension. I couldn't get away from the bloke. The Bradford game was always going to be a brutal one. I knew only too well going into it that Fenech would be out to make a point - to say: "I'm here because an incident involving *you*!" Fenech had stoutly denied the gouging charge. "I wouldn't mind (being sent off and suspended) if I had done what I was supposed to have done, but I'm innocent," he was quoted as saying.

Heading to Odsal Stadium, Bradford, on the tour bus I knew I was going to be in for a tough game, but I was comforted by the knowledge that I had the cream of Australia's rugby league players around me. I knew there weren't any better allies when the going was tough.

The match was all I expected, and more. It was a weird and fiery night - with a thick fog descending on the deep bowl that is the rather remarkable Bradford ground. Rex "Moose" Mossop, who was calling the game for Channel 10 in Australia, just about gave up trying to identify the ghostly figures flitting in and out of the mist. Mario, playing prop that night for the first time in his career, made it as tough as I expected he would. As Blocker Roach has put it, we stalked each other through the fog, and clashed repeatedly.

Fenech, in his first game for two months and his first

professional game at anything but hooker, called that fog-bound match: "The strangest experience I have ever had." Afterwards Fenech told an English pressman of his rivalry with me: "He does just the same things to me; it's just that's he's a little less obvious. I reckon I'm entitled to hit him as hard as I like, as long as it's within the rules."

It was a night that demonstrated the quality of Wally Lewis, footballer. Halfway through the first half we were just plodding along, basically going nowhere. Then Wally stepped in and took the game by the scruff of the neck. He just took charge - and we won 38-nil. I remember thinking to myself after one flash of magic: 'Geez, this bloke really is a genius.'

I have enormous respect for Wally Lewis. I take people as I find them, and I have always found him to be as good as gold. He has his own funny ways, but that's just Wally. I doubt that people have any idea at all of the sort of pressure he is under day after day, and has been for years. He's the most recognisable face in Queensland, and one of the most recognisable in all of Australia. He is on constant public show. He can't hide away in hotels like pop stars do. When he is out and about he's at the mercy of the public and if he gets a bit disgruntled, a bit short-tempered at times ... well, it's not hard to understand. He was a great player - a really great player.

With two aristocrats such as Lewis and Sterling at the helm, that '86 tour could not have been anything but successful. Sterlo is the greatest player of my experience, the modern master. No-one matched his field vision in a game, although Wally ran him close. On that tour I'd be pulling on a jersey before a game, and I'd glance across and see Wally or Sterlo pulling on theirs and I'd think to myself ... how great is this, playing with blokes like that!

Throughout that tour there was pressure on all of us to keep the unbeaten record intact. The record of the Invincibles loomed large over all of us - and we sure didn't want to be the next Aussie team to lose a match.

Only in France did things turn sour. I just don't fancy the place. The weather is colder than England, the food is terrible, the referees are dreadful, the football is bloody awful and the people are arrogant. At the games we played there was barely a quorum of spectators. It was a big downer, going from the comparative professionalism of the game at its top level in England, to that.

At least the French leg of any tour is guaranteed to provide some extraordinary tales for old players to tell their grandkids in years ahead. The match at Le Pontet, near the walled city of Avignon, was a case in point. Twenty minutes or so before kick-off the lights failed, plunging the ground into darkness. When the power was finally reconnected only half the lights were working. So the match went on in gloom, and descending fog. We won in a hand canter, 42-5, and at the end of it there was a wild brawl in which our big prop, Martin Bella, inadvertently clocked Wally Lewis, and in which our trainer, Larry Britton, was stomped upon. Blocker Roach almost triggered World War III when he gave the crowd a "fingers up" sign after he was sin-binned near the end.

The match we played in Paris was a joke, unpromoted and played on a suburban ground before a crowd of 700. The place was so obscure that a taxi driver bringing the touring press to the game had no idea where the ground was. After getting copious advice from various bystanders along the way he finally dropped the press gang at an entrance gate. They were promptly escorted in - to a basketball match! The French President's XIII was bolstered by three globetrotting Aussies that night (Ken Wolffe, Terry Stevenson and Will Tarry) and coached by another Aussie, Tas Baitieri. We beat them easily, 36-4.

Notwithstanding my lack of affection for France, I rate the Kangaroo tour the number one reward rugby league can offer. It beats everything else the game can put up.

While in France, I knocked back a $30,000 offer from Warrington to play eight games with them after the tour. I was tempted, but not too much. There are times when you have to draw the line and take a rest. As my old man says, a footballer's body can be equated with the soil; you have to let the soil lie fallow now and then to get back its nutrients, and ensure a good crop the next year. So it is with football players. The evidence surrounding players who have spent times with English clubs and then come back to the next Aussie season is that their form almost inevitably plummets. I said no to Warrington without too many regrets, and came home to the Australian summer.

It had been a wonderful year, despite the traumas at its beginning. I will not dwell at length on the season that followed so swiftly on the heels of the '86 tour - when my life dipped to its lowest ebb as I outlined in chapter one. Football-wise it was largely a blur for me. I was like a robot, going mechanically through the motions week by week, although there is tangible evidence that my form held together pretty well.

Inside, I was struggling though, with my enthusiasm level for football as low as it has ever been. Even getting to training had become a chore, reflected in an incident in July, when our new coach Billy Anderson dropped me for being late for training. Anderson told the *Sydney Morning Herald's* Roy Masters that it was the third time I had been late. Keith Barnes, who was doing his best to ease me through difficult times, intervened, and I held my spot.

Even after the relief of June 23, when the sexual assault charge against me was dismissed, it took a long time before I was anywhere near right again mentally.

When I look at the pages in my scrapbook covering the football side of 1987, it's almost as if I am seeing a stranger. There is one shot of a group of jubilant players after we won the $140,000 National Panasonic Cup (14-12 over Penrith at Parramatta Stadium). I'm right in the middle, celebrating with all the rest, jubilant like everyone else.

I was certainly entitled to be happy. That night I was somewhat stunned to be named the winner of the $20,000 series superstar award (of which I donated $8000 to charity). Not everyone approved. *Rugby League Week's* "Man on the Hill", Clive Galea, wrote:

Even the most one-eyed Tigers were embarrassed at Benny's award last Wednesday night.

It seems Benny needs only to run onto the field, kick the ball out on the full twice, miss a couple of field goals, make no breaks from dummy-half and abuse the second-marker rule to gain the critics' praise and man-of-the-match points.

Acid-penned Clive was entitled to his opinion. But like all the Tigers I was delighted to have won the cup, in a tough and fiery contest - and certainly welcomed the unexpected $20,000 award. The only difference was that I had something gnawing away inside me. Even that night, after a thrilling victory, I was awake at 4am, agonising over what the future held for me ...

The Frank Stanton era at Balmain had ended in 1986. His successor, Bill Anderson, was an excellent analytical student of the game. Bill was an academic among the coaches, with a really thorough knowledge of rugby league and how the game should be played. He just seemed to fall down a little when it came to putting his theories into practice. That's not a criticism - I have plenty of respect for him - and he could be judged unlucky to lose the job after only one year, and a pretty fair year at that.

Under Bill we had a very competitive season which at least maintained the momentum initiated by Stanton. We ran fifth, but failed by a fraction in the knockout semi, beaten 15-12 by the old foe, Souths. Phil Blake, who had gained a new lease of life after moving to Redfern, scored the try that provided the shade of difference, while the two kickers, Ross Conlon (Balmain) and Mark Ellison (Souths) kicked six and five goals respectively.

For 78 minutes the battle hung in the balance. There were never more than four points separating the two teams - and four times the scores were deadlocked. Ross Conlon kicked his six goals in succession - a wonderful effort in the pressure-cooker atmosphere of a semi-final. But with three minutes to play he missed one from a wide angle. A successful kick would have given us the lead, 14-13.

A penalty (for a deliberate forward pass) signalled the end for us in the 78th minute, as Ellison slotted over his final goal.

This time it was Mario Fenech's turn to enjoy the sweet taste of victory. "Today erased the bitter memory of what happened to me against Balmain last year," Mario told the media. "I'm still dirty about the way I was treated ... They couldn't prove I gouged so they got me on something else ... I've had to live with that ... the stigma of such a serious charge ... knowing that I let my team-mates down."

And me? Well, I would have loved to have gone on to a grand final and a premiership. But to tell you the truth I wasn't too sad the season was over. It had been an endurance test for me, although there were some sweeteners along the way - especially the winning of the Superstar award in the mid-week Cup. But to finish with football for the year meant a chance to fade back into obscurity, to heal.

It turned out to be a case of healing in more ways than one. I had had trouble with a groin injury throughout the year, and none of the umpteen bouts of treatment had helped much. My physio recommended that I fly to Adelaide to see a bloke who was reputedly the best in the business - a Dr Hyde by name. So I duly flew to Adelaide, and caught a cab to Dr Hyde's surgery. There I met him, a bloke in T-shirt, sweater and jeans, and sporting a beard. Frankly, I wasn't too hopeful. But he put me up on the table, and within a few seconds of investigation pushed a spot which almost put me up through the ceiling it hurt that much. "Sweet," said the doc. "I'll get that fixed for you in 10 minutes."

My problem was a muscle which was detached from the bone. I flew back to Adelaide around Christmas time and had the operation. Dr Hyde kept his promise - the operation was an absolute success.

Late in the year the news came through that Warren Ryan, the coaching mastermind of Canterbury's premiership wins in 1984 and '85, was to take over at Balmain in 1988. We had a fine side, one good enough to win premierships. Ryan had the reputation of being a prickly character, but he was a proven winner. Along with the rest of the Tigers I awaited his arrival with a mixture of cautious enthusiasm and sharp-edged interest ...

9

Grand Final Bribe!

ON THREE SUCCESSIVE nights, in the week leading up to the 1988 grand final, I received telephone calls offering me big money to throw the game. The bloke who rang (it was the same caller each time) told me he was a runner for a bookie. "There are big dollars for you if you're 'crook' on Sunday," he said. "It would be very much worth your while to meet me sometime this week."

I told him to piss off. But he was persistent - and he rang back twice in the next two days with the same message. It was frightening, and unsettling. I told Barnesy (Keith Barnes) about the calls and we agreed to keep it quiet. There were no advantages in going to the media, although I'm sure they would have killed for the story. We chose to let it lie, and get on with business. "Just ignore it," said Keith. "There is no way of knowing who the bloke is, and there is nothing to be gained by taking it any further."

It is a story I have never before told publicly, but it is something that has always nagged away at the back of my mind when I look back on 1988 - the Balmain year of so near and yet so far. Obviously a Tigers win in the grand final that year would have been enormously costly to someone ...

We were the fairytale story of the decade, the darlings of the media and, increasingly, just about everyone's favourite team as we strung together a succession of sudden-death wins under the burden of increasingly crushing pressure.

It was a fabulous time to be a Tiger. We built up a momentum which we thought would never stop, much of it based around the wild card in our line-up, the mercurial Ellery Hanley, Great Britain captain and rugby league's "Black Pearl".

At the end of the competition proper we had to beat the then competition leaders, Penrith, and Brisbane to even be sure of qualifying for a play-off for the semis. We beat the Panthers 16-14 in a desperate game at Leichhardt, and then the flashy Broncos, 20-10, also at home. The win over Brisbane completed a satisfying double. We had faced them at Lang Park in round seven, when they were unbeaten leaders and looking nigh-invincible. In a great match, it seemed as though they had winning momentum up when they fought back from an early deficit to level 18-all. But 13 minutes from the end, I pinched a try with a dummy and we went on to win 26-18.

I remember that try well. I half-saw one of their players break away from the marker position, and instantly decided to "go for it." They were thinking field goal - and were out to get the first receiver. I saw the glimmer of a chance - and luckily it came off. With Wayne Pearce sidelined, fighting a bout of viral meningitis, I captained the team that day, and was lucky to get through the game after taking a fairly nasty corked thigh into it.

In the Penrith match, their powerful centre, Brad Izzard, hit me with a tackle which set every bone in my body jangling. It was an enormous hit - a classic example of one of those perfectly-timed wipe-outs that you see about half-a-dozen times in a season. I thought I was in a bit of space at the time and it was like being hit by a runaway semi-trailer. Brad is no midget, and he got this one just right, causing me to further damage an already torn rib cartilage. I had needed four pain-killers to get me on the field for that game after a very uncomfortable week. I could have done without the Izzard special. From that point onwards to the end of our premiership campaign I was on pain-killers. It's a funny thing that when you're out on the paddock and something like that happens, you don't think about it too much. You just try and clear the cobwebs and get on with the game. It must be to do with the pumping of the adrenalin, because when you see it on the replay later you think: Christ!!! Was that me?? This was one of the daddy of all big hits, an express train job; my legs were thrown a metre off the ground.

Rugby League Week called it: "The most devastating tackle seen in Sydney for years."

I needed pain-killers to get me through training sessions in the week after that, and plenty on the match days that followed. At the time I quipped: "They have to find a new spot every time they give me a needle. When you add the holes from the acupuncture, I'm going to look like a dart-board."

The wins over Penrith and Brisbane gained us a toehold - a play-off against the Panthers to decide fifth spot in the finals. Both teams were sore and struggling, but we had clearly the better of it this time, winning 28-8. The bad news came a day or two later when Blocker Roach, our front-row cornerstone, was outed for four matches for an illegal tackle on Penrith's Chris Mortimer. I watched the replay of the "incident" again and again, and I thought it was a very tough penalty handed down by the Judiciary. No touch judge ran in at the time, and there was no action taken by the referee. I know that Blocker believes there might have been a sinister agenda in his suspension - that a club apart from Penrith may have had some influence in having him cited a day or so after the match.

I don't know about that, but I know that Balmain looked

at every possible way of getting the big bloke cleared - including the sensational scheme of flying him to England to sit out a game there with Warrington, the club Block was joining at the end of the season. The plan was that they would then fly him back in time for the grand final. Blocker would serve three matches in Sydney (the two semi-finals and the preliminary final of the Winfield Cup), plus the Warrington game. It was an inspired plot but it didn't come off. Apparently pressured by the NSW and Australian Rugby Leagues, Balmain belatedly stepped away from the scheme, and our hopes of having Blocker on deck for the big one were gone. Roach's bitterness about the whole thing intensified later, when no action was taken against Canterbury's Terry Lamb for the tackle that put Ellery Hanley out of the grand final.

The loss of Blocker Roach was disastrous - an immense blow, physically and mentally. But this Balmain side, under the firm hand of Warren Ryan, the inspiring captaincy of Wayne Pearce and bolstered by the injection of the champion Hanley, was a very tough outfit indeed.

One of our main men might have been missing, but in no way were we beaten yet.

My own form was extremely pleasing. The mixture of hard work and the crust of experience that was now on me produced some of the best football of my career. Ray Chesterton wrote in the *Daily Telegraph*:

Elias' performances for Balmain in the latter part of the season have re-written the dimensions of the hooking role. Never before - and possibly never again - has a hooker been able to boast skills that include kicking field goals, skilled ball distribution, elusive running, deft passing and winning scrums against the feed.

We pushed on minus Blocker, against the odds and defying the critics. We never looked like losing the preliminary semi-final against Manly, and beat them 19-6. We played beautifully that day. Among the goals Warren Ryan set us in matches was to get to 25 sets of six-tackles in a game, to make 25 "completions" in the modern jargon. On that day we got to 33, which was the best we had ever done. The following week came probably the pinnacle of the entire run - a wonderfully controlled performance against Canberra which brought us a 14-6 win, and glowing praise for the quality of our play.

We came back to win that one. Down 6-0 in the first half, we didn't find the front until the 62nd minute, when Ellery scored out wide to make it 8-6. A Ross Conlon penalty goal inched us further clear with five minutes remaining, and then Gary Freeman scoring the clinching try in the dying seconds.

We had one step to go before we reached the grand final, one hurdle to leap - a tough one - to beat Cronulla, the front-runners for most of the season, in the final. No team had even won a competition from fifth spot, but the feeling was growing that, just maybe, we could do it. The feeling of togetherness in the side by that stage was extraordinary. For weeks we had known that each 80 minutes we played could be our last; we just wanted to keep winning and winning.

Canterbury had cruised past the Sharks with surprising ease in the major semi-final (26-8), but it was a much more resolute Cronulla that lined up against us. The final developed into a particularly gruelling match, a real war of attrition with every yard gained an accomplishment. With the wear-and-tear factor taking effect, we were a fraction down on previous form, but a superb individual try by Ellery in the 71st minute rescued us, and we won 9-2, and thereby robbed a couple of admirable Sharks veterans - David Hatch and Dane Sorensen - of *their* dreams of winning a premiership. My own field goal (the 21st of my career) in the 59th minute had played its part, breaking a 2-2 deadlock. Our defence was great, and three times in that game we won scrums against the feed through the sheer power of the push. We had made it ... we were in the grand final!

In the dressing-room our super-supporter Laurie Nicholls was in tearaway form. "Ellery eats celery" he was shouting, and "Ben-knee, Ben-knee!" And, of course, the Nicholls catch-cry which signalled any match featuring the Black and Golds: "Tigurs!" "Tigurs!". Laurie is very special at Balmain, the best supporter in rugby league.

In the week that followed, coach Ryan did his level best to keep us steady, to keep us on course. He tried to defuse the enormous hype that had built up around us. Warren told us not to believe what we read in the papers, just to focus on what we had to do. His previous grand final experience was a great bonus for the club at that time.

But in retrospect, I'm not sure the club handled it too well. It had been 19 years since Balmain had been in a grand final and the expectations and pressures were enormous. Our magic run from the play-off to the grand final had given the team superstar status, and I don't think we handled it as well as we could have in that final week.

The big mistake was a gala Balmain luncheon - the day before the game! That was the worst move - it was pandemonium there, with our jumpers being raffled off, and grand final fever raging at unbelievable levels.

Psychologically I believe we blew the 1988 grand final right there. It was *exactly* what Warren Ryan had been trying to keep us away from. But there was an obligation to our supporters - and we fulfilled it.

After the dust had settled on the '88 season, I remember reading of Parramatta's gaffe back in 1976 when the team had a cavalcade of honour, a ticker-tape parade through the streets a few days before the grand final. I know that the Eels coach of the time, Terry Fearnley, always regarded that as a major mistake. I look back on our 1988 grand final luncheon in exactly the same way. The losing of the grand final began that day. We were acclaimed as heroes - and yet the job had not been completed.

The grand final turned out to be a flat game, and a bitterly disappointing event for us. We started well - I put up a bomb in the 21st minute, and scored a grand final try after Mick Neil was there first to knock the ball back - with his head! The Bulldogs' prop and captain, Peter Tunks, stood on me early in a tackle, and earned 10 minutes in the sin bin for his misdemeanour. But if any match has ever turned on one event - then this was that match.

Twelve minutes before halftime, our gamebreaker, Ellery Hanley, was caught in a joint tackle by Andrew Farrar and Terry Lamb. The tackle brought no great roar from the crowd. It didn't seem to have hit with any extraordinary impact ... it seemed a run-of-the-mill sort of moment at the time, not an unusual tackle in a big game, long before the League's welcome clamp-down on high shots.

But that one moment, that one tackle sure did change the 1988 grand final. One day I'll bring myself to have another look at it. So far I have never wanted to watch the video of the match. The theory is that it was Lamb who went in high in the tackle on Hanley.

Whatever happened in that moment, Ellery was in dreamland, escorted from the field on rubbery legs. Hanley, proud captain of Great Britain, was one of the toughest men I have ever met in football, a tremendously durable player able to soak up extraordinary levels of punishment. I can still see Paul Sironen hammering him with absolute block-busters in the Test series of 1990, and Ellery coming back for more and more.

On this fateful day there is no doubt we all expected he would be back in the match with us after halftime. By then he would have had more than 20 minutes to clear his head. With that clearly in mind, Warren sent Ellery back on the field for the final two minutes of the first half, in the belief that the halftime break would be sufficient to clear the cobwebs away.

But Ellery never came back, and his non-appearance

after halftime was the psychological boost that carried Canterbury onwards to their decisive win.

In the dressing-room at halftime, when I learned that Ellery would not be rejoining the match I went across to him and put my hand on his shoulder: "Come on, Ellery," I said. "Do it for us, mate. There's only 40 minutes to go, and we need you out there. Even if you're not right - just you being there on the field is going to make the difference. We can win this ... just 40 more minutes. Think of what we've been through ... there's just 40 minutes." I positively pleaded with the bloke.

He looked up at me and said: "Honestly Benny, I'm knackered. I can't go on, I can't go on ... I don't know what I'm doing."

We went back out there and got beaten 24-12. The magnificent charge of the previous six weeks finally crumbled away in the last little bit, when all aspects of our play fell away. At halftime we were down only 12-6, and the game was absolutely in the balance. I will be convinced to my dying day that at full strength, with Ellery Hanley on the paddock, we would have got home on adrenalin and enthusiasm in the second half.

I have never attempted to hide my personal disappointment at the fact that Hanley did not come back out for that second half. I respect the fact that he had taken a knock but ... Christ! ... this was a grand final!

That day was about the only time Ellery Hanley disappointed me. I had a lot to do with the bloke after Keith Barnes brought off the giant coup of signing him. I picked up Ellery and his fiancee, Debbie, at the airport on the day they arrived, and I organised a house for them, just around the corner from my place.

I remember the drive from the airport very well. All Ellery wanted to know about was Sydney football. He wanted to know about Warren Ryan, about all our moves, about how we played the game.

I left him and Debbie at lunchtime, then picked him up again later. This time Ellery did the talking. He had absorbed everything I had told him; he ran through all the players, the moves. By the time we trained that night he knew all the calls. I had never struck anyone quite like him. He was the supreme footballing professional. I thought: we've been working on these bloody things all year and this bloke's been here five minutes and knows them all already! Gee, I was impressed. He turned out to be a fabulous player for us.

I liked the guy a lot. I found him a pleasant and intelligent bloke to be around, and that will probably come as a surprise to members of the British media who have been in a situation of open warfare with him for years. I have plenty of sympathy for Ellery in that area. I think the press treated him really badly - they intruded on his privacy to the extent that he finally put up a wall. His attitude was: "Stuff you - if you're going to treat me like that I won't talk to you anymore." And he didn't.

A complex man, Ellery - very sensitive, very loyal when he gets to know you, and very cautious of people. He had a hard upbringing and he tended to be wary of people until he had assessed them as "okay".

In 1988 he brought Balmain alive. I doubt that any single player in the history of the game has had such a sustained impact in such a short time. He was black, he was athletic, he was quietly spoken and gentlemanly, and a good-looking bastard - an *extremely* marketable product.

On the paddock he was just a great player - a dynamic package, who played with enthusiasm and a shrewd sense of what was going on and what needed to be done. His footwork was sensational and he had this tremendous upper-body strength, even though he never did any weight work. He was one of the best-balanced players I have ever seen. It was a very, very positive feeling to have him in the team in 1988.

Along with all his other qualities, Ellery, in my opinion, was powerfully motivated by money. When he left Balmain in 1988 he gave his word that if he came back to Sydney, he would come to Balmain. But the following year he joined Western Suburbs on a huge contract.

After we had lost the grand final of '88 we went back to Balmain Leagues Club. If you hadn't heard the score you'd have thought we'd won the game for sure. The crowd was amazing. Picture if you can, Victoria Road (one of Sydney's biggest thoroughfares, which runs past the Leagues Club) with cars parked all the way up the median strip. Inside, the club was jammed with supporters. The applause when we walked in was genuinely deafening. We had stumbled at the last hurdle, but the fans were very proud of what we had given them, of what we had achieved. And we were too.

We had given it our best, and we could walk with our heads held high.

It was a milestone year in my career. My form had been as good as it had ever (or has ever) been. Max Krilich called me the best forward in the game. Warren Ryan was quoted as saying I was the best forward in the world, and the respected scribe and league historian, George Crawford, picked me in his all-time great Balmain team. After the miseries of 1987, it was a great year to be alive.

The season finished on a magical note when I won back the Australian jumper. Greg Conescu had played all three Tests against Great Britain that year, but a sensational and unexpected win by the Poms in the Third Test, at the Sydney Football Stadium, meant that changes were certain for the World Cup Final, to be played against the Kiwis in New Zealand at the end of our premiership season. A broken hand had affected my chances for the home Tests, but now I was ready.

I played two State of Origin games that season - two losses, unfortunately - the second and third games. The second game, before a baying Lang Park crowd of 31,817, turned out to be one of the most controversial of all Origin nights. The tasteful pre-game entertainment consisted of a belching cane toad consuming 13 battery-operated cockroaches. It set the scene nicely. On the football side of things it was the match in which Blocker Roach strayed temporarily from the tracks and flattened Maroons second-rower Bob Lindner off the ball, setting up a howling in the bleaches. And it was the game in which NSW prop Phil Daley roughed up Conescu in a tackle, prompting Wally Lewis to sprint in, thereby sparking a near all-in brawl. With order more or less restored, referee Mick Stone gave Conescu and Daley 10 minutes each in the sin bin ... then added the brave and monumental step of dispatching King Wally as well (for five minutes), for abuse.

At that point World War III broke out as cans - full and empty - rained down on Lang Park. One (empty) can collected me on the scone. With the match temporarily suspended, most of us retreated to the relative safety of midfield, although the thought was always in mind that the mob would very likely be over the fence and after us. It was a scary feeling.

Finally the football resumed, and Queensland won 16-6, to wrap up the series 2-nil. It was a very tight, very close game, in which the NSW performance redeemed a poor Blues effort (18-26) in the first game in Sydney.

It was one of those games in which a brawl was the psychological turning point. I have some memory of the infamous Newtown-Manly semi-final stoush in 1981. That all-in roughhouse, which featured one of the worst one-on-ones ever seen - Newtown's Steve Bowden v Manly's Mark Broadhurst - unsettled the favourites, Manly, just long enough for Newtown to sneak away and win the game. At Lang Park that night in 1988 I reckon the brawl, followed by the can-throwing, was enough to bring undone NSW's winning momentum. They settled better than we did after the resumption, and the game slipped away from us.

There was general agreement that the 16-6 scoreline was an unkind one to us, judged on the ebb and flow of the game. None of that mattered. The series had been run and won ... and we had run second.

Things didn't improve in the third game, either. This was a free-wheeling, open sort of match in which we led 18-6 before getting steam-rolled 38-22. The Queensland strongman, Sam Backo, capped a great series by scoring two tries in the game.

NSW coach John Peard copped plenty of flak after the whitewash, most of it undeserved. The selectors chopped and changed with the teams they handed him that year, making his task difficult. Plus we were up against a brilliant Queensland side - a team right at the height of their powers.

I thought Peardy did the very best he could. Matched against a Queensland team who were nigh-unbeatable, he was in the wrong place at the wrong time. But I never had doubts about the bloke himself. He knew the game well, and he had the ability to convey his thoughts clearly and precisely. His rapport with the players was excellent. He was just a bit stiff to be coach *that* particular year.

Heading into Auckland for the World Cup final in October of that year was just like going to Brisbane for a State of Origin match. The whole city was revved up with World Cup fever. They were going to *smash* us! They reckoned they had their strongest side in history, plus the bonus of having had a number of their players hardened and toughened by a season in the Winfield Cup. Balmain had six reps on duty in the game - Sirro, Junior, Blocker, Jimmy Jack, Gary Freeman (NZ) and me.

Well, as it turned out we smashed them - got them early in a match played in tremendous atmosphere and on a beautiful surface at Eden Park. We won 25-12 after galloping away to 25-nil. The new halfback on the block, Queensland's Allan "Alfie" Langer (tagged the "Ipswich Imp" in one paper), had a great game, scoring two tries and winning the man-of-the-match award. Our captain, Wally Lewis, suffered a broken arm in the first half, but battled on until halftime. We were never going to let it go, although they came back with consolation late tries by the Iro brothers, Kevin and Tony. It was a supremely confident and satisfying performance, and especially for me - considering that my previous game for Australia in New Zealand had been in the same town, in the disastrous Third Test of 1985.

That day represented probably the most outstanding performance by any team I have ever been associated with.

How sweet it was - to finish such a year like that.

10

Wozza

MY FEELINGS ABOUT Warren Ryan, the man who coached Balmain in three tumultuous years, 1988-89-90, are genuinely mixed. I don't like him as a human being, but I think he's a terrific football coach. Simple as that. Notwithstanding the second point, I think that if history is one day fair dinkum it will eventually attach the tag "Ryan's Folly" to the 1989 grand final. It was a game that Balmain should have won, and to my dying day I will remain convinced that we threw it away when the coach chose to replace our forward kingpins, Paul Sironen and Steve Roach, in the second half.

Keith Barnes took a gamble when he signed Ryan, the successful coach of Canterbury between 1984 and 1987, late in 1987 for the 1988 year. At Canterbury there had been long-running dramas surrounding the coach, and it seemed that he had thoroughly outstayed his welcome. Keith did his homework thoroughly. He was well aware that Ryan had a reputation of being a difficult bloke to deal with at times, but he also had a record which left no doubt he was a hell of a coach.

In the short term he was the perfect man to build on the professionalism that Frank Stanton had planted in the club. We awaited his arrival with interest and some trepidation. In his typically blunt way he told us early: "I'm not here to make friends, I'm here to make premiers." He was absolutely true to his word, with the invaluable capacity (for a coach) of being able to push aside any personal feelings in the interest of securing winning football. You could be his best buddy - but if you weren't good enough for first grade in his judgement, then you weren't going to be there. He stamped his authority on the place from day one. Warren was only interested in one thing - winning.

I don't think there's any doubt that Warren sees himself as the great analytical mind of rugby league. There was an arrogance about him - but he was, and no doubt still is, an outstanding coach. And despite that arrogance - that personal confidence that he was, without doubt, the "Greatest" - he had a mind open enough to welcome anything new that he felt might benefit the cause. He was always ready to take in any creative ideas. He'd listen, and if he didn't like it, he'd say: "No thanks". But if he liked what he was hearing, then he'd incorporate it. That was part of his secret as a winning coach.

Warren's mind was switched on to football at all times. You'd say: "Hello Warren, how are you?" and he'd be talking football straight away. I recall an early trial game we played at Cessnock, after which we got together for a few beers. Before long he had all the empty middy and schooner glasses shuffling around the table, and we were full-on into a tactical discussion about rugby league.

For much of his stay I thoroughly enjoyed the training sessions. Warren was tremendously innovative; contrary to popular opinion, he was not a restrictive coach who programmed things too much. He certainly gave me leeway to be creative around the rucks. "I'm not going to tell you how to play," he said to me. "You do what you want."

He had us all playing our particular roles, all doing something - preaching the belief that when everyone was doing something the opposition would be uncertain of what was going to happen. He was a brilliant analyst of a game.

He'd show us on video where an opposition team was weak, and then we'd go out and train and play towards the aim of targetting that weakness.

I'll never forget a game we played against Canterbury at Leichhardt, in which we were down at halftime. At the break, Warren said: "Look, the winger on the short side is dropping back to support the fullback. The first set of six you get at them in the second half, play out the six, and play them on the short side." So out we went - did exactly what he suggested - and scored a try down the short side!

Things like that had us really believing in him. He was such a practical coach; he'd show you visually what had to be done, then coach you physically towards achieving that goal. We'd play the Broncos and he'd say: "You're never going to beat the Broncos out wide with that backline of theirs. The only way to go is through the middle. I'll show you." And that's what we'd work on.

Oh, he knew the game alright. But geez, he could be a difficult bastard - abrasive and arrogant. It reached the stage where I just didn't like him at all. I hated the bloke. We soldiered on with this love-hate relationship. I liked the coaching ... but I sure didn't like the coach. When he finally left Balmain the timing was right. He'd run out of friends. Funnily enough, I think the bloke has mellowed in recent times. Maybe he's realised there's more to life than football.

As I have recorded, it was Frank Stanton who brought professionalism to the club, plus togetherness and a feeling of mateship. Ryan, the hard professional, built on that. If training started at 4 o'clock, you had be to there at a quarter to. He preached the gospel of hard work, of extra work if you wished to succeed. He was the one who introduced the extra weight training, the extra sprint training.

The general belief in the game is that players make the coach. Warren saw it differently. In his eyes it was the coach who made the players. His influence on the club was considerable, and yet ...

In 1988, we had our backs to the wall. Halfway through the year we were struggling to make the semi-finals, but we eventually did. It was Ellery Hanley, rather than Warren Ryan, who turned it around. Ellery was our "X" factor, and the credit for his arrival, and the monumental successes that followed, belongs to Keith Barnes. Coach Ryan has been loaded with praise for what we achieved. And yet the fact was we had a bloody good side. We had umpteen internationals, including one of the world's best halfbacks in Gary Freeman, the world's best fullback in Garry Jack, and the world's best goalkicker in Ross Conlon. Plus Junior, Sirro, and Blocker. It was a great mix, and without question the difference between a fair year and a near-great year was Ellery Hanley ... not Warren Ryan.

After our fabulous second half of the season in 1988, season 1989 was always going to be a year of excitement. The feeling was there all along that this was going to be *our* year. Twenty years on from the last Balmain premiership, it was time.

As often seemed to be the way with me, I was off to a bumpy start. In a match against Penrith at Penrith Park, a screwing scrum, which twisted at an awkward angle, left me with a sore neck. Later in the first half, I heard a distinct "crack" when I positioned my head badly for a tackle. I finished the game, in which we took something of a shellacking, 28-8, but my neck was hurting, and I had pins and needles down my left side. It was a scary experience. They took me off the paddock, and then to hospital by ambulance, with my neck in a brace and with sandbags (borrowed from a television crew) packed around my upper body so that I wouldn't move.

They kept me in Nepean Hospital until midnight and did all sorts of X-rays and tests. Fortunately all was okay - but it was a jolting experience. At the same time we had a major problem with my mum. She had flown to Lebanon to visit her mother, who was very ill. Planning to be there only two weeks, Mum had been trapped by the intensifying war, which had caused the closure of Beirut Airport. She was there at the time the fighting in the capital was at its worst, and for seven weeks there were no commercial flights out of the country. Back here in Sydney, so far away, we were worried sick. There'd be daily reports of numerous people being killed, and it was just about impossible to make contact with her. The phone system was chaotic, and we just couldn't get through. Dad was distraught, and we all felt pretty helpless. Finally, in May, mum managed to hop on a plane in Beirut and get out of the place. It was a wonderful reunion when she finally touched down at Sydney airport.

Amid this family trauma, I had a problem of a vastly different kind. One night I received a phone call from Maurice Lindsay, chairman of the Wigan club in England, who made a simply sensational offer. Wigan wanted to sign me for two years, and the offer was extraordinary - around $400,000. It was tempting - to join one of the best club teams in the world ... the chance of travelling ... the chance of playing in a cup final at Wembley in front of 80,000 people. I talked to Keith Barnes, who I count more as a friend than a club official. I talked to my family at length, and to my employers. It was an immensely tough decision. An extended deal with Wigan could have set me up for life. And it wasn't just the money. Wigan were very special in the rugby league scheme of things, and it was an honour to be invited to join them. It's a pretty exclusive club. Maurice rang me one night to re-inforce Wigan's keenness. "Look mate, we want you at all costs ... *whatever* the cost," he said.

Finally, I said no. Keith Barnes talked about what lay ahead for us all at Balmain - and things certainly looked great at that time. And he made the point strongly that the English option could always be "on hold" - a career move later in my footballing life. So, after much agonising, I signed a new deal with the Tigers, one that cost me thousands of dollars. A *Daily Mirror* headline suggested "Benny's $120,000 sacrifice". They weren't too far off the mark. But money isn't everything, I told myself.

The Balmain offer was outstanding in its own right. They doubled my contract money for 1989-90, and extended my deal with the club to the end of the 1992 season. Keith Barnes and I sealed it with a handshake. With a bloke such as "Golden Boots" you don't need anything more than that.

The truth was that I never really wanted to leave Balmain. I have had a variety of "nibbles" over the seasons, but the place is too much in my blood. When Laurie Freier was appointed to coach Easts in 1983, he called me over to his place at Maroubra one day and said: "I want you on my contract list. How much money will it take me to get you away from Balmain? I've got an open cheque ... all you have to do is fill in the figures." That was a time when Easts were throwing money at players as if they had their own personal mint at the club. Maybe they did.

Parramatta made me a very tempting offer early on. That was when I was living at West Ryde and going to Westmead College. It was a good and serious offer, but I said no. I've had various other calls over the years but my answer was pretty much a standard one: "Look, thanks for calling - but I'm happy where I am." The Wigan offer was the closest I ever came to leaving Balmain.

My father has had a strong influence on me declining offers to leave Balmain. Once he caught the rugby league (and Balmain) bug he has always been a passionate supporter of me staying a Tiger. He tells a story about an offer I had to leave the club in my early years at Balmain. At the time I was considering my future he was overseas, in the US. From there he sent me a telegram which basically said: "Ben, if they are trying to persuade you to go elsewhere, I'll give you the difference to stay at Balmain." I stayed.

At the end of the Kangaroo tour of 1986, when I was in strong demand to stay on and join Warrington, he was the one who ultimately talked me out of the temptation. He was aware of famous players who had been to England, but had been injured, affecting their careers. "There is no way I want you to even consider this offer," he said. "Even a machine has to have a rest or it burns out. You're a human being - blood and bone - and you've got to have a rest, too. Don't forget you're playing *sport* ... you're not just playing for a living to make money." I listened - and came home to Australia.

On the field in '89 I was in some strife. Twice in that season there were newspaper allegations that I had bitten an opposition player - first the Country Origin captain, Chris Mortimer, and then the fiery Penrith second-rower, Mark Geyer. A spectator brought a sign to one of the grounds - "Benny Elias, the Great Australian Bite".

"Louie" Mortimer and I, the opposing captains, were the centre of sensational headlines after the City-Country game on May 13. On field there were indications that Mortimer had been bitten, and furthermore, that I had been gouged in a tackle. Claim and counter-claim. Being a couple of old pros, Louie and I chose to leave it right there - on the field, and nothing more came of it.

With Geyer, I'll tell you what happened. The match was second-placed Penrith versus third-placed Balmain at Leichhardt in August, a game in which we smashed them, 33-6. The big bloke, who is now my team-mate at Balmain, had his fingers halfway down my throat as he made a tackle, ripping and tearing. I mean what do you do in a situation like that? I wear a mouthguard, but if someone's got a fist halfway down my throat, and is doing his best to choke me, then I'm going to bite him. I'd imagine anyone would do the same thing. The incident with Mark was a pure survival thing. As I have said, I believe gouging, spitting and biting are the ugliest offences in rugby league. There is no way that, as an aggressive and attacking act, I would grab someone's finger and bite it. But if a bloke's doing his best to re-arrange my face, well ... that's different.

I had long since been a target in the game. As dummy-half I was the focal point of the attack, and over the years I have become used to the message "Get Elias", with other verbs sometimes substituted for "get". That sort of pressure was at its most intense in 1988-89. I just had to learn to live with the constant sledging and the physical manifestation of the message: "Get Elias". I was in the survival business.

I missed the State of Origin Series in 1989 because of injury, with Mario Fenech getting the nod at hooker for the first two games, and Easts' David Trewhella for the third. In the City-Country game fans witnessed the unusual spectacle of the old buddies, Elias and Fenech, with their arms around each other. Mario came off the bench to play prop that day. Being together in the same side that week had broken the ice to an extent.

It turned out to be an excellent Origin series to miss. A fabulous Queensland team, one of the best state sides of all time, donkey-licked the Blues three-straight - 36-6, 16-12 and 36-16.

At the end of the series, there was a weird co-incidence. Mario Fenech suffered a broken thumb before the third Origin game, and thus lost his chance to tour New Zealand with the Australian team. I was in line to take his place, sharing the tour hooking job with Brisbane's Kerrod Walters. But in a match against Easts at the Football Stadium, I broke *my* thumb, and Trewhella got the tour spot.

So for me there was no state jumper in '89 ... and no green and gold. But there was still the supreme prize of the Winfield Cup and Giltinan Shield, and they were steadfastly in our black and gold sights.

Balmain had started the year flashily, winning the $90,000 Nissan Sevens tournament, at Parramatta Stadium, with me as captain. But our first half of the premiership season was nothing better than moderate. We won only six of our first 12 games and at that stage of the competition year had key forwards, Paul Sironen, Steve Roach, Bruce McGuire, and Kiwi halfback Gary Freeman on Test duty in New Zealand. The job of even making the semis looked a daunting one.

But we had shown in '88 that we thrived on pressure football and again in 1989 we dug deep to find the qualities we needed. From that mid-season point, we lost only two more of the 13 games we played - building tremendous momentum towards the semi-finals.

We finished third on the premiership ladder on 29 points, behind Souths (37) and Penrith (32), beautifully placed to go on with it. We faced our first semi-final hurdle with enormous confidence, playing Penrith, who we had thrashed 33-6 in the last round of the premiership proper. We beat them comfortably again, 24-12 this time, leading throughout and never looking under much threat.

It had been a difficult match preparation for me. I picked up a virus, and spent days in bed, as weak as a kitten. I could barely walk around the block on the day before the match. But mum's chicken broth helped get me through. That and the adrenalin rush of a big game. It's amazing how resilient the human body is. You can be way below par, and yet you can still find something for the big occasion. I helped set up a couple of tries against the Panthers, and was happy with my game under the circumstances. I had trained only once that week - briefly, on the Saturday morning.

The next week we faced the minor premiers, Souths, in the major semi-final for the prize of a grand final spot. Played in stifling heat, this match was true to the tradition of epic Balmain-Souths struggles over the years. We led them early, but they fought back to 10-all, 15 minutes into the second half, when Phil Blake put his winger, Ross Harrington, over for a try.

Thirteen minutes from time, there was a key moment in which I was fortunate enough to be the central figure. Souths' Mark Ellison was just a fraction slow with a clearing kick and I got to him, charging down the ball. I was then able to pounce on the ball as it rolled loose.

From the next play, our five-eighth, Mick Neil, scouted wide and put centre Andy Currier into a gap. Away went the big bloke from the English club side, Widnes, over for the try that changed the game. Currier, tall and lean, but constantly under fire for his supposedly soft defence, was a wonderful acquisition for the club in 1989. Balmain had planned to re-sign Ellery Hanley, but Ellery much preferred the quantity of the Western Suburbs dollars. Currier, a goalkicker and try-scoring opportunist, did a mighty job in his stead, playing a big part in everything we achieved.

We eventually beat Souths 20-10, and no doubt the fierce nature of the struggle softened them up for Canberra the following week in the preliminary final.

On that late afternoon of September 10, 1989, the major semi-final having just been won, we were in sight of our dream. In two weeks time we would play the grand final. Eighty minutes more of quality football, and the prize was ours ...

11

The Game That Got Away

IT HAS BEEN called the greatest grand final of them all. For me it will never be anything but the one that got away. Our 19-14 loss to Canberra at the Sydney Football Stadium on Sunday, September 24, 1989, will give me nightmares for the rest of my life.

Has ill-fate ever conspired so cruelly against a football team? A 12-2 halftime lead ... a freakish ankle-tap that robbed Mick Neil of a try just as he was about to put it down ... a Wayne Pearce fumble in the backline as we raided with a three-man overlap ... a field goal shot by me at 14-8 which needed just another two centimetres to climb over the bar. Geez! It hurts as much now as it did on that afternoon four years ago.

I wonder if Warren Ryan has nightmares, too? Even Warren, so seemingly sure of the expertise and correctness of his views on football, must surely agonise now and then over the fateful decisions he made that day ...

It is my view, and it will never change, that the coach's decision to take off Steve Roach (after little more than an hour) and Paul Sironen (just before Canberra winger John Ferguson scored the last-gasp try that sent the match into extra time) was the difference between us winning and losing that grand final. We led 14-8 when Ryan took Blocker off and were still clinging on when he called Sirro from the field. The replacements, Kevin Hardwick and Michael Pobjie, were honest journeymen footballers; Hardwick in particular was a wonderful servant of the Balmain club. That they were not in the same league as the two great international forwards they replaced is no reflection on them.

I'm sure that Warren will argue the coach's point of view for as long as he is asked about it. Give him an hour and he'll justify it brilliantly. I know, however, that he could never justify it in 100 years to the Balmain players who were out there on the paddock.

I'll tell you what it was like out there in the middle. When Blocker departed you could sense Canberra lift just a little. I couldn't believe it. We're talking about the best and most creative front-row forward in the world at that time. Out on the field someone commented: "Blocker's gone off ... what's wrong with him?" I suppose that's what we all presumed - that Steve was injured. Surely he wouldn't be taken off for any other reason. But big Blocker wasn't injured.

When he was gone you could sense a little psychological buzz on the other side. The Raiders big prop, Glenn Lazarus, was running a stride faster, the defence was a fraction keener. They sniffed that something good had happened for them.

And then the coach took Sirro off, too. The big bloke had scored a great try in the first half, and was sustaining his effort well - a worry to the Raiders' whether he was hitting the ball up, or crunching them in defence.

Another negative aspect of the decision to take Roach and Sironen off the field in the grand final was the apparent lack of feeling displayed towards two proud footballers. Week after week they had been such key men in our charge towards the premiership. Now we had the winning of the grand final within our grasp - and it was for sure that these two champion forwards wanted to be there in the 80th minute to savour that moment.

What was worse was that the changes in our line-up gave Canberra a reason for believing they could win the game. I'm damned sure I would have been pissed-off to the extreme if my coach had taken me off the field that day. Lazarus was to tell Blocker later: "As soon as you two went off we all just thought automatically - we'll win this!"

In my experience, successful coaches, almost without exception, are men of substantial ego. They like nothing better than to be seen to be in absolute control, to be able to dictate absolutely the terms of their area of expertise - the football field. It is my opinion that Warren, who is not underchanged in the ego department, was string-pulling in the manner of such men, showing that *he* was the one who knew what was best for the team at that particular stage, no matter that it meant pulling the plug on a couple of star internationals and Balmain stalwarts. The plan, perhaps, was to deliver the final coaching "masterstroke" on the day, by bringing on a couple of grafters to lock the game up.

Well, it didn't work. We were suddenly a far less confident side, and Canberra had the sniff of a chance. Within the Balmain ranks out in the centre that day the changes made created uncertainty ... where once there had been certainty.

The rest is history. I can still picture that horrible moment, almost frozen in slow motion, of Ferguson stepping off his left foot twice ... boom! boom! ... and jagging back inside to score his try 90 seconds from the siren. It was devastating. At 14-12 there was still the kick to come, but I remember thinking to myself: "We're in deep shit here."

I don't really want to talk about the rest. They got us in the extra 20 minutes, coming home like runaway green steam trains. In 1989 replaced players could not come back on, as they do today. Blocker and Sirro were gone for good, and so was the bloody game. The Canberra players seemed to grow bigger and stronger as the minutes ticked by. By contrast we were a diminished outfit.

Five-eighth Chris O'Sullivan's field goal and replacement prop Steve Jackson's try-of-a-lifetime were enough to get them in front. And then it was over ...

The feeling of devastation was overpowering. Around me, grown men were crying ... Junior and some of the others. I was fighting back my own tears. We stayed on the paddock to fulfil our obligations, then went back to a dressing-room as quiet as a morgue. In the room, David Brooks couldn't control himself. He snapped at the coach for what he had done - pretty much saying it for all of us.

In my opinion Warren Ryan got it wrong that day - simple as that.

It's something he's going to have to live with the rest of his life. If you cop the praise, then you have to cop the flak as well when things backfire. In years ahead, Warren Ryan will probably be remembered for a lot of things. He'll be remembered as a tough and uncompromising professional coach who won two premierships with Canterbury, and almost won a couple with Balmain and one with Newtown.

But he'll be remembered too - and as much as anything else - as the coach who gambled and took two champions prematurely from the field on grand final day 1989. If we could play it again, Sam - and I only wish we could - I'm sure that even the super coach of the '80s would do it differently ...

On grand final night, 1989, we dragged ourselves back to the Leagues Club for the second year in a row. This time it was different. In '88 it had been a festival - a celebration of what we had achieved in going as far as we had. But in '89 the expectations were different. We had been expected to win the grand final ... and we had expected to win it. This time the club was full, but the mood was sombre. Our supporters knew this had been the great chance, and that we had blown it ...

Before the game we had made a pact that we players were going to stay out together that night - win or lose. We would play the grand final as a close and united team, and we would play on afterwards the same way. We ate at about 11 o'clock, and stayed at Balmain Leagues Club until around 2 am, when all the wives and girlfriends went home. Then we headed into town - to the Bourbon and Beefsteak Bar at Kings Cross, where we partied 'til 6 am. From there we headed back to Balmain, bedraggled, tired and certainly the worst for wear.

By then the realisation was beginning to sink in that it was all over for '89. The sun was rising, and the booze we had drunk to help us forget the day before was wearing off. The dawning day brought us all back to reality, replacing the party mood with something altogether more sombre. But there still were some final fun and games - and garbled phone calls between incoherent players and their wives or girlfriends.

Our great fullback, Jimmy Jack, was one of the first to go, drifting off into the morning. Before long, the rest of us did the same.

We'd missed a chance that few sportsmen ever get, and we knew it. We were bruised for life. In summer, training started again, but for a long, long time it was hard to muster much enthusiasm ... real hard.

12

Blood Feuds

THE TROUBLE BETWEEN Mario Fenech and me goes back to the first time we ever met on a football field. It was a top-of-the-table round-five reserve grade match at Leichhardt Oval back on March 27, 1982. Mario and I were the opposing hookers in reserves that day, and we were at each other all match. Finally the game erupted, and a couple of props destined for greatness, Steve Roach (Balmain) and Peter Tunks (Souths) joined the fray.

In the aftermath, with control restored, the two hookers, being of a smarter breed, stayed on the paddock, while the two props were marched. As Blocker Roach related in his book, *Doing My Block*, he and Tunksie then continued their war in the tunnel. As far as Mario and I were concerned, it was very apparent from that first day that we didn't like each other.

On reflection, the sensational events of that game represented a very logical way for us to say howdy for the first time. In the seasons that followed we were to clash many, many times, sometimes sensationally - as in the 1986 minor semi-final at the SCG when referee Kevin Roberts sent Fenech off, and charged him with gouging me. A little later that season we both travelled 20,000 kilometres for a wild showdown at Bradford's Odsal Stadium. Fenech, suspended for four games by the NSWRL Judiciary, had served his suspension in England - and I tangled with him again in a Yorkshire fog.

Before Balmain-Souths games in the '80s we'd stand 10 metres apart, our gazes locked, glaring at each other. *Rugby League Week*, after the ferocious semi-final battle of 1986, wrote of the pair of us "sledging and snarling" - that's the way it was. The whistle would blow, and it would be on. In those matches the field of play was no place for the faint-hearted, I can tell you.

Fenech versus Elias has been the nearest thing to a blood feud that rugby league has had in modern times. Skin and hair was guaranteed to fly when we met, and it reached the stage where the crowd came to expect drama every time. The media guys certainly did; we have given them some easy headlines over the years. The hate that existed between Mario Fenech and me for years was surely as strong as that emotion can ever possibly be on a sporting field.

And yet, you know, the funny thing is that we probably could have been the best of mates under different circumstances. The problem, right from the start, was that we were too much alike - two intensively-competitive sons of proud and very close ethnic families, both of us with Latin passions and emotions coursing through our veins. Both of us chased the same things - fame and success at the highest level on the football field. At Souths they called Mario "Test Match" because of his intensely competitive spirit.

I'll make an admission now - I used to be frightened playing against him when things were at the lowest level in our feud. The bloke was twice my size and I used to think: 'Shit! what if he really goes berserk and loses it - he'll kill me!' The great comfort always for me was to have Blocker Roach around the place. On the football field he was my bodyguard. He'd always stand by me - he'd never leave a scrum until I was safely out. He was a very handy man, the big fella.

And yet it was Block who would more often than not stir it up with Mario. He used to gee him up all the time. He'd say, "who's the fuckin' Test hooker?" or "who's the fuckin' State of Origin hooker?" "Call yourself Test Match," he'd say to Mario. "You're fuckin' kidding."

I'd be right in the middle of this, and Mario would be steaming. Some of those games were a dangerous place to be, especially as we were at each other's throats at a time when scrums were still scrums. In the pattycake, rapid-fire scrums of today there's no chance for opposing hookers to get angry. But back then the ball was fiercely contested and the front row was a battle zone on some occasions.

Mario's most furious games were saved for the Tigers. A part of that was certainly his feeling for me; another part was the bad blood that has existed between the two clubs - Souths and Balmain - since 1909. These games are always especially hard. Whatever the reasons, Mario would be revved up, breathing fire - and his considerable judiciary record tells the tale of the ferociousness of his approach.

The problem with Mario and me was that we were two men after the same job. We were the up-and-comers among the hookers, and the chance was always there that the big prizes of the game were going to come to one of us. Luckily for me, more came my way than his.

I really felt for the bloke in 1989. He had the State of Origin job for the first two games that year, and even though NSW got a flogging in the series, he was still a certainty for the New Zealand tour and, at last, for the Australian jumper he had coveted throughout his career. Then Lady Luck dealt a wicked hand - Mario busted a thumb and missed the trip.

The Fenech-Elias feud has mellowed in recent times. I guess it started to change in 1989, when we were team-mates in the City Origin side. I was hooker and captain of the City side and Fenech the reserve forward. In the second half of that game he was suddenly on the paddock at my side, and we were packing into a scrum together, arms around each other!

Since his move to Norths in 1991 the atmosphere between us has changed further for the better. At North Sydney, Mario was no longer a hooker, and that is one certain factor in the improvement. We were no longer head-to-head. Probably both of us have grown up too, from those earlier firebrand years. I believe that at Norths, Fenech has played the best football of his life. He is a strong and damaging player, whether at prop or second row.

For all our troubles I can look at the bloke, and his career, with considerable respect. I have respect for all first grade players, because I think it's a big feat for anyone to make it to that level. I know that Fenech has made many sacrifices in his life in the cause of football, as I have. I know how competitive he is, how well he prepares for games. He is a tough and loyal footballer. The hate that I once felt for him has gone, although I know we will never be the best of mates.

Keen students of our feud will be disappointed to hear that there are no longer great problems between Mario and me. We see each other at social functions now and then, and we have shared a handshake and a chat at those times. We have never had a beer together, and perhaps never will. But maybe in years ahead people will look back on these two ethnic boys who grew up together - yet apart - in Sydney rugby league in the 1980s and '90s and say: "Well, they didn't like each other much - but they sure added some colour to the game."

My family have taken a very pragmatic attitude towards the feud between Mario and me.

"In the beginning we didn't think it was right ... didn't think it should be happening," says my father. "But as the years have gone by we have learned more about sport and about motivation. We've had to accept that sportsmen use such challenges as motivation. So we have nothing against Mario Fenech or any other footballer. We look upon it now as an interesting rivalry ... as part of the game."

My mother adds: "If I see Fenech get hurt I'm worried for him. For anybody - because I'm a mother. His mother would get upset just like I would."

I hold Mario in higher regard than a couple of other hookers I have brushed with over the years. The former Newtown, Canterbury and Parramatta hooker, Mark Bugden, and Canberra's Steve Walters are not among my favourite people.

Bugden always seemed to be out prove something when he faced me, and would go to any lengths to make his point. After one particularly spiteful game between Balmain and Canterbury at Leichhardt in 1987, our battle continued in the tunnel after we had both been sin-binned. I had had my nose smashed in an early tackle, and Bugden and I had sniped away in verbal and physical exchanges in the first 20 minutes, before we were given a 10-minute "cooling off" order. A policeman in the tunnel stepped between us as the war threatened to continue.

After that game Bugden shot off his mouth: "He's no angel. And I'm sick of getting the short end of the stick when I play against him," he told pressmen. "He likes to give it, but he doesn't like to take it."

Bugden was a hot-headed player who was as much a danger to his own team by his occasionally silly actions on the field as he was to the opposition. I had no time for the bloke.

Our battles lasted something like seven years. He was a competitive bastard, and would set out to do his best to knock me out every time we played. They'd wind him up all week, and by the weekend he only had to see my face and he'd go bananas.

The feud really blew up in a Canterbury-Balmain match at Parramatta Stadium in June, 1986. A heavy clash in a tackle sparked a real donnybrook, with other players rushing in. Referee Mick Stone sin-binned the pair of us for 10 minutes and the verbal exchanges continued all the way off the field and into the tunnel.

I always got on okay with the Brisbane Broncos hooker, Kerrod Walters, although in our tussle for the Test job on the 1990 Kangaroo Tour, there was no quarter asked or given. We were fiercely competitive, but it was never any more than that. When I won the Test jersey from him for the Second Test at Old Trafford in '90, he came up and congratulated me. "I'm going to get it back," he said. "Over my dead body," I replied.

It was the way things should be - intense competition, but congratulations and support within the context of a team situation as well.

Now, Kerrod's elder brother Steve is a different kettle of fish ...

I reckon he's a pretty fair hooker, but his brother is a better one. And Kerrod's a better bloke, too. Steve has tended to run off at the mouth, as he did before and after the 1991 Origin Series. In May that year the pair of us finished up on the front page of the *Sunday Telegraph* sports section, under a big headline: "Origin Feud". Journalist Phil Rothfield reported that Walters had triggered the likelihood of a fiery confrontation with me in the forthcoming game by claiming that I always looked for a sympathy vote by publicising injury problems before important matches.

"I'm expecting to read any day now about how he will be playing under duress with painkillers," the Queensland hooker had been quoted as saying. "We seem to get that from Benny a lot ... it's happened plenty of times before. I respect the bloke as a footballer, but ..."

I was fired up and ready to hit back.

"I've got no real wrap on him as a player," I retorted. "I'm surprised he's come out and said what he said. Most players at this level of football prefer to do their talking on the football field. Really, Walters is lucky to be in the Queensland side anyway. He had a shocker in the first match of series last season and the selectors dropped him from the team. This year he only got a start because his brother Kerrod was suspended."

In the same article there was a good plug for Steve from NSW (and Canberra) coach Tim Sheens. "He's been our most consistent forward at Canberra this season and we all know that he's a very good player."

Walters that year had further fuelled the controversy by making derogatory remarks about me in a television interview, claiming that I was unpopular with 95 per cent of my team-mates.

The third Walters - Kevin (a five-eighth) - gave an interesting insight into the depth of the feeling between Steve and me in a column in the Brisbane *Sunday Mail* in May, 1991. He wrote:

Older brother Steve said in a television interview with Bill Anderson on Friday that maybe he went a little overboard in his public slanging match with Ben Elias. Come off it Steve. You know you can't stand a bar of Benny.

Steve is a bloke who says what he feels, whereas a lot of players steer clear of controversy for fear of revving up the opposition.

I got along okay with Benny on the Kangaroo tour last year, but then again I don't have to play directly opposite him like Steve.

Our rivalry reached flashpoint in the second State of Origin game of '91, played on a Sydney Football Stadium quagmire. This was a match of some infamy, which ended with NSW's Mark Geyer cited and suspended, and featured the notorious Wally Lewis-Geyer confrontation - with me in the middle.

The press relished the fact that Walters and I had come to grips in a sensational brawl that broke out late in the first half.

The Telegraph Mirror headlined its report: "Feud Explodes in Wet - Elias, Walters turn on heat", and reported:

The old Benny Elias-Steve Walters State of Origin feud exploded again on the Football Stadium mud heap last night.

The NSW hooker and his Queensland counterpart make no secret of the fact that they have little time for each other - and they made it blatantly obvious to the 40,000-plus crowd in last night's spiteful encounter.

In the sensational brawl shortly before halftime, Walters and Elias separated themselves from the pack to have their own one-on-one bout ...

Elias and Walters weren't interested in the main event. Walters dragged Elias away and the pair wrestled on the ground and exchanged blows until other players raced in to separate them.

Steve Walters really has made some imbecilic comments about me publicly. He is one of the few players who doesn't have my respect. He's certainly not on my Christmas card list.

While on the subject of "feuds" and footballers who are not high on my popularity list, it's no secret that big Martin Bella and I are not the best of buddies. That traces back to something that happened on the Kangaroo tour of 1986. A few of us, including me, had had a big night out of our hotel - the Dragonara at Leeds - and had got home late. Very late. In fact we had arrived back just in time to go to breakfast. In the dining room I happened to be sitting at a table behind Bella, who was alongside our coach Don Furner. I heard Bella say to him: "What about Benny? ... He only got in half an hour ago." Martin obviously didn't know I was there. So I jumped in and said: "What are you talking about, Martin?" ... and after a bit of to-ing and fro-ing all was okay and there was no real drama.

But after that things were always a bit strained between Martin and me. The bloke is not my kettle of fish, and when we were away on subsequent tours I steered clear of him. I respect him as a player - he's a good player, a strong player - but I don't like him much, and I guess he doesn't like me. There have never been great dramas on the field. I may annoy him a bit - but nothing out of the ordinary.

The occasional feud between players is an inevitable part of the game. I would love to get on famously with every opponent I face, but I really don't think that is possible. Rugby league is a sport that, by its very nature, will sometimes create conflict between opponents. You can't have players pounding and plotting away, fighting for every advantage, without some bad blood rising now and again. This, I'm sure, is how it has been since 1908. I'm just thankful that for the few people I've met in the game who I don't get along with, there are countless more who I respect and like a great deal.

13

Sex, Drugs and Rock 'n' Roll

AFTER ALL THESE seasons I guess that anyone who is at all interested in rugby league would know a little bit about the life and times of Ben Elias.

But the coverage of rugby league is most often one-dimensional, focusing mainly on the getting ready for, the playing and the aftermath of football matches. Rarely does it tell you much about the *real* person - the human being behind the footballer. With all sports people there is another side, rarely seen - a side of private interests and private opinions. I thought you might be interested to know some of that "other side" of Benny Elias. In the pages that follow some of my thoughts and beliefs are revealed, on a variety of subjects.

SOCIAL DRUGS

With the tennis star, Pat Cash, the rock singer and activist, Angry Anderson, and some others back in 1991, I was involved in a "Say No to Drugs" campaign. I have never been more enthusiastic about anything I have done out of football. I had a friend at school who could have played for Australia, but drugs wrecked his life. His story is mirrored so many times in the society we live in. Drugs have never been part of my life, and never will be.

Just as footballers who take risks with drugs are putting their careers at stake, individuals who plays around with drugs are taking a real chance with their health, and their lives. My message is simple: Say No!

PERFORMANCE-ENHANCING DRUGS

I have no doubt that drugs designed to artificially improve a player's performance, such as uppers and steroids, have been significant facts of life in the game. I use the past tense advisedly. The NSWRL's strong drug-testing policy has put the squeeze on wayward players and clubs, to the extent that they can no longer take the chance. Players who run the gauntlet are risking thousands of dollars and perhaps even their careers.

I am convinced that a very successful team of not so long back was pumped up on steroids. Players in that team all of a sudden were very big, and very strong. In my view, the successes they achieved are tarnished as a result. What they achieved was gained with chemical help - and I can see nothing admirable about that.

PAIN-KILLERS

I lived on pain-killers on the 1990 Kangaroo Tour after I had ripped a rib cartilage in the Second Test. But those six weeks apart, and a spell during the 1988 finals series when I needed help to play and train, I have used them only sparingly in my career - and only when the medicos had advised me that I could do no further damage by taking them.

ALCOHOL

I have to say I love a beer. It's a legal substance and a good social catalyst when you're with friends.

But I treat alcohol with care. As of January 1 each year I go off alcohol and soft drinks for three months to clean out my system. I have done that for 10 years or more. During the season I don't drink at all during the week, but I'll have a few to let down after the game.

CIGARETTES

When I first started playing grade football there would have been half-a-dozen team-mates who would reach for a fag first thing after each game and training session. Now you wouldn't find a handful of smokers in the entire 16 Winfield Cup clubs. I don't smoke, and would urge all young people not to. It's a disastrous habit - a wrecker of health, and a killer. But I believe very strongly that there is a great hypocrisy in the Government ban on cigarette advertising. After all, we're talking about a legal product, in a free country. The Government are quite happy to reap their millions from the tobacco industry - and in my view their attitude is two-faced. What's next in the big clamp-down? Beer and soft drinks? I think Winfield have been excellent and committed sponsors of the game of rugby league over a long period, and I can tell you that never once have I, or any other player that I'm aware of, been asked to do anything to help directly promote their product.

SEX BEFORE SPORT

Make up your own minds, folks! Much as I love it I wouldn't get involved on match day and I doubt many professional sportspeople do. The need is there these days to be so focused *mentally* on what you have to do in the game that *anything* else is a distraction. I remember when Bill Anderson was coach at Balmain that the subject was raised, fairly delicately, when he talked to the players' wives and girlfriends at a team barbecue. His message basically was "do what you're comfortable with", and I concur.

FOOTBALL GROUPIES

Every club has its groupies, and that's apparent from the moment you walk out of a dressing-room after a game. Sex is very, very available in the high-profile world of rugby league and the temptations are considerable, especially for starry-eyed young players just making their mark. However, the advice has to be to be strong, and to be very careful. There are bad apples around - people whose motives are more than just being with a high-profile person/player.

WOMEN

I'm a dedicated Cindy Crawford fan, but I think if I had a chance of being on a desert island with anyone except my wife, Kelly - I'd pick Madonna, just to try and figure out what makes her tick. She's no stunning beauty but I think that she's about the second-most intriguing woman (apart from my wife!!) in the world. And Elizabeth Taylor ... I've always thought she was a bit special, too.

MUSIC

I was brought up on Elvis. Brother Leo was an Elvis fanatic - he had every album. I just love that old rock 'n' roll ... The Beatles ... The Stones, although these days I'm more into INXS and Jimmy Barnes. I admire Jimmy Barnes a great deal and count him as a good mate. I flew down to his farm by helicopter one day to do a promotion and took a signed football and jersey to his son Jackie. From that day onwards the young bloke was hooked on rugby league, and the Tigers.

My passion for rock music (and especially Elvis) helped push me into a nightclub venture at West Ryde a few years ago. With an old pal, Dave Lazarus, I headed into the business for a time, and had a lot of fun. We called it King Creole's and the Tigers helped christen the place with a big rock 'n' roll preview night. It was a late one ... *Blue Suede Shoes, Jailhouse Rock, Heartbreak Hotel* ... I really love that stuff.

BLOOD-BORNE DISEASES

I think all of us in the game are very conscious of the dangers of bleeding footballers these days. The introduction of the blood bin, where players are forced to leave the field to have bleeding cuts and gashes cleaned up, was welcomed by all players. We're all acutely conscious of the risks of Hepatitis B and AIDS. This is life-and-death stuff - and the players increasingly take matters into their own hands and are quick to identify a bleeding player to the referee. I'm very aware of the dangers. As a hooker packing into scrums I am more vulnerable than most.

DIET

When I was young and stupid I used to think that you could eat and drink anything, go out late at night - and it still wouldn't affect your football. Wayne Pearce had a lot to do with changing the way I prepared for games. I used to look at this bloke going like a maniac in the 78th minute of a match and think: what's he on ... and where can I get some?? I gradually tailored Junior's dietary advice to suit my own needs - aiming at a diet that would build up energy during the week, culminating in the maximisation of performance on game day. Once mum would cook me steak and eggs on the morning of a match. Now it's a progressive build-up ... no alcohol ... cutting down the fatty foods ... lots of carbohydrates, pastas etc ... lots of fruit. On match mornings Kelly makes me a beautiful big pasta dish, usually lasagna, and eggs on toast.

I break loose now and then with a visit to Hungry Jack's, McDonald's or KFC. And I love a pizza ... but only occasionally.

THE MENTAL GAME

One of the tools of my trade is mental visualisation. I have become very good at it over the years. I can actually picture myself in a game. I run through the match plays in my mind, getting them right.

I believe that the essential motivation for success in any sport, or in life, has to come from yourself. I remember Bill Anderson sending me to a sports psychologist one day. I sat there listening to the bloke, but I was thinking: this is bullshit! I know what I have to do - I don't need anyone to tell me how to set my goals. I'm the one who's in charge of my destiny.

But I don't discard outside motivation altogether. It still

sends a tingle up my spine to think of Steve Mortimer's passionate address before the first State of Origin game at Lang Park in 1985. And our current coach at Balmain, Alan Jones, is a tremendous motivator, able to touch a chord, to give you a lift with the things he says. Jonesy can make you walk tall. One certainty of sport in the '90s is that if you're going to win you're going to have to work at it mentally just as much as you do physically.

RELIGION

I grew up in a good Catholic family and my parents are still devoted church-goers. I sort of drifted away in recent years. Basically I lost interest in going to church - I just grew out of it. I'm sure my mum and dad regret that, and it probably is a shame. Anyhow, I still say my prayers at night, and I still believe in the Christian way of living, whatever name you want to put on it.

FAVOURITE PLACES

Phuket, in Thailand, is my all-time favourite. I reckon it's the best holiday spot in the world ... great weather ... beautifully clear water ... and it's cheap. Kelly and I have decided that when I finish playing football we're going to have three months or so over there. I like going up to Coffs Harbour, too. Kelly's folks have a place up there.

MOVIES

I like action movies and *Top Gun* is pretty close to my number one. I saw that with Kelly and it seemed to be a picture that drew us closer together. I love the movies and we make an effort to go every second week. I really enjoy the feeling of being in a darkened cinema, of escaping for an hour or two from the real world. They can't get to you at the movies - it's my Great Escape.

GOLF

Golf is an escape too - three or four hours in the sunshine, communing with nature, far away from the pressures of life. I love the game, and I'll take it up properly for sure later on when time is a bit more available. I have a hit now and then - usually at North Ryde, near where I grew up. I occasionally try to sneak a set of tennis and a bit of body surfing, too.

BOOKS

I've never been a great reader - I reckon Kelly reads enough for both of us. But she gave me *Kane and Abel* one day, and I couldn't put it down. I've read most of Jeffrey Archer's books since.

POLITICS

Politics is not something I would ever want to get involved in. I reckon it's a cynical business. The basic aim of politicians seems to be self-preservation. I especially hate the promises we are loaded with at election time. Basically they're bribes, to get the pollies back in. They are rarely based on the grounds of what's best for the country.

CARS

I'm a bit of a car freak, and I have a dream. One day I will drive a Mercedes 500 sports.

ANIMALS

I've got the *best* dog in the world - a two-year-old Border Collie named Muir (I got it as a pup from Rod Muir). I love that dog. I get home from work and training some nights, stuffed and struggling - and he's there to greet me with the biggest smile and the happiest welcome you could imagine. He's so happy he almost turns himself inside out. It gives you a lift straight away.

TRAVEL

Rugby league has shown me the world. I've been to England and France, New Zealand and Papua New Guinea, to Hawaii and Singapore and all over Australia. It's been a hell of an education and the travel bug is likely to be a chronic condition with me in the years to come. But, you know what? I always love coming home. I wouldn't swap this place for any of them.

FUTURE AMBITIONS

Probably the only certainty of my future is that I will always be involved in football, somewhere and somehow. England is one possibility when I get towards the tail-end of my career. That carrot has been dangling for a while. I've had some super offers from over there, and Wigan is the big temptation. I like England very much, despite the weather. The friendship and the spirit of the north is very appealing.

Kelly and I have talked about the possibility of us one day going up the NSW coast to live, and that's an option. Another is pursue my career in radio. I recently signed a new three-year contract at 2GB in Sydney and I get a real buzz out of my work there. I especially like being behind the microphone. Not too many players get the chance to work in the media when their playing days are over. That opportunity - if it comes - is certainly appealing. Much more so than coaching, which is not on my list of preferred options.

RETIREMENT

I always said I'd retire from football when I was 30. Next year (1994), I'll be 30 when I play the season with Balmain. I'll just see how it goes. If I feel I have something to offer, I may go on. But I don't want to knock my body around too much.

AUSTRALIA 50 YEARS ON

It took time for traditional Australians to accept the influx of Italians, Greeks and Lebanese in the 1950s and '60s. Now the country is going through a phase of learning to accept the Vietnamese, the Japanese and the Chinese. The Australians have to work at that - but the Asian people have to work at it too. When I went to university the Asian students tended to stick very much in their own groups. That is not the way; they've got to make the effort. But I'm sure it will come together very well in a wonderfully mixed society in the years ahead. The "new" Australians can draw on some of the traditions here, and the "old" Australians can enhance their own life and living by tapping in to some of the things that a new culture brings. By then Australia will be a republic, heading on its own course in the world as it should be. The future looks terrific, and I just hope I'm around for a long, long time to enjoy it.

14

Gibbo and Bozo

IT WAS IN season 1990 that I had my first and only experience with the Great Coach. Missing the 1989 State of Origin series, I had not had the chance of playing under Jack Gibson's hand that year. But in 1990 - as the memory of the agonising grand final day gradually faded, and the keen anticipation of a second Kangaroo tour grew in direct proportion - I played under Big Jack's direction, first as skipper of the City side, and then as captain of the Blues in all three Origin games.

By then Jack was long-since a living legend of the game, a figure at the same time mysterious and greatly admired. To get the chance to play in a Gibson team was special for me. I thought to myself: this is an important occasion in my career. I'm going to be able to look back one day and say: "I played under Jack Gibson."

I think plenty of us felt the same when the players from the two City sides met him for the first time that season, down at Heffron Park, Matraville, one afternoon. For about half of us it was our first experience of Gibson, and the air of anticipation was enormous.

You could have cut the breeze with a knife as Jack

gathered us around him. There was a pause, as there often is with Jack, and then he said quietly: "We've just got to score more points than them and we'll win." That was it. He turned and walked away, and we saw nothing more of him until the Origin side went into camp.

In its own way it was a classic Gibson one-liner. Maybe we were expecting more, but you couldn't argue with the logic, and the more you thought about it, the more you thought: well, yeah ... that's right, isn't it? The players that day probably felt a bit like the crowd at Parramatta Leagues Club on grand final night, 1981, when thousands of them hushed to a deathly silence to hear words from the coach who had just masterminded the club's first premiership win. Jack walked to the microphone and uttered six words: "Ding dong, the witch is dead." And the witch *was* dead, the monkey was off Parramatta's back. Jack Gibson has a way of saying simple things that stick in your head.

He has a strange way about him, but he talks fundamental common sense. He keeps it very, very simple. "I'm not going to try and teach you guys in 24 hours how to play football," he said to us. We focused on getting the simple things right, of being aware of the need of getting our own individual games right.

I liked him a lot. He was prepared to let the talent come out in the side - he wasn't going to restrict that, and he was dead honest. In no way was Jack in the business of proving himself a genius coach. He knew he had a heap of talent around him, and he just wanted to see that talent work as well as it could.

The bloke is a fascinating character, living somewhere inside the aura that hangs around him. Sometimes you'll hear a smart person talk for 25 minutes or so, and you'll take in about a fifth of it. With Gibson, I'd venture to say that in a 25-minute speech you'd soak up just about the lot.

It's one of the rewards of the game that, now and then, you get the chance to brush against people like him.

Without doubt, Gibson is going to be judged one of the most influential and successful people to ever be associated with the game of rugby league. No-one can take from me the fact that I played under his coaching - and helped win an Origin Series, as his captain, in the process.

It was before that series that I received a first-hand indication of how much support we Blues had from another important figure - the head man, the NSWRL general manager, John Quayle. He invited me down to his office one day before the series began, and for two hours we just sat there and talked about football and all sorts of things. More than anything else, I got a clear message as to how much he wanted to beat Queensland - to win the State of Origin series. He wanted to win as much, perhaps even more, than the players! It was a great message, coming from the top, and one that I took back to the team.

When we fronted up to the challenge in 1990, NSW hadn't won the Origin prize since 1986. In the previous two seasons, the Blues hadn't won a single game.

The first match in 1990, an 8-0 win to NSW under a brilliant full moon at the Sydney Football Stadium, represented one of the most satisfying football days or nights of my life.

The match, which was preceded by a mock "war" at the SFS as artillery pieces were wheeled onto the ground, was ours all the way. The score was modest, but as John MacDonald wrote in the *Sydney Morning Herald*, it could have been 28-nil, so decisive was our hold on the game. Our major difficulty was converting field domination and a superb control of the game into points. Ultimately we had to settle for a try by centre Mark McGaw and two Michael O'Connor goals to get us home. We would have wished for more, but it was enough.

I won the man-of-the-match award, and in a slice of praise that I will always value, coach Jack Gibson told the press: "Elias could have left 10 minutes after halftime and he would have still been man of the match."

The *Sydney Morning Herald* wrote of a "performance of genius from Benny Elias", and commented:

The brilliance of his performance added weight to a theory that Elias has abilities unmatched by any *hooker in the history of the game in Australia.*

There is no doubt that Sandy Pearce, Snowy Justice, Kevin Schubert, Ken Kearney, Ian Walsh, Noel Kelly, Elwyn Walters, Max Krilich and others were wonderful players and great hookers.

But could any one of them come even close to matching Elias's all-round bag of skills?

He runs, kicks, feints, schemes, tackles, chases, backs up, hooks, directs.

It was immensely flattering.

In the midst of all the Origin hype, I was much in the spotlight, and there were many varied comments around that time on Ben Elias, the man and the footballer. They included:

Roy Masters, the former first grade coach turned journalist, who suggested that: "Elias, 26, is evasive, elusive, crafty, opportunistic ... on the field and off."

Steve Roach: "He's a sly little Leb ... but I love him. Benny's all the time pinching you, doing sneaky things, and when the coach looks around he has this look of an angel on his face."

Ricky Stuart, the Canberra, NSW and Australian halfback: "He has a switch. He can be talking loud, fooling about and then he is suddenly quiet and serious."

Paul Sironen, when asked by a journalist whether he believed team-mates were always aware of what I was up to on the field: "No, mate, we don't exactly. You get set for a run, you get the call and when you come flying through for the ball, Benny takes off by himself! What makes him look good is if his runners are convincing enough that it creates plenty of room for him. But he's just so sneaky, mate. You just don't know what he's doing, ever. It must be terrible for them (the opposition). He's a tough little bastard as well, you know. If you're small playing rugby league you've gotta be tough, regardless of who you are."

Ben Elias on Ben Elias (in the *Sydney Morning Herald*): "I was a real cheeky little bastard. I still am, but I am what I am, which is pretty harmless really".

Frank Johnson (1948 Kangaroo hooker): "I said to Benny one day: 'I've seen all the great hooker-forwards. You are the most complete. No-one had all your skills'. "

I especially appreciated that from the late Frank Johnson - an admirable man who did vast amounts of work for the game in coaching young players, and never made any fuss about it.

After my performance in the first Origin game, a pressman asked me where I managed to get all my energy from. "Mate, it's no secret - I eat heaps of bananas," I replied. And I did - six or seven of them before a game. It was true, and it was also good business. A month or so before I had signed a promotional deal with the banana marketing people. I was reaping the benefits of being a high-profile player in a high-profile sport. Earlier in the year I had signed a deal with the Nissan car company. Part of it was the permanent use of a 300 ZX sedan - valued at $63,000!

The second Origin match of 1990, the winning of the series for us was a piece of rugby league history. It was played in Melbourne, at Olympic Park, before a sell-out crowd of 25,800. A sell-out crowd in the middle of Aussie Rules country!! In a characteristically tense and see-sawing game, we got home 12-6, two tries to one.

The *Sydney Morning Herald* began their match report this way:

One moment of inspiration and 79 minutes of perspiration gave NSW the State of Origin series when they defeated Queensland 12-6 in their historic match at Olympic Park last night.

Half Ricky Stuart, a unanimous man of the match, provided the inspired moment 30 minutes into the first half. Stuart intercepted an inside pass from Queensland second-rower Dan Stains when a Maroon try looked imminent. He then showed pace he is seldom credited with to race 80 metres and give NSW a 6-0 lead.

Played on an uneven surface (I changed from short to long sprigs at halftime), the match was not a classic. And afterwards there were loud cries of protest from the Queensland camp concerning the refereeing of Greg McCallum. But, in the midst of our Blue celebration, we weren't too worried about any of that. In two controlled and proud performances spanning a fortnight in May, we had turned around the one-way traffic of 1988 and '89.

With our forward pack surging, we were going strong when we led the third match 10-4 after 24 minutes. But Queensland spirit can never be under-estimated at Lang Park (or anywhere!). The Maroons lifted as they so often do - and we simply ran out of possession. In the end they got us 14-10 and the crowd of 35,000 went home in great spirits, brandishing their Wally Lewis masks.

Jack Gibson's postscript to the press was typically oblique. Asked whether he would be back at the helm the following year, Gibson replied:

"So you know what you're doing next year? I might be in Darwin. Whatever I might say now I could change my mind about it in 10 minutes." On the match, he commented: "We seemed to get all the tough calls tonight from the referee (David Manson). I'll leave it at that."

A clean sweep would have been good. But, despite the stumble at the last hurdle, we Blues had accomplished what we set out to do. I am as proud as it's possible to be to have been captain of the winning team in a State of Origin series, and as the song says ... "they can't take that away from me."

It was a season in which I was genuinely "Captain

Hook(er)". At Balmain, our skipper, Wayne Pearce, was gradually succumbing to the wear-and-tear, bone-on-bone grating of a failing left knee, and played little football (he didn't start a first grade game until round 17). I was captain for most of the year, and it turned out to be a lively one in which we put 1989 well behind us, and made another solid charge to the semi-finals. We eventually ran fifth, winning 14 of 22 games.

But to get to the semis we had to beat Newcastle (12-4) in a mid-week play-off for the fifth spot. Blunted by the efforts of that match, and still sore, we were easy pickings for Manly the next weekend, and they beat us 16-nil, with their crafty five-eighth, Cliff Lyons, carving us up. The end of the season was hugely emotional, with the realisation sinking in that Junior, our captain, our idol, our inspiration and our mate had played his last game. Rugby league, for sure, was the poorer for that.

Wayne's last match at Leichhardt, against Parramatta in round 21, was surely one of the most emotional sporting afternoons that Australia has ever experienced. It was a magnificent send-off, with a tear in almost every eye, magnificent except for one thing - Parramatta spoiled the party by beating a Balmain team minus Paul Sironen and Steve Roach, 14-10. That game did us serious psychological damage. We were still in the running for the finals and had plenty to play for, while they were out of it. Yet they beat us. It was a grave blow to our hopes of going much further.

That we couldn't come up with a win for Junior disappointed us all. I'll certainly never forget the bloke - and I hope we're mates for life. He was a revolutionary in so many ways - at a time when the game was changing and needed strong and positive direction. I doubt that any era of rugby league has ever had a man more tuned to the needs of the times. He taught us all plenty about diet, about preparation, about new, sophisticated training, about gentlemanly behaviour, about the importance of doing the right thing, on and off the paddock. Apart from being a great player, he was also an educator. Along with Frank Stanton, and under the shrewd eye of Keith Barnes, he dragged Balmain into rugby league's new era.

The thing I'll remember most about Junior Pearce is the way he was towards the end of games. It didn't matter what the scoreboard read, he'd get harder and harder. He never eased off, and he never gave up. Rugby league handed him some dreadful knocks, yet he never whinged. He was a great player, and a great mate.

The glittering prize for all of us throughout that season was the prospect of a Kangaroo tour. My goals were set high: to win a spot on the tour, and then to win back my Test jumper. On the night of September 23, 1990, goal no. 1 was reached when I was named vice-captain of the 17th Kangaroos. Goal no. 2 had still to be worked on. Kerrod Walters had beaten me for the Test job against New Zealand during the season - and I knew I had some ground to make up.

To be named as vice-captain of the team, alongside a man such as that champion player and leader, Mal Meninga, was a source of great pride to me. Two touring teams in a row (1982 and 1986) had come home unbeaten, and the pressure on coach Bob Fulton's boys of 1990 was heavy indeed. But we left with happy hearts, and hopes high for another wonderful tour.

I had been in the shadows for a long time as far as Test football was concerned. My only official Test had been back in 1985, although I had played the World Cup Final in New Zealand in 1988. I was determined to make every post a winner; I was starting second, but I planned to finish first.

"I'm not going over there for a holiday," I told the *Telegraph's* Jon Geddes. "I'm there for a reason - and that is to win the Test position."

As can be the way of things in football, my chance came swiftly on tour, in the wake of an unexpected defeat in the First Test - at the ground which had become something of a hoodoo venue for Kangaroo teams, Wembley Stadium. Revved up by the rousing strains of *Land of Hope and Glory,* Ellery Hanley's Great Britain side played splendidly, before the largest crowd to ever attend a Test match in England, 54,569.

With Hanley, Garry Schofield and their halfback, Andy Gregory, the powerbrokers, the Poms won 19-12 against a team rated 5/1 on favourites. As they had done in 1973, the Aussies stumbled in the wide open spaces and extraordinary atmosphere of Wembley, playing just enough below their best to open the gate for the first British Test win over Australia in England since 1978.

It was after this match that I received the call I had waited so long for. Key Test changes made by Bob Fulton included Ricky Stuart for Allan Langer at half, B. Elias for Kerrod Walters at hooker, and the call-up of the enigmatic Cliff Lyons at five-eighth. The challenge for the new boys was a big one - to try and rescue the Ashes two weeks hence at the famous Old Trafford ground in Manchester.

In the crowd of 46,615 at the ground that day were my mum and dad, who had decided to grab a northern hemisphere holiday - and were subsequently to extend it further to take in the Third Test at Elland Road, Leeds.

The Second Test is by now safely enshrined in rugby league folklore as "The Miracle at Old Trafford". After 70 minutes of the battle - and what a battle - we Australians grouped behind our posts at 10-all, as Great Britain kicker Paul Eastwood lined up a simple conversion shot. The British centre, Paul Loughlin, had just intercepted a Ricky Stuart pass and raced away for a try that levelled the scores. On the conversion perhaps lay the fate of the Ashes. Hexed by 13 Kangaroos, Eastwood sliced his shot wide.

The rest is history. Ricky missed a field goal shot, then I sprayed one too. Finally, 42 minutes and 30 seconds after the second half had begun, the miracle: Stuart dummying and breaking clear 75 metres out, Mal Meninga elbowing himself through a traffic jam of players, shouting for the ball - and scoring!!!

At that moment I was back up the paddock, trailing the play, but unable to keep up. Finally I just stood there and watched. It was a beautiful sight - a feeling I just can't put into words.

What a game it was, featuring what has been called the most spectacular Test match try ever scored - Cliff Lyons' touchdown in the 55th minute. The ball whipped through 14 pairs of hands, then touched the right boot of Andrew Ettingshausen as he centre-kicked, before Lyons pounced to score.

It was one of the great days of my life. With the winning back of the Test jumper I had made a promise - that I would play till my last breath ran out if need be. I revelled in the game, relished the cut and thrust of a tremendous contest. At the end of it I was awarded a gold medal as man of the match. The whole day sticks in my mind as pure magic.

We had no doubts after that great escape that we would go on and retain the Ashes. Britain had had their chance - and failed by a fraction to take it. Mentally and physically we were in the ascendancy, and they were in decline.

Back in the Sydney press after that memorable Second Test, I even got a wrap from Ian Walsh - the man who had, some years before, expressed such severe doubt about me because of my size. Walsh wrote:

I thought he was too small. I thought he would be killed in the rucks, and in my day he would have been. But the game has changed dramatically. He is now a great player with unbelievable skills.

Before the Third Test, my old Balmain team-mate and now Great Britain vice-captain, Garry Schofield, called me a "bloody nuisance". Confirming that the Poms would target me in the Test, Schofield said: "He's the man we have to stop this time. He showed in the Second Test what a world-class player he is in any standard of football."

At Elland Road, on a freezing afternoon two weeks later, we won the Third Test 14-nil. Pain-killers were our companions and comforts in that game. Half a dozen of us had pain-killing injections to get us through the Test, and I was one of them. I had ripped a rib cartilage late in the Second Test, but there was no way I was going to give Kerrod a sniff of the Test spot again. I needed pain-killers to help me through each match from then onwards, including the two French Tests at the end of the tour.

The Leeds Test was grim and hard and very demanding indeed, as an icy northern wind blasted down the ground. What I remember most of all from that game is Paul Sironen smashing Ellery Hanley time and again with thundering tackles. "Who gives a stuff about club bloody friendships - this is an international," said Big Sirro later. Hanley showed how tough he was that day. I have never seen one player smash another so consistently - yet Ellery just kept picking himself up and trying again.

I remember too, the try I scored with eight minutes to go, to wrap it all up. I had trailed a break upfield, and was positioned one off the ruck on the right-hand side of the field. Steve Roach fired me the ball, and from 10 metres out I had enough momentum to reach the corner. Ellery Hanley gave me a smack in the mouth as I scored, and I remember that. But I recall even better the feeling of getting there, of being over the line for the try that wrapped up the series. It was my first Test try.

It was a grand tour, with much fire and colour. I especially remember the match against Wakefield Trinity where three Aussies (Mark Carroll, David Gillespie and Ricky Stuart) were sent off. Carroll, Souths' tough forward, got his marching orders after he flew in to give me some assistance. Following the break-up of a hotly contested scrum, I was copping something of a bashing, and Mark came in swinging, to help out.

The experience of the 1990 tour will live on in my memory, although France provided its traditional low-point at the tail-end of the campaign. I survived some nasty moments along the way and won back the Test jumper that I coveted. My worst scare came four or five days after the drinking binge that followed the Second Test win. I was in my room in the hotel in Manchester (the captain and vice-captain get their own rooms on tour), when I developed an agonising pain in my back.

I got up to try and walk downstairs to the foyer, but I was almost paralysed. The pain was unbelievable. I could barely manage to pick up the phone to call reception: "Put me on to Dr Gibbs' room, quick!" It was a training morning and, unfortunately, half the team accompanied the team doc, Nathan Gibbs, up to my room after I had dragged him away from his breakfast. I was there doubled up in pain - and crowded in the room were half the 1990 Kangaroo touring team, laughing at me. The doc shot off to his room, found me some pain-killers, and then rushed me to hospital. Turned out it was a kidney stone, which I was able to pass fairly quickly. I have never suffered pain like it.

The damned thing caused a misunderstanding between my girlfriend (now wife) Kelly and me. She had rung up from Australia early that morning just as the pain was really starting to concern me, and I had been very short with her. I just said: "Kelly, I'm so crook ... I've got to go." She probably presumed I'd had a night out drinking with the boys, and was suffering the consequences. The next thing she knew I was all over the back page of the newspapers in Sydney with the story of me being taken to hospital. "Elias Rushed To Hospital - 'I thought that I was going to die'," screamed the back page headline in the *Telegraph Mirror*.

The French leg was more farcical than ever as we galloped over very poor opposition, and counted the days 'til we get could on the plane home. I did it fairly tough - thanks to my rib problem. On a long bus haul from Paris to

Lyon early in the campaign, I had all sorts of problems even breathing. I doubted I would make it to the First Test, the following weekend, but I picked up. On a ground outside the famous walled city of Avignon, we thrashed the French 60 points to 4, with "Brandy" Alexander picking up 26 points. After the game the French League president, Jean-Paul Verdaguer, publicly branded his players "nincompoops" - which wouldn't have been all that helpful to morale.

The Second Test, played at Perpignan, near the Spanish border, was closer - but we were down about four gears by then. Playing on one of the few grounds in France that wasn't under snow we won 34-10, with big Sirro running riot.

The sustained achievements of that tour, and the success under pressure, were a tribute to the coaching ability of Bob Fulton. I consider myself fortunate in recent seasons to have come under the representative coaching wing of Fulton, and then Phil Gould with NSW. Fulton is a superb coach for a tour. He's been through that mill himself as a player, and he knows what works, and what doesn't.

He's a true professional - he does his homework really, really thoroughly. And he's a coach for his players. The footballers in a Bob Fulton team know they are going to be well looked after. He understands very well the value of having players who are happy and motivated to do well.

A shrewd man ... a very shrewd man. He's strong on statistics, strong on detail, and a very hard character indeed. But "Bozo" knows when to ease the reins too, knows that there must be some fun along the way on any campaign.

I think his coaching effort in bringing us back from one-nil down after Wembley to win the Ashes, and every other game, was of the highest order. He was under enormous pressure after we were beaten in the First Test. But he didn't flinch. He made the changes that he believed needed to be made, and we headed on. There was plenty at stake, and he had the guts to set a new course, and stick to it.

The off-field behaviour of the Kangaroos in 1990 was the subject of a good deal of media attention - more so after the tour than during it. The occasion of the celebration drink at a cricket centre outside Manchester is sure to take its place high up on the list of notorious stories from Kangaroo tours.

It happened the day after the win at Old Trafford, and caused no end of controversy. For starters, there was great drama about us *not* being at another function, a luncheon put on for 500 members of *Rugby League Week's* various supporters tours. These people had paid something like $6000 or so each to come over there and give us a cheer. The luncheon was attended by various ARL bigwigs, including Ken Arthurson and Bob Abbott. Only one player turned up - Bob Lindner, who arrived more or less by mistake. As far as I was concerned the arrangements surrounding the *RLW* function were always pretty vague, although we copped some flak about not being there. I think we were very good at fulfilling our official social obligations on that tour - but this one was a big ask, on the morning after a Test match. It was not on our official schedule ... it was sort of an optional thing, and we decided to go elsewhere. Bobby Lindner had been out of the hotel when Bob Fulton had called a meeting of players that morning. At the meeting it had been decided that we would go to Duke Mink's Cricket Centre at Stockport to have our let-down celebration get-together.

Duke Mink was a mate of mine from Australia, and we went to his place with the intention of playing indoor cricket. However, there happened to be a fully stocked bar at the centre so we brushed the cricket and decided instead to have a drink. Before long there were some lively drinking games underway ...

We were drinking straight spirits and the fact was that none of us were used to drinking straight spirits. Within a couple of hours things started to fall apart rather badly.

What happened was that one of our group really went crazy. Behind us at the bar was a mob of soccer supporters watching the soccer on TV and cheering for Leeds United. Leeds were going pretty well, and these guys were singing songs the way English soccer fans do, and making plenty of noise. One of our guys became increasingly narked by them and was shouting out: "Shut up, you fucking idiots."

Unfortunately, as the scene progressively deteriorated, Leeds scored a goal. This was the breaking point. Our man detached himself from the group as the cheering and singing broke out again, and advanced on the Poms. Singling out the loudest of the soccer mob, he hollered: "I've had enough of you, you Pommy bastard!!" - and went *booom*, and decked the bloke.

At this point, the man behind the bar intervened. "Hang on, hang on," he said. "There's no need for that kind of shit."

Next thing our bloke was over the bar, cornered the barman - and clobbered him. The brief scene that ensued could genuinely be described as "wild". A few of us, including coach Bob Fulton, intervened to break it up.

The police were called, and the Kangaroos beat a hasty tactical retreat in taxis. Next day we were big news in the London *Sun*, under the headline "Aussie Yobs Riot in Bar", which carried quotes from an un-named guest at the cricket centre along the lines of: "They were absolutely drunk and going bananas" and "they were maniacs". The story was sent back home by the travelling press corps. It was one of several of what the press like to call "incidents" on tour.

In Sydney, the *Telegraph Mirror* headline was "Roos Deny Wild Party", followed by a stiff defence mounted by the tour manager, Keith Barnes. "There was a very minor incident that has been blown out of all proportion," said Keith.

At other times, there was some damage done at our hotel in Manchester, and a size-12 inadvertently found its way through a plate-glass window in one of our hotels in France.

In cold black-and-white print, things like that don't look good. And I'm sure those sort of "incidents" helped age our manager about 20 years on tour. Barnesy was trying to achieve the impossible - to guide 28 fit, healthy athletes through three months' touring without problems. To manage a Kangaroo team has traditionally been seen as a "plum" appointment in the game. In one way it is. But in another it's a horror - perhaps the most stressful job in the world.

To explain the occasional problem to people who have never been part of the tour experience is not that easy. The frustrations can be immense at times. The weather closes in on you, you're 20,000 kilometres from your loved ones, and you're living in each other's pockets day after day. Back home, you might be missing some of the great events of your life. I can recall Louie Mortimer crying with frustration on the 1986 Kangaroo tour. He hit the roof one day: "Shit!! My kid walked for the first time the other day ... and I wasn't there to see it". In 1990, I was missing Kelly (a lot). But the married blokes were in an even more difficult position. They were missing their kids growing up. In France, towards the end of the three months, that can cut really deep - and there are times when you just have to let it go. The fracas at the cricket centre in Manchester was one of those occasions.

The bad days fade quickly in memory when you come home, and the tours grow into a glowing and unforgettable experience in your mind. That one in 1990 was a beauty. There's wasn't a moment's animosity between the players, or a hint of any division between the New South Welshmen and the Queenslanders. We confronted the hardest football any Australian team had faced there in a long time, and we triumphed. Along the way I picked up a "Golden Kangaroo" award, after being voted as the most valuable Australian player on tour by readers of England's leading league magazine, *Open Rugby*.

It was a bloody great tour.

Geez, I was unlucky though. If I'd been just a little bit smarter at positioning myself in the shower I might have been $350,000 richer. Laurie Daley and I were the blokes who flanked Andrew Ettingshausen in what was to become the most famous (and most expensive!) rugby league photo ever taken.

ET of course took *HQ* magazine to court and was awarded $350,000 damages. Good luck to him.

I received nothing - and all I want to say is that I'm pretty crooked at what went on. I mean, Brett Cochrane was the official photographer on tour, having been given the approval of the Australian Rugby League, and generous acceptance by the players. He was around most of the time, and that was fair enough. But for these shower photos - we presumed he was taking head shots ... but in fact he was taking full frontals! I saw the portfolio at the time the trial was on. Full frontals - from head to toe! I'm dirty about that. I'm sure Cochrane would never be welcomed back on a Kangaroo tour.

ET was my roomie in France in 1990 - a good bloke, a humble bloke, and a bloke with no airs and graces about himself.

The settling of the nude photos controversy early in 1993 (pending appeal) made it a pretty sensational start to the season for him: A thumping new contract with Cronulla, running way into six-figures, and $350,000 damages!

The backs have all the luck.

15

1987 Revisited

ON THE KANGAROO tour of 1990 I was the subject of a foul and vicious whispering campaign. The rumours first reached me ears around Third Test time, when I had a phone call from my brother Joe. He told me that a story was spreading like wildfire through Sydney that I would be facing sex charges when I returned home. The rumours were all over town.

I was shattered. It was one of those situations where I could not believe what I was hearing. Not again, I thought. Not again.

"It's outrageous," I told Joe. "It's bullshit ... there's not one grain of truth in it."

Depending on which club or pub you happened to be in, the stories had me sexually assaulting my girlfriend's sister, or the sister of one or other of my Balmain club-mates. Some miserable bastard was out to get me. Someone who was jealous or just plain vindictive. Someone who was a real sicko.

The stories even reached Kelly (then my girlfriend, later my wife) in a very direct and disturbing way. Around that time, Kelly had some weird phone calls about the alleged trouble I was in. I didn't find out until a long time later that even Kelly had been roped into this monstrous web of lies and whispers. Counselled by Junior Pearce, who provided advice and loyal support during that unpleasant time, Kelly kept quiet about the phone calls. She didn't want to worry me further.

The worst thing for me was the reality of the Sydney grapevine. Sydney must be the best rumour city in the world. Drop a word of scandal about someone in a pub somewhere and it'll be all over town in a day or two, regardless of whether it's true or not. While I was doing my best for my country on the playing fields of England and France, loaded up with pain-killers so I could keep going, back home my reputation was being torn to shreds.

For the second time in three years *everyone* knew the real story of Benny Elias.

On the French leg of the tour I was champing at the bit. I just wanted to get home and get to the bottom of this new horror in my life. When the rugby league job was finally done, we flew back via Singapore where we had an R & R stop to break the trip. It was in Singapore that the *Telegraph Mirror's* Ray Chesterton pulled me aside.

"Mate, the story is hot stuff back home," he said. "The rumour is around that the police will be there to meet you at the airport. You'll have every television station and every newspaperman in Sydney waiting for you. I wanted to let you know so you'll be ready for it."

It was incredible. This bastard of a thing had happened in my life again. A vicious rumour, started by some unknown mongrel had spread and spread until it was out of control.

Now, all of Sydney was waiting for me to be arrested.

No superstar has ever had a bigger reception than the one I received at Sydney's Mascot airport the day we came home. It was a bit like that Alfred Hitchcock film, *The Birds* - you know, when all the birds are waiting silently, menacingly. The media was at Mascot in those sort of numbers, waiting, watching my every move. I was furious, happy to be home, but just boiling inside.

Press guys there that I knew told me that the stories had been around, and that they had been sent out to the airport "just in case".

"Well, I'm sorry to disappoint you," I said. "You're wasting your time."

Nothing came of the rumours. There was no arrest, no court case - because *nothing* had happened. But that doesn't mean that Benny Elias wasn't torn to shreds for the second time in three years, all but destroyed by the rumour mill of Sydney.

I would really love to be able to get across to readers how cruel it was, how vindictive. But words will never be strong enough to do that. One of the most disturbing things was when friends told me that even the police had been relating these rumours. There were stories about police who were on the case, police who had seen the reports, police who were going to be at the airport to intercept me. A pal of mine rang me one day and told me of something a certain detective had said about me at a party a few days earlier. I was filthy - and I rang the bloke's superintendent. I told him I had three witnesses and was ready to begin action for defamation. The bloke went to water. Within a day or two I had a letter of apology.

My legal people believe that the rumours of 1990 were no more than a spin-off from what had happened in 1987. Undoubtedly there were people who were unhappy to see me cleared of the charges I faced in '87. But the depth of the malice still astounds me. While I was 20,000 kilometres from home, I had been ruined again in a flurry of wicked lies and deceit.

Something that horse racing's highly respected AJC Chief Stipendiary Steward, John Schreck, said in 1993 pretty much summed up my situation back in 1990. In a passionate defence of the fairness of Sydney racing against a savage attack by turf journalist Ken Callander, Schreck declared: "I am afraid it (Callander's criticism) is an example that the knocking syndrome is alive and well in Australia ... and 90 per cent of the people slot into the category."

In 1990 I was a victim of that "knocking syndrome", the Aussie "tall poppy" syndrome.

It was a sour ending to what had been a great sporting tour. The rumours evaporated as quickly as they had come. They were absolute bullshit, based on nothing but the imagination of some cretin. But it's stating the obvious to say they did me no good.

16

Enter Alan Jones

THE WARREN RYAN era at Balmain ended one day in the spring of 1990. On that day, Warren and his right-hand man, Brian Satterley, strode purposefully into Balmain Leagues club for a scheduled meeting. Soon afterwards they departed - and it was not long before the news was around that Warren would not be coaching the Tigers in '91.

The feeling was strongly through the place by then that the Ryan era at the club had run its course, that Warren had worn down his welcome enough for the club to bid him thanks and goodbye. He had brought considerable, if not ultimate, success to the Tigers - two grand finals and a semi-final appearance - and had maintained and built upon the momentum established by Frank Stanton.

But Balmain had discovered, as had Canterbury before us, that Ryan could be a hard man to live with in the football club context. There was also a deep undercurrent of feeling against him relating to the events of the 1989 grand final. I don't think the club ever forgave him for the fact that we lost that game when we seemed to have it won.

That will always be seen as his Great Mistake. But I don't think, in terms of his overall contribution to the club, that Ryan could ever be judged too harshly. He brought expertise, toughness and ultra-professionalism to Balmain, and the years of his coaching were years of considerable success and great hope at the club. Ryan fired a parting shot at Balmain in his bitter comment that he had left the club because "the orange had been squeezed dry". There was a bit of juice left on the day that we whipped Ryan's Western Suburbs 21-8 in 1991.

The rumours had been around for a long time that Ryan was going to Wests. Hot on the heels of that one was the other rumour - that the former Australian rugby union coach, Alan Jones, would take over at Balmain. Jones had close ties with a great Balmain stalwart, John Brennan, through their business association at the Sydney radio station, 2UE. It was an amazing situation - the possibility that a man who had coached rugby union at the highest level might switch and become a first grade rugby league coach. This was something that had never happened and *could* surely never happen in the game, considering the wide gulf that existed between the two codes, and the animosity that had been a fact of life over the years - largely on the rugby side of the fence.

But Alan Jones, of course, is a pretty remarkable bloke - genuinely one of Australia's great achievers, and a man with an immense capacity for work. Before long the rumours of late 1990 were a lot more than just rumours ...

Barnesy called the senior players together one day and talked officially about the possibility of Jones taking over as coach. Soon after that, Alan Jones came down and met a group of the senior guys. He made a great impression on all of us - so good in fact that when we met Keith Barnes the next day the vote of support for him to take over as first grade coach was 100 per cent.

I guess we all appreciated the risk factor - of a coach who had not paid his dues in rugby league, a bloke who was completely untried in one of the most constantly demanding jobs in the world of sport. But we had faith. Jones was straightforward, highly intelligent and preached messages of success ... and success was what each one of us was looking for.

His lack of experience in rugby league did not seem such a problem. When Alan Jones was signed - the signal for blazing headlines - he brought with him one of the greatest and most knowledgeable of rugby league men, Arthur Beetson. It seemed a sensational package: Jones the motivator, the inspirer of men, and Beetson, the football fine-tuner who had done everything there was to do in rugby league, and whose knowledge of the game was unsurpassed. We should be able to win with that sort of formula, we reckoned.

We started our pre-season training with great expectations for the year ahead. The training was fine - though different from anything we had done before. We trained down at Blackmore Oval at Leichhardt - innovative, interesting sessions which only served to heighten the air of anticipation for what lay ahead.

But before long Beetson was gone - for reasons that I am still unsure of - a slightly unsettling development so early in the beginning of a new era at the club. Coach Jones brought in Parramatta lower-grade coach Ken Shine as his new right-hand man, and we pressed on, hoping for great things.

In mid-February, I received one of the great thrills of my football life when I was appointed captain of the Tigers for 1991. It meant the world to me. "It is one of the greatest things that has ever happened to me in rugby league," I told the press. "When I first started playing football I used to think how terrific it would be to play for Balmain, let alone be captain. I am really honoured."

I was well aware of the tradition of that job - of men such as Keith Barnes, Peter Provan and Wayne Pearce who had preceded me - and I was determined to give it all I had.

But our season was plagued by ill-fortune, beginning with the unexpected but unavoidable absence of the coach, who was forced into hospital for a time early in the year with a severe back complaint. This put us on the wrong foot before the trial matches were over, and then our first two premiership games were disasters - 16-26 and 4-44 losses to Canterbury and Cronulla respectively. The Cronulla game, played down at Caltex, was a major embarrassment - representing one of the worst Balmain efforts I had ever been associated with. We had three internationals in the pack that day - Roach, Sironen and Elias - yet we folded like a deck of cards, conceding eight tries. A draw against Newcastle (12-all) the following week provided only a brief respite, and we sank deeper into the mire in the rounds that followed.

Controversy was often our travelling companion. We had a coach who believed in saying exactly what he thought, and at times there were fireworks. When Illawarra beat us (12-9) in controversial circumstances in round 5, there was an almighty blow-up. Jonesy launched into a 20-minute tirade against referee Chris Ward, during which he referred to Ward's performance as "Al Capone stuff". Pressmen stood open-mouthed as he ripped in.

"There were so many mistakes by the referee I stopped writing them down," he said. "You can't go on provoking people like my players were today. It's not fair that players make all that effort - and then get that sort of treatment. No game can survive with any credibility when it conducts itself like that."

I broke ribs that day, we lost a game we probably should have won, and the club was fined $10,000 for the coach's remarks. It wasn't a brilliant day for the Tigers.

The pressure grew through a difficult first two months of the premiership. We didn't win a game in that time - the draw against Newcastle the only dividend in eight week-ends of football. The media was howling for blood -

someone's - and the pressure built week by week on all of us.

A Sun-Herald investigation in May served only to stir the pot a little more. It was headlined: "Tiger Bosses Blame The Players" and included such items as:

- A Balmain director claiming that the players were unhappy with my captaincy.
- A leading executive of our major sponsors, Philips, declaring that he believed Gary Freeman, and not Benny Elias, should be captain.
- Keith Barnes denying that either halfback Gary Freeman or coach Jones would be leaving the club before the end of the season.

By then Gary Freeman, the champion New Zealand halfback, was in reserve grade, and his status at the club continued to be the subject of ongoing controversy through the year. He played out the season, mostly in the lower grade, and then left for Eastern Suburbs. Balmain's loss was to prove very definitely the Roosters' gain.

Freeman was on the outer at Balmain for *philosophical* reasons rather than any personal gulf between he and the coach. Alan Jones wanted a different kind of player at halfback - someone who was an outstanding kicker of the ball, and a good link-man. The talented rugby union international, Brian Smith, had joined us - and Smith, who is a magnificent kicker of the ball, fitted the job description better than did Freeman. Brian has probably the best kick in the game after Ricky Stuart, and the best hands in the game after Wally Lewis. I didn't agree with the decision that put Gary Freeman in seconds - but it was most certainly not my decision to make, and I fully accepted that reality. I was paid to play for the Tigers; Alan was the coach. That's the way it was, and had to be.

It just seemed to me that we penalised ourselves by not having Freeman in the side. The bloke is an extraordinary player, a winner. Any football club would count itself fortunate to have such a player around. There is no more competitive player in the game of rugby league than "Whiz" Freeman. His philosophy is that you're never beaten, and he plays that way every time. His attitude presents a tremendous role model for any young footballer.

Gee, he's a tough player too. I remember a day at Leichhardt in 1989, in which Freeman found himself on the wrong end of Greg Dowling's knee in a Balmain v Brisbane game. The knock was a bad one which cut his gums badly and knocked out teeth. I can still recall Freeman, scrambling around on the ground, calling on team-mates to give him a hand as he searched for a missing tooth. He played brilliantly that day - before and after the kneeing incident which earned Dowling an early shower - and we won the game, 24-6.

I had a great understanding with Freeman on the paddock. Of all the blokes I have played with, only he and Scott Gale had an unfailing and uncanny sense of knowing when I was going to have a shot from dummy-half. They'd be up alongside every time, calling for the ball. Freeman is in the Terry Lamb class when it comes to backing up. The turn around at Easts that co-incided with his arrival there was no chance event. A bloke such as Freeman brings instant pride, competitiveness and will to win. He's a special player - and I was sorry to see him leave the Tigers.

The 1991 Balmain year certainly finished a hell of a lot better than it started. After our disastrous beginning we came home strongly, scoring resounding wins over semi-finalists Wests and Manly. The drought-breaker had come at Leichhardt on May 19, a round 9 win over the classy Broncos, 14-4. Brian Smith played halfback that day and was a key figure with his powerful kicking game. The broken thumb I suffered against Manly in round 13 was the end for me. By the end of the 22 rounds, we had mustered 16 points, to finish 12th on the ladder. It had been a solid comeback effort after a disastrous start and the announcement was made that Alan Jones would be coaching us again in 1992.

Readers of my book no doubt will want to know my views on Alan Jones, football coach. He's such an extraordinary figure, a man of such diverse talents, that I hardly know where to begin.

The fundamental thing is that Alan Jones arrived with, and as part of, a new era at Balmain. The old order was finishing, with the mainstays of the 1980s - Wayne Pearce, Steve Roach, Bruce McGuire, Kerry Hemsley, Garry Jack, John Davidson, Gary Bridge and others - all gone, or going. These people had been the backbone of the club for a decade, and now it was time to start all over again. New Tiger cubs were coming through, and Alan Jones was the man charged with the job of developing them, and the side.

The great thing about Alan Jones as a football coach is his determination to develop his players into better, more rounded human beings. He doesn't only want to see them progress as footballers. Through his coaching, and his interest in the players, he provides optimism and opportunity for the sort of passage they can have through *life* via football. In no way does he want to see his players complete their careers, and then head for the scrap-heap.

He opens doors for young players, educates them in some of the finer things in life. Blokes who have never been in anything better than a leagues club bistro suddenly find themselves at team dinners in fine restaurants. They meet people they would never dream of meeting, are offered unexpected job opportunities and learn social skills that will unquestionably help them through life. He provides opportunity and incentive. His beautiful house at Newtown has always been and open and welcoming place for Tiger footballers.

I know, though, that Alan has found the job of coaching

a first grade rugby league side much tougher than he expected. He said to me one day that to coach in the Winfield Cup was like preparing the Wallabies to play the All Blacks - every week. It was an interesting analogy.

Not surprisingly, as one of Australia's most sought-after speakers, he is the most "verbal" of all the coaches of my experience. In that capacity he can be tremendously inspiring. You can go into a Monday team meeting, down in the dumps after a loss at the weekend, and leave absolutely jumping out of your skin and ready for the next match. You can't wait until Sunday comes. Sometimes, when you've had a loss, he can make you believe you've had a win.

If there was a serious deficiency with Alan Jones, rugby league coach, it lay in the technical area in the earlier days of his tenure - and that's not so surprising when you consider that the coach came to league in his middle years, having had no hands-on experience of the game in his life. Probably when people look back and tell the story of Alan Jones, his appointment at Balmain in 1991 will be judged one of the most extraordinary things to ever happen in the game of rugby league.

With his acute intelligence and ability to absorb, Jonesy learned the game well, and quickly. But I think he was unlucky he didn't have a man with the depth of league knowledge of a Beetson, a Freier or an Anderson by his side in those early times, on a game-by-game basis. A mix of Jones' exceptional motivational talents with such football experience would have been a winning prospect. As it turned out, Ken Shine developed into a terrific sidekick for the coach as his confidence and experience in the game grew. Ken is an intelligent bloke with an acute feeling for, and knowledge of, the game. Like all of us he wants success - and he has worked hard towards that goal.

Ken Shine is typical of the breed of highly committed and talented "background" men that successful football clubs must have. Our long-time trainer/conditioner, Les Hobbs, was certainly one of that breed. Les was head trainer at the club from the day I joined in '82 until his departure in early 1993. Work commitments forced him out, and I'm sure all of us regretted him leaving. Les was a hard man, but with a great depth of compassion and care for Balmain club and its players. Doing the "extra" things to help a player was never a problem for Les. I thought he was a terrific trainer/ conditioner and a great bloke. A fierce loyalty for Balmain positively shone out of the man. I hope he can clear the decks enough in his working life to come back to the Tigers one day.

Lady Luck certainly did not smile on Alan Jones' keenly-anticipated introduction to rugby league coaching. Looking back to when he joined the Tigers in season 1991, I'm sure that most people have long forgotten just how unfortunate he was at that time. We had only just got going when he was rushed off to hospital with that serious back problem. The operation that he needed, and the recuperation period, meant that we were without him for six weeks or so at a vital period of the season. That unfortunate start hijacked Jones in his new role as a rugby league coach - and it wrong-footed the team, too. Shine, fresh from Parramatta under -21s, had the testing job of trying to steer the ship, dealing with a team which was laced with hardened pros. It was a tough beginning for all of us.

Alan had come from a code of football (rugby) in which there was not the same emphasis on defence as in rugby league. Even in some league circles he was hailed as a new Messiah of attacking football. But the reality of league in the 1990s is of a game which requires a powerful and well-organised defence as one of its foundation stones. This was one area in which Jonesy had to make some directional changes in his philosophical approach to the game. I'm sure he'd freely admit he had things to learn in those early stages, and in some instances he learned them the hard way, through mistakes made.

The anticipation at Balmain in early 1991 had been for success. As a football team we had been winners in the 1980s, contenders since Frank Stanton had picked us up by the bootstraps after the wooden-spoon year of 1981. Alan Jones was a winner too - coach of a triumphant, winning Wallaby team, one-time speech writer for a prime minister, outstanding motivational speaker and a budding star in a new field, as breakfast announcer on 2UE. He wanted to win as much as we did, and that we didn't get the early success we hoped for was a disappointment to us all.

Sometimes the dramas that surrounded him have been unsettling for the football team. All of us were tip-toeing around on eggshells late in the 1992 season, when a campaign was on to sack him from the club.

Throughout that difficult period the players just kept their heads down and did their best to focus on the job of winning football matches. It was hard going - there were so many rumours, so much back-biting, so much bickering and arguing behind the scenes. The media simply revelled in it.

They asked for my opinion on who should be coach in 1993 and for one of the few times in my life I answered "no comment". I am a footballer, paid handsomely to play the game to the best of my ability. I was not then, and am not now, interested in the politicking. Decisions about coaches are made by directors - in boardrooms.

In August, 1992, Balmain voted to re-appoint Alan Jones as coach for 1993. I had no problems with that. Over the years the appointment of this coach or that has never swayed my resolve to prepare as well as I could for the season ... and then to give it everything I had.

I looked forward to 1993 as I had to all my footballing years, knowing that we had the potential to be among the real achievers of that season.

17

Mr Sheens

THE EVENTS AT the end of the State of Origin series of 1991 left a sour taste in my mouth - and I'm not talking about the fact that we lost the battle to the Maroons. It hurt even more that the NSW coach, Tim Sheens, showed what I considered to be gross disloyalty to me as captain.

Sheens had won the appointment as the NSW coach after Jack Gibson decided not to continue after the triumph of 1990. Having steered the Canberra Raiders to premierships in 1989 and 1990, Sheens was not an unexpected choice for the Blues job, and I was confident that the Origin crown could be retained by NSW. But things did not turn out as I had hoped.

After the desperately-close, series-deciding third game, which we lost 14-12 at Lang Park, Sheens chose television as his forum to have a crack at me. I had copped some flack already, from an un-named NSW selector who bagged me in print for the way I had played in the third game. The selector was quoted by the *Telegraph Mirror's* Phil Rothfield as saying: "Benny tried 110 per cent but we were disappointed with his overall game. He took the wrong option on quite a few occasions. He probably went himself too often, trying to break the line from dummy-half. You can't blame one player for a loss, but I think he would have been better playing more of a team game than as an individualist."

I was stung by the criticism. I didn't think I had gone *that* badly, and I had not been aware that the selectors, or the coach, had been disappointed by the way I had played. Replying to the criticisms of the selector, I stated that I played in accordance with the instructions from the coach. "I did what the coach told me to do. Tim told me to run as much as possible from dummy-half to relieve some pressure on the forwards. He emphasised that for the three matches."

On Channel 7's *Sportsworld* the following Sunday, Sheens had his say: "I didn't tell him (Elias) to throw flick passes in our own half. I didn't tell him to miss tackles or ignore calls for the ball to go out to the backs," he said.

I was privately ropeable, although publicly diplomatic. My belief is that the relationship between a coach and his captain, especially at that level, is sacrosanct. I certainly had not been critical of Sheens when I had spoken to the press. Publicly the player should stick by his coach and vice-versa. Now here was the coach, finger-pointing at me through the television screen after we had lost. Whatever happened to the brotherhood of the Blues? It was a classic case of sour grapes. Tim Sheens was looking for a scapegoat.

I'll go on record right now with the comment that I believe what Tim Sheens did and said as NSW coach after we lost was unprofessional, poor sportsmanship ... and from my point of view as skipper, just plain pathetic.

Sheens had seemingly impeccable credentials for the job as NSW coach, but I must admit I had my doubts about the bloke right through. He seemed to have a chip on his shoulder from the start. My opinion is that the task was too big for him. The NSW Rugby League provided some substance to that theory when they did not re-appoint Sheens in 1992.

I am not looking to paint myself as the hard-done-by Golden Boy in the 1991 series. We were beaten, I contributed some mistakes - and I was as disappointed as buggery that the Maroons had won. I am by no means the perfect player. If I take 10 options and seven of them are right and I stuff up on three - then that's the way I play the game. I *do* take risks now and then, but they are not extravagant risks, they are *calculated* risks. I am not a robot. And I'm the first to admit that I do take wrong options on the football field at times. For a bloke who's touching the ball on 95 per cent of the plays, you'd expect that to happen. I have never played the perfect game, where I have taken every right option. But even players of genius such as Sterlo and Wally used to take bad options occasionally.

And another thing - I'm not prepared to cop the rap for something that happened after the third game ... something that brought criticism down on the entire NSW team. We copped more than a little flak for walking off the Lang Park arena before the presentation was made to the Queenslanders. I want to make it clear that it was our coach who said "let's get off here" when we were milling around after the game. People felt we had displayed poor sportsmanship in not waiting while the winners bathed in their moment of glory. I'll admit, it didn't look too flash - but if you want to get the full story as to why it happened ... ask the coach.

Sheens to me always seemed a fairly unhappy and morose bloke, although I thought that he and I worked together reasonably well during the series. Mind you, there wasn't all that much communication between us. I was certainly supportive of him. He was not out to restrict individual flair and I told the *Courier-Mail* during the series: "That's one of the good things about Tim's coaching. He allows the enterprising players to use their skills."

As with most high-profile (and successful) coaches there was a fair slice of ego in the man; he'd won a couple of competitions with Canberra, and I'm sure he perceived himself as a "super coach" (one of many). The fact was he had won competitions with an array of simply outstanding players - Gary Belcher, John Ferguson, Mal Meninga,

Ricky Stuart, Laurie Daley, Bradley Clyde, Dean Lance, Brent Todd, Steve Walters, Glenn Lazarus and co. There would have been something wrong if a coach *hadn't* been having success with that lot. To Sheens' great credit, he unshackled the talent he had in that superb line-up - and the result was a team which ranks as one of the most exciting the game has ever seen. I'm sure Tim Sheens is very proud of his Green Machine, and he should be.

I do not seek to underplay Tim Sheens' achievements with Canberra. As a coach he has premierships hanging from his belt, plus the reality of many brilliant performances from a brilliant team, and it's entirely reasonable to presume that his input has been a strong contributing factor to the success gained. In this chapter I set out to do no more than relate the story of my own comparatively brief dealings with Sheens and my personal observations on the man - based on our shared roles as captain-and-coach of the 1991 NSW team.

In the 1991 State of Origin series I don't believe the NSW team ever had the necessary feeling of comradeship and togetherness. When you're in the camp the building of that sort of quality must come from the top man - the coach, but this time we had a tutor who was something of a loner. Jack Gibson built the right sort of spirit the previous year. If Jack is a bit distant himself, he has blokes around him to handle the areas where's he's not so strong. Johnny Peard, a decent bloke and a shrewd football man, was a tower of strength during the 1990 series.

As he had done with Canberra, Sheens chose to shut the team away from public view, and especially from the media. When we went to Brisbane, he and I (as captain) were the only two Blues representatives to whom the local media had access. "The media distracts players, and this is a very important match," Sheens told the Queensland pressmen.

As you may have gathered, coach Sheens didn't endear himself to me much during that series. Part of it I suppose was the fact that he was the club coach of my opposite number and intense rival, Steve Walters. Rightly or wrongly, I had the feeling throughout the series that Sheens was promoting Walters. It was Walters this and Walters that - publicly and in-house, and it became very boring. I was the NSW hooker and captain, and the incumbent Australian hooker, but it seemed to me that my coach was not the ally that he could have been.

Anyway, that's gone. In my view, Sheens proved that he was not the right man for the job in '91. I wish him no ill - he has had some fine successes in premiership football and good luck to him. But I can say that I received very little enjoyment out of my association with him. I have no desire to renew the acquaintance. Probably he feels the same.

It was a fiery and extremely controversial series that year. I struggled to make it at all. I busted a rib against Illawarra and missed the City-Country game. But I received a marvellous vote of confidence from the top.

John Quayle rang me on the day of the State team selection and asked: "Are you available for selection? If you're okay, you're in the side."

I could barely get the words out: "Yeah, I'm as right as rain."

Before a ball was kicked, I was headline news in Queensland over a light-hearted magazine article I had written the previous October. The article re-surfaced - and how - before State of Origin I.

"Benny Stirs Up Hornet's Nest - 'I Hate Queensland' - Magazine Story Fury" shouted a monster headline on the backpage of the *Telegraph Mirror* of May 8. In the story that followed, journalist Ray Chesterton described the article I had written as a "brutal spoof". "NSW captain Benny Elias has lit the fuse to Queensland's motivation for tonight's Winfield State of Origin clash," he wrote.

The article was just that - a spoof - but was treated as a deadly serious motivational tool by the Queenslanders.

In the piece, headlined "Why I Hate Queensland", I popped my tongue firmly in cheek and:

- Called Queensland women over the age of 30 "leather ladies" because they spent so much time in the sun.
- Described going to Brisbane as a step back in time.
- Criticised the Brisbane Broncos for their sacking Wally Lewis as first grade captain during the 1990-91 off-season.
- Suggested that planes flying over Brisbane always had a rocky trip because of all the hot air rising from below.
- Claimed that Queensland players had to come south to make their marks before Queenslanders would applaud their ability.

"I'll never forget the 'Benny is a suck' chant which greeted me for State of Origin 3 (1990), " I wrote. "It made me doubly keen. I loved holding the shield aloft before the crowd in Dodge City."

I saw (and still see) the article as no more than a bit of fun. But in Brisbane at State of Origin time it was, of course, like a red rag to a bull

"The outburst has caused a furore in the Queensland camp, with players and officials incensed at what they see as a deeply hurtful attack on their way of life," reported one Brisbane paper.

Preceded by this storm in a teacup, the first match of the series, at Lang Park, was as tight as a drum. Queensland got us 6-4 with Wally Lewis (as usual) a major contributor. Lewis, who was by then in the veteran class, had been under fire before the game. In the *Telegraph Mirror*, Ian Walsh had written:

It's time for Wally Lewis to answer the beckoning call of Old Father Time and quit rugby league with his reputation still intact ... I simply don't want to see Lewis ... show that he can't cut the mustard anymore.

In fact King Wally cut the mustard quite handily, and

the Brisbane newspaper headlines the next morning trumpeted the fact. "King Wally' Reigns Over Rivals Again" one paper proudly roared. Wally had put on the match-clinching try, scored by Mal Meninga. It was a game in which we had failed to convert pressure into points, but gone desperately close all the same. After the hooter, our fullback, Greg Alexander, fell short with a long-range penalty shot which would have salvaged a draw.

The crunch match in Sydney two weeks later was a real timebomb of a game, with the first half laced with flare-ups. It was the night that Mark Geyer really stepped into the spotlight. Although, as it turned out, he stepped straight out again when he was suspended for six matches - for a second-half high-shot on Queensland's fullback, the skyscraper Paul Hauff - an incident which sparked a major brawl.

As captain I was caught smack bang in the middle of the now famous chest-bumping duel between Wally Lewis and Geyer after the halftime hooter had sounded. Things had livened up late in the half when Geyer - whose full-on approach to the game was likened to that of a "stormtrooper" by one paper - niggled Steve Walters. Queensland forward Andrew Gee moved in to force Geyer away and the pair traded punches. Wally Lewis flew in, and so did plenty of others, and it was on. Not surprisingly, considering our pre-series verbal tussle, Steve Walters and I were singled out for our own little war.

"NSW captain Ben Elias, a bitter rival of Walters, made a beeline for Walters as soon as the skirmish started," wrote Brisbane journalist Paul Malone. "The pair were locked in combat for several seconds."

Order was eventually restored, and referee David Manson called out Lewis, Geyer and myself. It was a flashpoint situation as Manson tried to keep Lewis and Geyer from each other's throats. I'm sure he was thinking: "Shiiit ... what am I going to do here?" Wally and MG were like a couple of raging bulls as they bumped and threatened. It was Lewis at his inflammatory best/worst.

Back in the dressing-room after the pin had been replaced in the grenade, the atmosphere was electric. I think we were all nearly as fired up as Geyer. We were supporting him all the way. We couldn't wait to get back out there and prove our point.

We won that night, 14-12, when Michael O'Connor kicked one of the greatest pressure goals that the game has ever seen. Snoz was as cool as The Iceman as he knocked it over from the sideline, with a wonderful kick which curled in, and flopped over. John MacDonald in the *Sydney Morning Herald* wrote: "It was equal to any goal in history."

I didn't get to see the goal. Frankly, I couldn't bear to watch. I just turned my back - I knew the reaction of the crowd would tell the story. When this tremendous roar went up I swung back round. You little beauty!!!

The mighty O'Connor goal converted a 74th-minute try in the corner by centre Mark McGaw. Not long before that it seemed the match had escaped us when Alfie Langer and Lewis combined to put Dale Shearer over the line for 12-8.

Controversy about Geyer and the brawls deflected attention from the thrilling nature of the game. Queensland really blew up on Geyer and their coach Graham Lowe produced a famous quote:

There were 25 players in a fair contest and one lunatic running around getting away with murder.

Lowe later apologised to Geyer and his family for the "lunatic" reference. But the Queenslanders went right on with their pursuit of the big bloke, and MG copped what I thought was a tough suspension a few days later.

The Geyer hearing, on the last day of May, was front and back page news. Both Steve Roach and I went to bat for Geyer at the hearing at the NSW Leagues Club - and Graham Lowe confirmed that Hauff had not been injured in the incident involving the big second-rower.

Ray Chesterton's strong report in the *Telegraph Mirror* of the Judiciary hearing added to the theory that Geyer had been harshly dealt with. Chesterton wrote:

Geyer was the victim of a complaint from the losing Queensland side and stands alone as the only player singled out in a night of enormous mental, physical and verbal turbulence.

There were several all-in brawls, Queensland players ran up to 20 metres at times to throw punches, Queensland captain Wally Lewis engaged in an ugly, provocative shouting match, pushing past the referee to continue screaming at one stage - all without censure.

Geyer does not claim to be a saint - but his deeds in the State of Origin clash deserved to be treated with the same leniency shown other players, or the Judiciary committee dock last night should have been bursting at the seams.

The total evidence mustered against Geyer last night was an ambiguous video film and a statutory declaration from Hauff saying he felt "a stinging blow to the jaw".

Geyer pleaded not guilty to three charges last night of attacking the head, and had the first two - for incidents involving Queensland winger Michael Hancock and Queensland forward Andrew Gee - dismissed.

The hearing lasted two-and-a-half hours and at one stage Geyer demonstrated a shoulder charge on one of his legal team. It was a colourful night - but a cruel one for big MG.

The third match was a classic, but one that had us limping home with our tails between our legs - losers at Lang Park yet again. Ten minutes from the end of a fabulous, see-sawing game the announcement was made over the PA that the game was to be Wally Lewis' last in State of Origin football. The timing was perfect for the Maroons. They led 14-12, and kept us at bay to win by that score. Apart from one highly controversial incident, it was a match free of the spite that had marked the Sydney battle

- and a game which showed very clearly the fickle side of the game of rugby league. Only one goal was kicked in eight attempts (by Mal Meninga) and our Sydney hero, Michael O'Connor, missed with all four of his shots.

The one note of controversy involved O'Connor, who was on the receiving end in an incident which sent shock waves through the league world for weeks to come. Flattened in the course of a tackle by his Queensland opposite number and Australian captain, Mal Meninga, O'Connor suffered bruising of the brain, a broken nose, a split lip and blackened eyes. Meninga subsequently rang O'Connor to offer an apology, but the high-principled NSW centre remained furious that the NSWRL did not take any action - particularly after Queensland's relentless pursuit of Mark Geyer following State of Origin II.

The night of State of Origin III belonged to Wally Lewis, and afterwards the crowd sang: "For he's a jolly good fellow" as the Queensland captain slow-walked around the ground, soaking up the atmosphere. Lewis later called that match "the greatest Origin match ever". It was certainly a cracker.

After it came the flak, the sniping by coach Sheens and that NSW selector hiding behind his veil of anonymity.

One should never forget the contribution of the referees to these fabulous, drama-charged State of Origin matches. By the end of the 1993 representative season I had played 16 Origin games, and in that time had played under a number of refs, most of whom were excellent - men such as Mick Stone, Kevin Roberts, Bill Harrigan, Greg McCallum, Eddie Ward and David Manson. But there was one referee, who was involved in the second and third Origin matches in which I played (in 1985), who I could never put in the same class. I consider myself fortunate in that I missed most of the refereeing career of the man they called the "Grasshopper", Queenslander Barry Gomersall.

There's not a lot I can say about Barry. Let's just leave it at this - that in France they call such referees *patriotique*. In his own way, Barry was a colourful part of the State of Origin story. Whether he deserved to be there, and whether he was good for the game, is another matter entirely.

He was certainly a confident bloke, and to be a good State of Origin referee you'd need to have to have ice in your veins. It can be a terrifying experience just being out there as one of 26 players. To be the ref, all on your own, would be a shocker. I remember well the second game in 1988 when Mick Stone showed courage above and beyond the call of duty and sin-binned Wally Lewis. That was the signal for a rain of beer cans, one of which struck me on the head. I think we were all genuinely scared that night - the ref, the players ... all of us. It felt like the joint was going to explode, that any minute the screaming hordes would be over the fence and into us. They call Lang Park "The Coliseum" among other things. I reckon that's fair enough.

In the wake of the Origin Series of '91, I lost my Test spot to Steve Walters. I suffered a broken thumb in Balmain's 24-8 win over Manly at Leichhardt in late June (the first Test was scheduled for July 3). Officially I made myself available for selection in the Test against the Kiwis if required - but the Australian selectors chose not to consider me. Newspaper reports indicated that the vote would have been 6-nil against me anyway if my name had come up for consideration at the meeting. Not for the first time in my career, I was "off" with the selectors.

As it turned out the thumb injury was a bad one, providing an apt ending to the 1991 season for me. We had struggled at Balmain, I had busted a rib, I had blued with the coach in the Origin series, Queensland had beaten us and I had lost my Test jumper. It had been a "flat" and disappointing season. Perhaps I was suffering from lingering post-Kangaroo tour blues. Chances were, after my sequence of misfortune, that the year was going to finish on a low note for me. And so it did.

The broken thumb required surgery, and then a lengthy recuperation period. The operation came just as Australia crashed 8-24 to the Kiwis in the first Test, in Melbourne. Fit and well I guess I may have been some chance for a recall. But it was over for the year for B. Elias and the off-season began earlier for me than it ever had - right in the middle of winter. I played only 10 games for the Tigers in the entire season. I had hoped to be back in time to be in the running for the Australian tour to Papua New Guinea in October - but I missed the boat there, too.

When 1991 had dawned back on January 1, I probably should have stayed in bed ...

18

Sacked

IN 1992 I was sacked as captain of both Balmain and NSW. I had taken over as skipper of the Tigers in 1990, filling in for Junior Pearce as he fought his long battle with a failing knee, and then been given the job officially in 1991, even though injuries reduced my season to 10 games that year. I was proud to be captain of Balmain. The club was so much part of my life - to lead the team was the ultimate honour.

To lose the job, for reasons that I thought were questionable, cut me to the bone. The rumours that I was going to be replaced as captain were around town for some time before Alan Jones broke the news to me one morning in early 1992 at his house in Newtown. In fact they went back to early December of '91, when the *Telegraph Mirror* reported that our new halfback buy, the ex-union international Brian Smith, had been appointed captain for the Nissan Sevens tournament in February.

I conceded then I wasn't too confident about hanging on as skipper in '92. "It's probably not looking too good," I told the paper.

After I had been sacked as Balmain skipper, Alan Jones told the *Sunday Telegraph's* Phil Rothfield that constant pressure from critics (on me) was a major reason he replaced me, with Blocker Roach.

"It's very sad that Benny's been placed under so much

Above: A snapshot from my greatest day — the day Miss Kelly Crawford became Mrs Kelly Crawford-Elias.

Below: My parents, Norman and Barbara Elias, to whom I owe so much.

RLW

News Ltd

Right: Celebrating with Blocker after I had scored a crucial try in our defeat of Penrith in the 1989 major preliminary semi-final.

Below: With our marvellous full-back, Garry Jack, a week later, after we'd beaten Souths to reach the grand final.

RLW

RLW

News Ltd

Above: The Balmain team during the playing of the national anthem before the 1989 Grand Final. Left to right: Bruce McGuire, Garry Jack (obscured), James Grant, Andy Currier, Steve O'Brien, Tim Brasher, Gary Freeman, Steve Roach, Mick Neil, Paul Sironen, Steve Edmed, Ben Elias (obscured), Wayne Pearce.

Right: The feeling of utter despair after the same game.

Both pics RLW

The two greatest footballers I played with or against were Peter Sterling, (left) the best of them all, and the long-time Queensland and Australian captain, Wally Lewis, pictured below with me after the historic State of Origin match in Melbourne in 1990.

RLW

Above: With the master coach, Jack Gibson, after winning the 1990 State of Origin series.

Below: On the fly during the first match of that series. The other players (from left) are: Steve Roach, Steve Walters (on ground), Bruce McGuire, David Gillespie (obscured), Dan Stains, Wally Fullerton Smith and Laurie Daley. The referee is David Manson.

News Ltd

Above: Three Tigers among the Lions. Sirro (no.11) has played the ball, while I send Blocker at the Great Britain forwards during the 1990 series, when Australia recovered from a Test down to retain the Ashes.

Below: With our inspirational captain, Mal Meninga, after clinching the Ashes at Leeds.

Both pics Andrew Varley

Right: Benny Elias, 1990 Kangaroo vice-captain, and, for the final four Tests of the tour, first-choice hooker.

Below: With Mal Meninga (left), Brad Mackay ... and the Ashes trophy.

Bottom: Celebrations at Leeds: The players in picture are (left to right) Brad Mackay, Mal Meninga (obscured, with cap), Greg Alexander, Des Hasler, Ben Elias, Mark Sargent, Dale Shearer, Gary Belcher, Laurie Daley, Paul Sironen (obscured, at back), Bob Lindner, Ricky Stuart, Steve Roach, Cliff Lyons.

All pics Andrew Varley

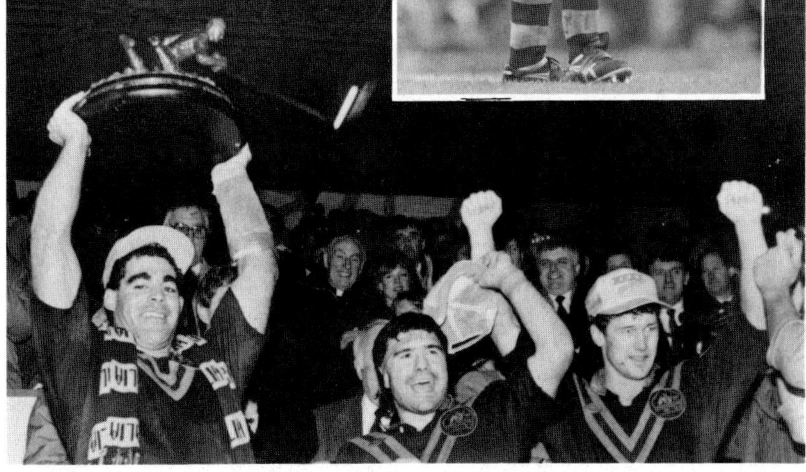

RLW

Above: Interviewing the Canberra, NSW and Australian five-eighth, Laurie Daley, for Sydney radio station 2GB.

Right: Struggling for form during a charity tennis day at White City.

Below: With AFL star John Platten, during the filming of a special episode of the TV game show, Family Feud.

News Ltd

Above: Providing an autograph for that amazing American rock star, Tina Turner, during the production of the now-famous TV commercial that promoted the game during 1990.

Below: With another famous singer, Jimmy Barnes, who I first met in 1991 and now count as a good friend.

Bob Barker

Craig Golding

Three photos from one of the most dramatic matches I ever played in — the second Origin match of 1991, which NSW won 14-12 after Michael O'Connor kicked a goal from the sidelines with six minutes left.

Left: I burst away in the pouring rain.

Below: The infamous confrontation between Wally Lewis and NSW second-rower Mark Geyer. The referee is David Manson.

Opposite page: With big Blocker after our amazing victory.

Martin Johnson

RLW

Above: Alan Jones (left), Balmain coach from 1991 to 1993, with his assistant Ken Shine.

Right: 1991 NSW coach Tim Sheens.

Below: The Canberra, Queensland and, since 1991, Australian hooker, Steve Walters.

All pics RLW

RLW

I was named man of the match after NSW's tough victory in the first Origin match of 1992, but most people only remember the bad head gash I suffered. At right, I'm escorted to the blood bin early in the second half.

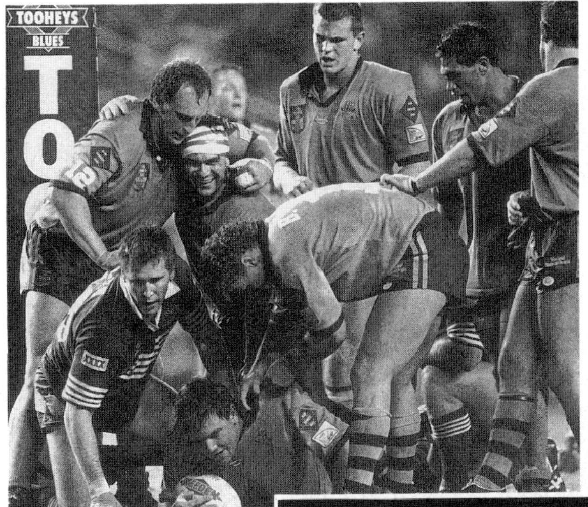

News Ltd

Left: I was back in time to be on hand when NSW's Craig Salvatori crashed over for the game-breaking try. The other players pictured are Queensland prop, Gavin Allen, and NSW's (left to right): John Cartwright, Rod Wishart (at back), Brad Mackay, Paul Harragon, John Simon and Brad Fittler.

RLW

Right: Being interviewed after the game by 2UE's John Gibbs.

Left: Getting a pass away, despite the tackle of Penrith's Mark McGaw, in early 1993.

Below: Doing the right thing by a Tigers fan, after playing in a testimonial match for Wally Lewis on the Gold Coast in September, 1992.

Below: Balmain players pictured during a loss to Norths in 1991. Left to right: Garry Jack, Ben Elias, John Elias, Craig Izzard, Steve O'Brien and Gary McFarlane.

All pics RLW

The only time I have ever been sent off in grade football occurred on May 9, 1993, when referee Graeme West marched me (above), right on halftime, for allegedly abusing a touch judge. Watching the second half from the stands (below) was a bitter experience. The subsequent two-match suspension, which meant I missed the second Origin match that year, was one of the greatest disappointments of my career.

Both pics RLW

Above: NSW players celebrate winning the 1993 State of Origin series. Back Row: Brad Fittler, Brad Mackay, Glenn Lazarus, David Gillespie, Scott Gourley, Andrew Ettingshausen, Graham Mackay, coach Phil Gould, Paul Harragon, Terry Hill, Paul Sironen, Jason Taylor. Front: Ricky Stuart, Laurie Daley, Tim Brasher, David Fairleigh, Ben Elias, Rod Wishart.

Both pics RLW

Right: As Balmain's 1993 season rolled on, there were still mountains to climb, dreams to pursue...

pressure, and that's one of the reasons I took the captaincy away from him," Jones said. "Everywhere the guy went he found himself under attack for some reason. That smear stuff is disgraceful. I just felt, even though it was disappointing to Benny at the time, that if we reduced some of the pressure it would help him."

In the same interview, the coach was very positive about my role with the Tigers:

Every week he plays as if his life depends on the result. It's his ambition and commitment to the game that carries everyone along with him. Very inspirational stuff.

Jonesy has always played down the importance of the captaincy role. I see it very differently. I think that the captaincy is an all-embracing and important job at a football club. In my view the captain is the bloke who has to show the way, on and off the field. He's got to be a leader on the field - and at training. Junior was the perfect captain because he was always leading from the front, no matter what we were doing.

I took it hard - it knocked me around a fair bit psychologically. But I had toughened over the years. I set aside my disappointment, and got down to business. A professional approach had to be the fall-back situation, despite the disappointment I felt inside. The captaincy thing created an awkwardness between Blocker and me for a time - and we had been team-mates and pals for years. There wasn't much we could say; I congratulated him, he said thanks and we put our heads down and went back to trying to build a winning football team. Ultimately it didn't affect our relationship at all. At the time, Blocker said: "If Benny was captain he knows he'd have my full support, and I know that I will have his." He did.

I was never given an "official" reason for my sacking as captain. As vice-captain of the 1990 Kangaroo tour, captain of NSW for the previous two seasons and Balmain captain in 1991, I thought I at least deserved that.

I don't want to put Jonesy down in any way. He has been tremendously supportive of me, and I am greatly appreciative of that. It's just when people ask me the question that I get asked from time to time - "Why weren't (aren't) you captain in 1992-93?" - I can't give them an answer which can go close to fully explaining it. I haven't got one.

Not long after this little storm in Tigertown had blown away, my neck was on the chopping block again - this time in my capacity as incumbent captain of the NSW Blues. I had been skipper in 1990 and 1991, and we had won one and lost one - going down 14-12 in the third game of 1991 after the tightest series on record.

As soon as the representative season began, the stories started appearing in print - and obviously from the right sources - that I was heading for the axe as captain.

Bradley Clyde was the first bloke touted to take over, but he later pulled the rug from under himself with an honest assessment that he wasn't ready for the job. Then Jack Gibson was quoted as saying that Laurie Daley should get the captaincy.

Then it was ET. The *Telegraph Mirror* came out with a front-page story that Andrew was to be captain of the City side, and was the front-runner for the state job. This story obviously came from a very high-up source, and it certainly signalled the thinking in Phillip Street at that time - even if it did turn out to be wrong. All the time I was wondering: what have I done? I must have either played five shockers in a row or told a member of the League hierarchy to get stuffed!

I retained the City captaincy, despite the "leak" to the *Tele Mirror*, but if officialdom needed a further excuse for giving me the shove, it came in the match itself. Country Origin beat City for the first time, 17-10 - and Country skipper Laurie Daley had a whale of a game. That night Laurie was named captain of NSW. Sources from within Phillip Street subsequently told me there was no *one* reason for me losing the job. One official put forward a theory that I was not popular with the players. Another said that I was not going to be in the Australian team (that Steve Walters was going to get that job) and therefore there was a strong case for me not to be picked as NSW captain. Mainly it seemed that a powerful push from the country was the key development. I'm told that a great deal of politicking went on from a day or two before the time that ET was mooted as City captain.

I can throw no further light on it. As incumbent NSW captain I believe that I was entitled to some support (I barely received any, apparently!) - if only out of respect for the position and the tradition of the role of Blues' captain. Not for the first time in my life, I received not very much more than rumours and hints. The lack of support was disappointing, but life went on.

John Quayle was good about it. He called me in and explained the mechanics of the decision - that the captaincy was decided by the NSWRL Board of Directors. "It was a decision for the future," he said. "We're looking at youth."

I appreciated John taking the time to at least talk me through the thing. "Look", I said. "That's fine - I'm just glad to be part of the side." Which I was. Later Laurie came up to me and said: "Mate, I need all the help I can get. I've captained nothing." I gladly pledged my 110 per cent support. I've always had a good relationship with Laurie. There was no way I was going to let my disappointment erode the team in any way.

But I *was* disappointed. You set yourself high-achieving goals and you try to reach them, and it has to be disappointing when you miss. Rejection is not easy for any of us to take. I suppose I was puzzled as much as anything. I thought I had done a pretty fair job as captain for two years and there was no indication I hadn't (apart from Tim Sheens' sniping in 1991). The NSW situation was possibly a flow-on from what had happened at Balmain. I couldn't see any other reason.

The suggestions which finally surfaced in print that I was allegedly unpopular with other players really angered me. The ammunition for that theory had perhaps been provided by Steve Walters in a television interview 12 months before. I resented it, and disputed it. "There is one person who has said that I'm unpopular and he's the hooker for the Queensland side," I told the *Sunday Telegraph's* Phil Rothfield. "When asked to name the players, he doesn't have the answers. I don't have any problems whatsoever in that area. I enjoy everyone's company, and I get on well with other people."

A further theory touched on by Ray Chesterton, in an article in the *Telegraph Mirror*, was that the decision was an indirect result of the vicious campaign of whispers and innuendo that had been levelled against me since 1987. Chesterton's theory was: "Eventually the cowardly rumour-mongering created a climate in which it was seen as more discreet to end his captaincy of NSW"

Chesterton made reference to the rumours which plagued me on the 1990 Kangaroo tour, and wrote:

Senior rugby league officials, concerned at the viciousness of the rumours and their potentially disastrous effects on the game's image, made their own discreet enquiries at the highest police level.

Police gave solid assurance Elias was not being sought and said they were mystified at the stories.

It was a smear campaign that smeared Elias more than any cut he suffered on a football field.

... The knives have been out for Elias all season and his removal as state captain was pre-ordained.

By that time I'd had a lot of disappointments in my life. I was pretty good at picking myself up and dusting myself off. The game was still the thing; I just wanted to get out there and play it.

It's funny how things can turn out. Blocker was missing for a time, injured, at Balmain and I was given the captaincy. We won five straight games, then lost the sixth after the bell when Penrith's Andrew Leeds kicked a monster goal at Penrith Stadium. Block had a difficult year, owing to a bad knee injury and then a chronic back problem, and played only nine games, so as it turned out I was skipper for a fair lump of the season.

Our win over St George less than 48 hours after the City-Country game was a beauty. The Tigers had Paul Sironen and myself backing up, and at halftime at Kogarah we were on the ropes, down 16-2. But a big second-half fightback brought us storming back to win 22-17. We had to climb off the canvas twice in that game. After fighting back to 16-all, Saints' Andrew Walker banged over a field goal - a big psychological moment - for 17-16. But a runaway try by winger James Grant near the end won it for us.

Controversy and me were very close running mates in 1992. I got badly cut in the first Origin game in Sydney, and received all the flack in the world when the photos and TV images appeared of the end of the game, of mum (who had run onto the field at fulltime) and me covered in blood.

I'll tell you how it happened. The game was like trench warfare, a real bruiser. Queensland's Steve Jackson and Gary Larson both got flattened and had to leave the field. I copped a bad cut going in for a tackle - a real nasty slash on the top of my head, and had to go off. In the dressing-room, after I made it clear that I was going back out there, our doctor Nathan Gibbs worked flat-out to try and patch me up. Halfway through it, with 30 minutes still to play, Laurie Daley appeared in the room. Our captain was gone - he was badly concussed. We were going down like flies. Shit! I just had to get out there again. Laurie mumbled: "Mate, you're in charge" - and I hit the tunnel running, with eight stitches in my melon, and some fluorescent green tape wrapped haphazardly around my head. "Control the middle," were the final words ringing in my ears from new NSW coach, Phil Gould. Near the end of the game the cut opened up again, and the blood was coursing down my face. In the heat of battle, referee David Manson neglected to send me off the field again to the blood bin, and so I was there at the hooter, as stand-in captain. The scoreboard read: NSW 14, Queensland 6.

In a flash my mum was there on the field with me. Dad had told her to sit down, and not to worry. My mum tells the story this way:

Norm said - sit down ... but I said: "No, I want to go." When I got there I said: "Benny, don't worry, the blood is nothing." I saw the blood coming out and I tried to clean it. And I kept saying to Benny: "Don't worry". I knew the whole family was watching the game and when you see blood, you get scared. I asked Ben if it hurt and he said: "No, mum". I was just trying to get the blood off his face.

My father can give a deeper insight into that night, into why my mother felt she had to be by my side.

The town that my wife comes from is called Zgharta. It is in some ways the "Northern Ireland" of Lebanon, and is a famous place in Lebanon. The inhabitants of Zgharta are stubborn and determined and bitter; if they want something, they will do whatever they have to do to get it. They stick to their principles, generation after generation. For 150 years or so there was feuding among families there, and some killing took place. Some of it still goes on. When people from other parts of Lebanon hear the name of somebody who comes from the town, they look twice.

I believe that Benny has got a lot of that Zgharta determination planted in his mind. One of the mottos of the town - the way people were brought up - was that when husbands went off to be involved in a fight, their wives would go and help out.

What happened on that State of Origin night was a sort of genetic thing. There was Ben covered in blood, and

Barbara went down there to encourage him, to cheer him, to *boost him. It was a reaction that was planted deep inside her. On this occasion, the whole nation got to see it.*

It was an emotional night in many ways. Phil Gould had said to us at halftime: "We've heard about that Maroon jumper for years. Take a look at your own. It's time to stand up for it."

Afterwards Gould said simply: "Courage is such a small word to describe what the players did out there tonight."

I felt great in the moments after the game, but I looked bloody dreadful. It was only later that I realised just *how* bad I looked. As soon as the match ended the television and radio people surrounded me - I had been voted man of the match - and all of a sudden my mum was alongside, giving me a hug. She was a typical mother that night, concerned for the welfare of her son. She just couldn't hold back; she had to run down from the crowd and see if I was okay. So these pictures were beamed everywhere, and I must admit they looked pretty gruesome.

I took a pasting over it. People accused me of "grandstanding". In Queensland, former Test centre Tony Currie wrote in a column in a Brisbane newspaper: "Bloody Benny, who looked like he had been in a car wreck without a seatbelt, did more to bring the game into disrepute than any coach ever did by bagging a referee." I resented his stupid comment, and I fired back that Currie was just a frustrated reserve-grader trying to make a name for himself. I mean I would have liked to have been as clean as a whistle, with my hair nicely brushed. But I had been cut, and when you get cut, you bleed. I particularly resented the criticism made of my mum that night. There could have been no more human response, surely, than a mother checking on her child in the excitement and drama of such a situation.

My individual performance had been a very satisfying one. In a *Sydney Morning Herald* feature "The Game

Breaker", journalist Daniel Williams wrote:

Elias was the team man last night. Mostly he kept things simple, feeding his forwards, but when the strike players were off and the forwards began to suffer from the speed of the game, Elias ran a little more, tried a little more. And he talked and talked.

Writing in the *Telegraph Mirror*, Mark Geyer called Origin I, 1992: "The toughest game I have ever seen."

Coach Phil Gould's introduction to Origin football in 1992 confirmed him as one of the great coaching talents of the game. My experiences with him in '92-93 have left no doubt in my mind that he's one of the finest coaches I have ever been involved with - and I've experienced the varying skills of a few of them over the years.

Gould has an outstanding relationship with his players, and he is a brilliant communicator. He seems to be always able to dig out some unusual motivational tool. It could be from a book he's read, or maybe a film he's recently seen. He'll draw on sources like that, and then relate the message back to the team and to the job at hand. Gould is right up there alongside Bob Fulton and Jack Gibson as the best representative coach that I have ever been involved with.

His knowledge of the game is pretty extraordinary, too. "Balance" is a key word with Phil Gould. Under his coaching control, there's time to muck around and have some fun, but he knows just when to rule the line and begin the serious business.

The battle that was Origin I, 1992, and some carnage in our following game, against Norths, prompted 5an outburst from me in the media. At Leichhardt Oval the Sunday after the state game, our big centre, Ian McCann, was caught in a high shot by Mario Fenech, and finished up in hospital. In the same game, the Bears' Peter McPhail was sent off, as Fenech had been, for another high tackle. There was further drama when Fenech claimed he had been gouged in the match - although the complaint was not pursued.

Rugby League Week quoted me as saying I feared someone would be killed if a violent trend that seemed to be on the rise in football at that time was not arrested.

"Football isn't that important when you see a team-mate knocked out, bleeding badly from the mouth and the trainers calling for the stretchers," I said.

There is no question at all that the game has become physically harder and faster since I started in grade back in 1982. The players are bigger and stronger, thanks to scientific weight programs, and the aggression level is extraordinary - even though the League has done a mighty job in their drive to exterminate blatant foul play. It's kamikaze stuff out there these days - players launching their bodies at each other, at full pace. Often it's like hitting a brick wall. And it's all done with a minimum of protection, although that's starting to change.

Now we're starting to see chest protectors, back protectors and thigh guards to go with the more traditional aids such as mouthguards, headgear and shin pads. The protection is needed, although I'm sure it won't ever get to the stage of American football's armour-plated warriors. I think anything a player can use to protect his body is good, as long as it's legal and he's comfortable with it.

In 1993 I was approached to try out an additional piece of equipment - "grip" gloves. I have seen old photos of English players wearing gloves - but they were merely a protection against the cold. These new gloves are designed to help your handling. As a bloke who handles the ball a huge amount in any game, I'll probably give them a go at some time. Like everyone in the game, I am constantly seeking that extra "edge" that might make me a better player, might give me a start over the blokes I face up against.

On May 19, Queensland levelled up the 1992 Origin series when Allan Langer kicked a field goal with two minutes to play at Lang Park, to squeak the Maroons home,

5-4. It was a tough, slogging game which came under some criticism for its lack of adventure and flair. Both coaches, Phil Gould and Graham Lowe, went stoutly onto the front foot over that one, but I'm not sure everyone was convinced. It was certainly a dour series in '92, and one which imposed enormous physical demands on the players. In the final call there wasn't much between the teams, but I always felt we had the edge.

My young Balmain team-mate, Tim Brasher, played a big hand in confirming that theory when he produced a terrific second half in the deciding game at the SFS. Called on for the second half to replace our injured winger, Rod Wishart, Brasher pulled off two try-saving tackles, on the Queensland centres, Mark Coyne and Mal Meninga, and made several incisive dashes which stretched the Queensland defence. Steaming home in the second half, we converted a nervous 4-2 halftime lead into a 16-4 triumph, to clinch the series. I had a hand in the try which kicked us away to 8-4 in the second half, steering the play down the blindside with a short dash before Daley, Illawarra centre Paul McGregor, and Daley again combined to put ET over. It was a fabulous experience to win the series-decider in front of such an exuberant and supportive home crowd and, for me, easily the highlight of what - the NSW victory apart - was an extremely frustrating football season.

The triple play in my year of disappointment, 1992 - having already lost two captaincy roles that I cherished - came when I failed to regain the Test jumper from Steve Walters for the home series against Great Britain. A controversial two-week suspension of his younger brother Kerrod, for taking a poke at Wests' Graeme Wynn in a premiership match in 1991, had opened the gate for Steve to make the Queensland side that year, and the Canberra hooker went on from there, winning the Test spot for the matches against New Zealand in 1991, and keeping the job for the Ashes Tests in '92. I thought I was unlucky to miss out against the Poms. NSW won the Origin series 2-1, (14-6, 4-5, 16-4). I was man of the match in the first game, and Walters and I competed fiercely throughout. After my success in England in 1990, I was perhaps entitled to believe I had done enough. But the selectors saw it otherwise and went for Walters. While I was back in the shadows, he played the three Tests and Australia retained the Ashes 2-1, despite losing the second Test at Princes Park in Melbourne, 33-10, in one of the most stunning upsets in the game's history.

Steve Walters retained the spot for the Test against Papua New Guinea in Townsville in July, and then Steve and Kerrod got the nod for the World Cup campaign to England in October - with Steve taking man-of-the-match honours in the cup final at Wembley. Kerrod was in the selectors' sights all the way through the finals series as Brisbane rampaged through to take the premiership, so I could understand them taking him. He was training four days a week and playing, while I had long since disappeared from view. I wasn't over the moon about being left out, but I understood.

I married Kelly Crawford the day before the team was picked. We had the honeymoon on hold, just in case. But I missed the flight to the north of England and went instead to Thailand where the new Mrs Elias and myself had a fabulous three-week holiday.

I at least managed to achieve one football milestone in this season of disappearing opportunities. My 21 games for the Tigers carried me past the landmark of 200 first grade games for the club (including games where I came on as a replacement). At the end of the season I had 205 on the board, second only to Garry Jack (229). By then I had played more grade games than any other player in the history of the club. My tally stood at 253, nine ahead of the record that had been established by John Owens in the years 1980-88.

During the year I signed a contract which may well see

me out at Balmain. It takes me to the end of 1994, and it's at that time that I will pause, talk to Kelly and consider my options. I don't think there was ever really a chance that I was going to leave Balmain. Without doubt, I have sacrificed many tens of thousands of dollars over the years by staying put. But there's a lot more to life than money. You have to be content and happy where you are.

I remember in early years working alongside my boyhood idol, Greg Cox, in a wood-turning business owned by John O'Brien and Kevin Smyth. Greg had just made the City side, and he was truly Balmain's Golden Boy. Everyone loved him, and for me it was a real buzz to be working alongside him.

One day I took a phone call for Greg, from Cronulla coach (and St George legend) Norm Provan. Greg had recently been married and at the time was angling for the security of a three-year contract with Balmain. They had offered him only two years. Eventually Greg took the bait of a three-year deal offered by Cronulla, and left. His football life seemed to be a struggle from that point onwards. At Cronulla, and later at Wests, he never looked as happy, as settled, or as *effective* as he had been at Balmain. If he'd stayed he would have been a Junior Pearce at Balmain - good-looking, tonnes of ability, a hugely popular local hero. I always thought about Greg whenever temptation was calling me to leave Balmain. I accepted that if I was happy, then I should be content with my lot.

The Balmain year in 1992 was better than '91 - but ultimately disappointing. We finished up 10th on the ladder on 21 points, just a couple of wins out of the five. Our five-match winning charge in the first round had us third after nine rounds. But we lost our next three, including that "miracle" defeat by Penrith, and stumbled often enough in the second round to put ourselves out of the running. The Penrith game was something of a watershed in the year. The loss in such dramatic circumstances, as fullback Leeds kicked his after-the-bell goal, seemed to drain our confidence for what lay ahead. We lost our next two games (to Manly and Brisbane) and in July turned in a shocker at home when we were beaten 26-14 by lowly Gold Coast. A 30-10 thrashing at the hands of Canterbury late in the year - a game in which Terry Lamb cut loose - was the final nail in the coffin for us.

For the second time in three seasons there was an emotional ending to our year at Leichhardt. In our round-21 match against St George we farewelled three outstanding Tigers - Steve Roach, Garry Jack and David Brooks. We lost the game (20-14), but there was barely a dry eye in the house as more than 17,000 people turned out to say goodbye to three great players.

All three had been mighty contributors to Balmain's successes of the 1980s. In their absence we would look to the new breed of young Tiger cubs - such players as Jacin Sinclair, Will Robinson, Matt Munro and Paul Davis - to help build a new dynasty in the 1990s.

The months of August and September, 1992, were among the most traumatic in the history of Balmain club - with coach Jones the man at the eye of a continuing storm. Gary Freeman's book *Tiger, Tiger, Kiwi, Rooster*, released in early August, contained scathing criticism of the coach, and added fuel to an already touchy situation as an anti-Jones lobby gained strength at the club.

The pressure continued throughout August, culminating sensationally in a *Daily Telegraph* poster story on Friday, August 28, headlined: "Jones Sacked - Pearce Tipped To Coach Tigers". Ray Chesterton's story began:

High-profile Balmain coach Alan Jones will be sacked just 24 hours after the club completes its last match of the season against North Sydney on Sunday.

Balmain's committee is lined up eight votes to two, or at worst 7-3, against Jones being re-appointed after two years in the job.

Former Test and Kangaroo star Wayne Pearce will be appointed as Jones' replacement although he has yet to be formally approached.

The story created an immense storm in Sydney sporting circles that weekend - and especially at Balmain, where there was a flurry of activity. By Sunday, the opinions which had provided a solid foundation for Chesterton's story were wavering. Balmain strong men, George Stone (president) and Keith Barnes (chief executive), were 100 per cent behind the coach, and intense lobbying worthy of Parliament House in Canberra began. In the *Sun-Herald*, Alan Clarkson sounded a warning to the club:

Before the board votes on this highly emotional issue, they should listen intently to some of the rumblings from the public about their proposed action.

We drew that last match 14-all, after frittering away a 14-4 lead. Even as the game was being played, behind-the-scenes discussions about the '93 coach were continuing, and by late on that Sunday afternoon the *Telegraph Mirror's* Friday story was starting to look sick, as support for the coach steadily grew.

The *Telegraph Mirror* of the following Tuesday morning carried a headline of the same size as "Jones Sacked", but one which carried a vastly different message ... "Alan Jones Coup - Tigers Retain Coach".

The Ray Chesterton story that followed under that headline began:

Beleaguered Balmain rugby league coach Alan Jones last night pulled off a stunning coup when he was swept back for another season on the unanimous - 10-nil - vote of the club board ...

It was an amazing turnaround. From an 8-2 or 7-3 vote against him (presuming Chesterton's information was correct), coach Jones had gained a spectacular declaration of confidence from the club. He told the media he felt as if he had been reprieved from death row, and was extremely critical of those pressmen who had written of his sacking prematurely. The following day, Chesterton was cheekily back in print, claiming credit for saving Jones' neck via his now-infamous story that had appeared on the previous Friday.

We players survived as best we could in the seething atmosphere of the time. As the turmoil raged around us we focused on doing what we were paid to do - playing football. I supported Steve Roach's public declaration when the "Jones Sacked" story first surfaced. Blocker said:

It's a bit weak that the cat has been let out of the bag.

We're on the same number of competition points as Canberra and no-one is calling for Tim Sheens' head.

It seems that Alan is just a victim of his profile. He's brought all these youngsters to the club and a lot of attention to the club and all that will be lost. He's done a good job and deserves another chance.

There was a hefty sting in the tail of Garry Jack's departure for England, where he was joining the Sheffield Eagles club. On the day he flew out, *Rugby League Week* published a article in which Garry launched a scathing attack on coach Alan Jones.

We live in a democracy, and I will always defend the right of people to say what they honestly believe. In one way that's very much how I feel about what Jimmy Jack chose to do. But in another I feel that he comprehensively did the wrong thing, in the *way* that he fired this blistering parting salvo.

It was common knowledge at Balmain that Garry Jack and Alan Jones didn't get on. That happens in every football club - there are differences of opinion between strong-willed men - and sometimes they can blow up into barely-concealed warfare. So it was with Jones and Jack.

There is no doubt that Jimmy Jack believed every single word of what he wrote in *Rugby League Week*. But people saw what he had done as a "hit and run" episode. The day the story hit the streets, Jimmy was on the plane and off to England to join the Sheffield Eagles.

I thought he did it in the wrong way, and I've told him so. If he felt he had to say what he said then he should have gone to the coach and said it face to face. Then, if he had decided to press on and go public as he did in *RLW*, he should have remained in Australia, for at least a day or two, to respond to the fall-out.

I spoke to him on the phone about it not long ago. I told him I thought he'd cut his own throat. If he had to do what he did, he should have then waited, and met the press to answer all the questions that arose. He could have simply told them: "The article represents the way I feel. It represents my honest view of things at Balmain. If it is a crime to come out and say what you honestly think - well, I'm guilty, and you can arrest me now."

Garry Jack's motivation for what he did was honourable. He honestly believed he was helping the club by saying what he said. He loved Balmain - still does no doubt - and in his view the coaching style of Alan Jones was not what the club needed.

Football and feudin' was the last thing on my mind on Saturday, October 3, 1992, when I married my sweetheart, Kelly. You can't believe how nervous I was. Over the years I'd played Test matches, grand finals, Origin games - but this was far more nerve-wracking. We were married at St Peter Chanel's Church, Woolwich, and Father John Keeble told us: "A grand final is only 80 minutes, this is for life."

The emotion of the day got to me, and I shed a tear or two.

It was a wonderful day. The sun shone brightly, everything went perfectly and Kelly looked a million dollars ...

We had first met in 1989. Kelly was the receptionist at the Sydney radio station, 2 Day FM, at a time when I was doing regular reports for the station. We used to chat over the phone, but it was a long time before we actually met. I went into the station one day, but she was off work.

"What about this Kelly?" I asked the station manager, Noel McGurgan. "She seems like a lovely girl."

"Mate - you should meet her," said Noel. "She's a knockout."

Anyway, some time later 2 Day FM had a party to which I was invited. Just about the first person I saw was this beautiful blonde girl.

"You've got to be Kelly," I said.

"And you've got to be Ben," she replied.

"Yeah."

Kelly had a steady boyfriend at the time and it was quite a while before she agreed to go out with me. Finally that happened, and we started going out regularly. I met the Crawford family and pretty much fell in love with them - even though her old man, Terry, is a fanatical St George supporter. I used to love going to their place after training, just sitting around the table having a bit of dinner, and talking.

Kelly's father told her: "Any footballer who comes into my house, I'm going to break his legs" - and she told me about it. I presume he meant any footballer *not* from St George. So the first time we met I shook his hand and said: "I hear you're going to break my legs!"

I'm a very lucky bloke to have found Kelly Crawford. She's just terrific. Of all the great things that have happened to me in my life, she's the best. Our marriage is built on trust, honesty and love. I like to think of us as a great team. We discuss and plan things together, and I have no doubt I am a better person for having met her. She loves me for what I am. She's not really into football, but she comes along to give me a cheer anyway.

The day I met her was the best day of my life.

19

The Best of My Time

I DOUBT I'LL tackle many harder tasks in my life than trying to rate in order the many champions I have played with and against in my football career. A word comes immediately to my mind when I think about what I have experienced these past 12 seasons - "privileged". It's exactly how I feel about having had the chance to share the playing fields of the 1980s and '90s with the men I will list in this chapter. The great thing about rugby league is that its champions come in all shapes and sizes. In my top ten you'll find smaller players of subtle skills standing alongside giants who stride the fields as if in Forty League boots.

The greatest difficulty in listing a top ten, of course, lies in the players left out. In my eyes each one of them - and I have listed them at the end of the chapter - can genuinely wear the tag "champion" too. And so can some others not even mentioned. But, you can't pick 'em all - so after many hours of consideration and much crossing and re-crossing out ... here goes.

1. PETER STERLING

Sterlo had the best field vision of any player I ever played with or against. The bloke was a genius. He had a sense of what could happen three or four plays ahead - and the capacity to then *make* it happen for whatever team he was playing with. Sterlo was a conductor, an orchestrator of rugby league. I loved watching him play, and I loved playing with him. I was nowhere near as keen on playing against him.

There was nothing flash about Sterlo. He did the hard graft every game, and although he lacked genuine speed, he had all the rest of the requirements. His kicking game was superb - short and long - and so was his passing game, whether he was easing a forward through a gap from close-in, or sending a wide pass to Brett Kenny, Mick Cronin and the rest. In just about every match he played he was the focal point; some afternoons it seemed that every single thing on the football field revolved around him. To a hesitant defence, he was mesmerising - creating uncertainty which signalled their doom. I reckon if you could do a career check on the options he took, he'd come up right 95 per cent of the time - an extraordinary fact when you consider the vast number of times he would handle the ball. He was a truly great player, and the field vision that made him great (along with courage, intelligence, excellent tackling technique and so on) was one of the modern wonders of the game.

Sterlo also was (and is) a terrific bloke. Off the field on Kangaroo tours he continued as the orchestrator, bringing a spirit of cameraderie and togetherness to the team. Tours need a livewire organiser - and Sterlo was that, on and off the paddock. He was a special player.

I know in the years ahead it will be with great pride that I'll be able to tell my kids and grandkids: "I played with Peter Sterling."

2. WALLY LEWIS

There was always enough drama surrounding Wally Lewis to suggest that he could have been a leading Shakespearean actor. But with Wally it was all part of the package; with Wally you didn't ever just get football - you got drama, controversy and pathos. State of Origin football would never have been what it is today without him. The statue of him that stands at Lang Park is no more than he deserves.

I had a lot of trouble separating Sterling and Lewis at the top of my list. They both possessed a vastly wider vision on the football field than most players. And they shared the quality of time. Both seemed to be able to slow down the passing of the seconds; there was always the impression with them that they had the luxury of heaps of time as they wove their magic.

Lewis played most of his career under the weight of extraordinary expectations and enormous pressure. In Sydney he was hated, and he had to carry that burden in any match he played. In Queensland he was regarded as superhuman, and he had to carry that burden as well. Yet, under pressure, he never flinched; he would *always* produce.

Lewis had extra qualities of size and strength over Sterling. Like Sterlo he was a great leader on the field - a constructive talker who could brilliantly sum up the trend of the game, pinpoint the weaknesses that needed to be targeted. He was also a genius at fine-tuning referees. I'm sure his ability to get over the top of referees was a plus for Queensland many times. He wasn't afraid to call them every name under the sun - and unlike some, he'd get away with it.

Lewis polarised the fans as few players ever have, but whether you loved him or hated him you'd have to agree - the bloke was a champion.

3. ELLERY HANLEY

The "Black Pearl" was a genius of the football field, a supreme athlete and a consummate professional. Balmain fans will never forget his short season with the Tigers in 1988 - and neither will the players who were there alongside him. It was Hanley who swept us along, on the crest of a wave, all the way to the grand final. In virtually every match he played (except the grand final) he pulled out amazing tricks and special qualities to get us through. He added an "X" factor to Balmain that hadn't been there. Without him I don't think there's any way we would have made the grand final.

Hanley is one of the greatest "naturals" to play the game. He didn't do gym work, and he didn't practise his sprints, yet he had this great natural speed and strength which lifted him way above the pack.

I'm sure one of Ellery's secrets as a footballer was his tremendous balance. He seemed to have a low centre of gravity, and was very hard to topple once he was in full flight. That balance, added to his raw strength and very fair speed, made him a nightmare for would-be defenders.

The other big plus about Ellery the footballer was his attitude to training and playing. It was inevitably professional, and positive. He was a good bloke to be around, and his attitude rubbed off on Balmain in '88. He was magic.

4. MAL MENINGA

The big fella. I doubt I can add much to the millions of words spoken and written about Mal Meninga's many years in football. The bloke is a man of dignity, a gentleman. He's had his share of knockers over the years, but he just goes out and answers them in the best way, on the playing field.

Mal has always had the happy knack of producing his

best on the big occasion. I can still see him now, up the field like a runaway express as he chased Ricky Stuart's break in the Second Test at Manchester in 1990. Nobody could have stopped his progress that day, as he charged upfield to take the pass, win the Test, and save the Ashes.

Because of his power, he's one of the most feared players in the game. He's nearly impossible to stop one-on-one from anywhere close to the line. I rate him a great captain, too. He's a skipper who doesn't say all that much - but what he says is quality. As a player he's like a fine old red wine; he just gets better and better with age.

5. GARRY JACK

Jimmy Jack was the hardest man I ever saw in football. Iron hard. It didn't matter who he was playing, Jimmy gave every ounce of sinew, bone and muscle in his body. It might be Brisbane before 40,000 or Gold Coast before 4000, Jimmy would be ripping in from fullback at 1000 miles an hour, putting life and limb on the line.

Jimmy Jack was a great example of a bloke playing right up to his potential. He was mentally tough, very focused, and fear never held him back. He had a job to do out there on a Sunday afternoon, and nothing would deflect him from it. I'll never forget a day we played North Sydney and he had three teeth knocked out. He just rounded them up, stuck them in his sock, and kept playing. A normal person would have come off.

It was wonderfully re-assuring to have him at the back, whether with Balmain, NSW or Australia. His catching of the high ball at times was unbelievable. When Jimmy was at fullback you knew things were okay, that in the last line you had a man you could trust with your life.

6. STEVE ROACH

Blocker Roach would often generate a certain quality in the ranks of the opposition. It's called fear. Blocker knew only one way to play - *very* hard and *very* tough. He'd give it to the opposition verbally and he'd give it to them physically. He would thus create a climate in which his own team was free to fully expound its skills.

Blocker was a wonderful mix - a big, bruising bloke who just happened to possess the best and most subtle ball skills since the great Arthur Beetson. He turned many a game with his wonderful off-loading of the ball. He would hit ... and then slip, and some fortunate runner alongside would be away.

A little bloke like me was always very happy indeed to have him at my side in the scrums. Blocker's mere presence seemed to generate an air of respect from opposing forwards, leaving a little hooker free to try and work his tricks.

I always reckoned that Blocker read my game better than any other player. We played a tonne of football together and he developed what was almost a sixth sense about my play. Those times when I would have a go from dummy-half, Blocker would always be up there alongside to carry it on.

I'm delighted that I was lucky and played my career with him ... and not against him.

7. WAYNE PEARCE

In many ways Junior Pearce was the greatest model of all for budding young footballers. Junior certainly did not possess the skills of many of the players mentioned in this chapter, but in that fact lay the essence of the message he gave out. What he *did* have he made the very most of.

Of all the footballers I have seen he got closer to consistently playing right up to his potential than anyone. I think it was Albert Einstein who suggested that human beings only use five per cent of their capacity. Albert hadn't met Junior.

The Pearce influence on rugby league extended far wider than the field of play. Through the 1980s he set the pace in the many associated areas of the game - diet, sophisticated training, links with the media, off-field standards of behaviour, and general lifestyle - all of it geared to success on the football field.

None of that should obscure the fact that he was a hell of a footballer, too - a lock or second-rower of untiring quality, who was able to sustain his effort almost unbelievably throughout matches. Possessor of a wonderfully generous spirit, Junior was always ready to give a hand, or a word of advice to young blokes coming through the ranks. He was the game's Mr. Positive.

Everything he received from the game he deserved, and when it kicked him in the teeth, as it did now and then, he simply picked himself up and got on with his life. He was very special.

8. GARRY SCHOFIELD

Scoey, who graced Balmain between 1985 and 1987, was something of a freak. There aren't many players in the game who would have the guts or flair to put over a little chip from within their own quarter. When Scoey did it, he'd almost invariably get it back.

He was the bloke you looked to when the team was just about down and out and in need of something remarkable. He had a bag of skills that you couldn't hitch a rope around; he had all the kicking skills, and all the handling skills. And as his career developed he became stronger in defence. He was also a wonderful "reader" of a game, a lethal interceptor of any backline pass that happened to stray. Scoey had rare gifts. He could turn a game in the blink of an eye. All good football teams need at least one of these sort of people.

9. TERRY LAMB

Pound for pound, Terry's probably the greatest value player in rugby league, and has been for years. I'm talking both attack and defence. He reads both brilliantly, and reacts accordingly.

"Baa" is the ultimate club player, although his representative career has plenty of glitter too. It's hard to imagine the day that he won't be there in the no. 6 at Canterbury. I'll bet the Bulldogs find it hard to think about that, too.

Lamb is the greatest backer-upper in the game. That supreme quality he has, to *always* be there when a break is on, must have brought literally hundreds of tries to the teams he has played in over the years. He has scored plenty of them himself. Like all the great players he has outstanding field vision - an ability to see a little further than the ordinary player. If it's tackle one in the count he'll have something in mind for four or five.

The bloke has a terrific feeling for the game. He's a superb competitor, and a warm and happy character off the field. We were close on the '86 Kangaroo tour, and it was always a pleasure to be around him; with Baa there'd always be a joke or a bit of fun on.

If he hadn't belted Ellery Hanley on grand final day, 1988, he'd have been in my top five!

10. BRADLEY CLYDE

He's the player of the '90s - the first bloke you want in your team. I think of him a bit like Junior Pearce - except that he's bigger and has more natural talent. I reckon Brad is a fabulous player, and as the years go by his progress up the all-time greats list will only be one way - upwards. He'll finish up as a legend of the game.

I honestly can't imagine a better "package" of the modern footballer than Clyde. He's a superb player in both attack and defence, and the workload he carries in any match is extraordinary.

Only one thing can possibly beat him, and that's injury. He's had an unfair share of those, more than his quota. Injury-free, there are no limits on what he can achieve.

It's about now that I realised what an impossible task I faced in picking just 10 players. I mean, how could I leave out Brett Kenny or Laurie Daley, Paul Sironen or Glenn Lazarus, Michael O'Connor or Mick Cronin, Allan Langer or Ricky Stuart ... or Ray Price ... or Steve Mortimer... or Gary Belcher.

Kenny, the natural - a freak of a player ...

Daley, who seems to find new skills every week ...

Stuart and Langer, so different in their halfback skills, yet in the end so equal in ability ...

Sirro, simply awesome - and better and better by the year ...

O'Connor, a player of unlimited talent ...

Mortimer, dynamic, explosive - a match-turner ... Cronin, great centre, ruthless points-gatherer ... Lazzo, a man mountain - after Blocker, the best of the props ...

Price, the ultimate competitor - to have him in your side was like having two or three players ...

Belcher, whose classy, gliding play made him a such great successor to Jimmy Jack ...

And the rest ... journeymen, tradesmen and stars.

I respect them all. Well, almost all of them. And I know when it's all over for me in football that I'm going to file away my own memories of the players with whom I have been privileged to share the stage. When I think about them it will be with affection and admiration.

Thanks guys ... the pleasure has been mine.

20

Why Balmain Must Move

I believe the Balmain Tigers have two choices for the future: re-locate or die. My preferred option is for the Tigers to fully investigate the most radical of all the various possibilities - a move to Melbourne. The one certainty is that we cannot hang on too much longer at Leichhardt. If we do cling to that tradition it won't be long at all before we hear the soft tread of the executioner. Balmain will be bound for extinction, headed down the same path as Newtown, which departed from the premiership after the 1983 season.

I understand that some people will see my words as "heresy", that they will call me "disloyal". To them I would simply say that in setting out in this chapter my suggestions for the future of the Balmain club, I am spurred on by the purest of motives. I really love that place, that football club. Balmain has not just been part of my life, it has *been* my life.

I would hate more than anything else to see it die.

The great old club has never faced more important decisions than it does right now. As much as I respect such qualities as tradition, loyalty and local ties that go back over 85 years, the reality of Balmain is that it is a dying area from a rugby league point of view. The nature of the population has changed dramatically. Where once it was working-class and blue-collar you can now substitute the words “yuppie” and “trendy”. The suburbs that the club embraces are populated by a new breed who care little or nothing for rugby league. We are largely a cul-de-sac of non-league people, despite the pockets of support that still exist. Our own people have largely drifted away to other places, and that fact is reflected in the crowds we draw to Leichhardt, even when things are going well.

I am a footballing traditionalist, and love everything that Balmain stands for, but despite that, I know that Leichhardt in the 1990s does not go anywhere close to fulfilling the requirements of a modern football ground. The parking is abysmal, the public transport inadequate, and the facilities poor - especially on a rainy day. We can seat two-and-a-half thousand people in the grandstand - that's all. On a rainy day everyone else gets wet. Years ago people would put up with that, but not anymore.

Six years ago, when I was marketing manager at the club, I put forward a proposal that we play our home matches at Parramatta Stadium, about 20km west of Leichhardt. That idea still blows in the wind now and then. I thought we could share the place with Parramatta, and maybe change the Stadium's name to give Balmain at least a part-share of identity there.

Into the 1990s, I no longer believe that a move to Parramatta provides a satisfactory long-term answer. It's a band-aid solution. A move to Parramatta would provide Balmain with better facilities - and access to private sponsors' boxes that we don't have at Leichhardt. But it would do nothing to solve our fundamental problem of a lack of junior footballers. The juniors in Balmain have dwindled alarmingly over the years, and there is no chance of that trend being reversed.

The answer lies in the toughest of all decisions - a

radical physical re-location of the club. The Central Coast area, north of Sydney, has been mentioned, and that is an option. My preference is for the more adventurous step of taking the team and the club, holus-bolus, to Melbourne. High-profile businessmen such as Kerry Packer and John Singleton have an association with the club now. I believe it would be a magnificent thing for the club, and the game, for us to shift, with the support of men like Packer and Singleton - to take the game into the heartland of Melbourne. A new team of "Tigers", established in Melbourne's suburbs, could be as strong as the Broncos within five years. I'm sure the NSWRL would throw its full weight behind such a move, providing all the necessary support for the beginning of junior development programs, and all the grass-roots mechanics that would have to be instigated.

A "new" Tigers, based in the country's second-biggest city, would be very welcome from a television point of view, particularly in this age of TV networking when advertisers are looking for the widest possible national spread for their products.

The Melbourne option took on some sort of solid form in 1993, when the Melbourne-based AFL club, Carlton, invited Balmain to play several games in 1994 on their home ground, Princes Park. Carlton, one of Aussie rules' most famous teams, approached the NSWRL, before beginning negotiations with Keith Barnes. The approach from down south was potentially the something that might lead to a Sydney team eventually establishing a permanent base in Melbourne. "If an existing club was prepared to play games here, embraced it and promoted it, it (rugby league) would have a real chance of survival," said Carlton executive director Ian Collins.

A further intriguing option lies with Sydney's bid to host the summer Olympic Games in the year 2000. That bid, if successful, will result in the construction of a magnificent stadium at Homebush - the super stadium that Sydney should have had years ago. Homebush is just a few short kilometres west of Leichhardt. Perhaps the chance may come for Balmain to relocate there into the next century. The attraction of such a stadium would draw people in its own right, and perhaps build a whole new support base for the Tigers - while not taking the club too far from its current roots.

The big fear of our long-time supporters is that any move away from Leichhardt would automatically rob the club of its heritage and its identity. I don't see it that way. The club would still be Balmain, still be the famous black and golds. The tradition, the identity, the *meaning* of Balmain would just be shifted elsewhere - hopefully to build there for another 80 years or so.

Amalgamation is not the answer. There is no way you're ever going to get two clubs to agree to that. Take Easts and Souths; people talk about them blending into one club at some time in the future. You can get set with me. Easts and Souths have been at each other's throats for over 85 years. They are oil and water - there's no way you'd successfully get them to mix.

Decision time is right now at Balmain. There's no way we can survive on crowds of 6000-7000, no way that a battling leagues club can continue to provide the wherewithal in an increasingly expensive and competitive premiership. Under the Alan Jones regime, the club has been given valuable outside financial support, and I'm talking big dollars, from people brought to Balmain through their friendship with Alan. When Alan's term at the club is finished that support can be expected to dry up too.

In May 1993, Balmain unveiled a six-million dollar plan to redevelop Leichhardt Oval into one of the showpiece grounds of the premiership. Club officials met the members of Leichhardt Council and emerged confident that funds could be raised for the redevelopment within two years. The plan was for a refurbishment along the lines of the spectacular changes at North Sydney Oval - incorporating a new grandstand, better parking and a shopping complex.

I read the story with interest, and would love nothing better than the utopian dream of such a ground filled to capacity with people cheering for Balmain. My doubts remain - doubts that this part of Sydney that I love still has the numbers and the heart to support a major rugby league team on a permanent basis.

The key word in the whole thing is *survival*. When things are desperate and you are fighting for your life, then you must take desperate measures. The problem is not going to go away; there's no point Balmain sitting down and hoping that the Good Fairy will come along and fix everything up. The only fairy that will come along will be a big bloke with an axe who will lop off our heads.

We should study the US experience of teams re-locating lock, stock and barrel. That's the answer for Balmain - and Melbourne is the place.

The lack of forward planning at the individual clubs has been one of rugby league's deficiencies. We're talking about a multi-million dollar business, budgets of three million dollars or so per club. That's big business, but I'll bet few, if any, of them have done a financial projection for the next 10 years, or five years, or even *two* years. They operate year-by-year, hanging on in some cases by the skin of their teeth.

Things are changing fast in the once-exclusive Sydney premiership. The NSW Rugby League has done its best to impose standards of financial responsibility on the clubs - and it has certainly provided a vision for the future, of a genuinely national competition. Some of the old clubs are likely to die if they do not react to the changing times. There will be no sympathy - none of the old mates' act of the League hanging onto a club just because they've been around for 85 years and their officials are a good bunch of blokes. Professionalism has arrived, and some clubs are already at full stretch, trying to keep up ... and struggling to stay alive.

My club, Balmain, is one of them.

It is not just the administration of the game that is changing. As the football-athlete grows bigger, faster and stronger I predict there will eventually be revolutionary changes in the game itself. I'd like to see rugby league one day become a 10-man game. The men to go in my "futureleague" team would be the lock forward (sorry Junior) and the second-rowers (sorry Sirro).

In my 12 seasons in first grade football I have increasingly had the feeling of the field becoming more and more crowded, of the game closing in on its players. In that brief space of time the footballers have grown bigger physically, thanks to scientific training techniques, and there is no doubt they are fitter than ever before. In State of Origin games - which are truly rugby league's state-of-the-art showpieces - the field is like Sydney's Pitt Street at 5pm ... it's so crowded.

Ten-man rugby league would open the game up brilliantly. Demands on players would be enormous, and the use of the interchange would have to expanded to cater for the load. The emphasis on defence would be out the window. There would be many more tries scored - and surely that's what the fans want - and the best and most skilful team could be counted on to win just about every time.

In games at the highest level these days you may go 35 minutes or so before you even see a half-break. Then the fans are on their feet. That's what they want to see - breaks being made, tries being scored, flowing football. They don't want a switch back to those boring, low-scoring grand finals of the mid-1980s. Get six players off the field and you'd have entertaining football all the time.

Another problem the reduction would help get around is that of a very thin spread of first grade talent. In 1995, following the inclusion of teams from Auckland, Perth, Brisbane and North Queensland, the premiership will have

20 first grade teams - that's 300 players a week (including reserves). That's rubbish. We just don't have that many players of genuine first grade standard. At 10-a-side you'd have a quality 200. Lesser player numbers would also slightly help reduce the financial load on cash-strapped clubs.

The other big step I would advocate is for referees to be given electronic help. I have lived through so many games that have been won and lost on refereeing decisions - I reckon any assistance available should be used. The ideal system would be to have experts in the stand monitoring instant video replays of touchy decisions. It would be quite simple - a green light for a fair try, a red light for no try - or alternatively just wire the ref for sound so that he has direct contact with the box. The game of cricket has now begun to introduce the system of electronic assistance to umpires, and it's time that rugby league began to shift in that direction, too.

Rugby league needs to make these type of changes if it is to continue to prosper in this rapidly evolving world. Not change for change's sake, but progress, so that the people who follow the game are given what they deserve. League in 1993 is a far different game from that of 85, 25, even 5 years ago. Five years ago we didn't have blood bins, 10-metre offside rules and in-goal judges. No-one would have suggested the Sydney premiership would feature teams from Western Australia and New Zealand by 1995. The one certainty of football is that the game will continue to change - the challenge for players, coaches, and officials is to initiate and encourage such progress, without damaging rugby league's status as the greatest of all football codes.

21

Sent Off!

BEFORE THE 1993 premiership season, coach Alan Jones gathered us all together one night and offered us a stunning incentive to make the semi-finals - a trip for the team to Argentina.

Ole! If we could drag together all the talent we had in the side, and at last fulfil the potential of the "new" Balmain, South America was an enticing prospect. A trip to the Sydney Football Stadium in September would be fine - but Argentina was a further appealing goal to shoot for.

We began in hope, as Sydney's rugby league premiership teams have done ever since 1908. I soaked up my now-traditional blow to the solar plexus before it all began, when the coach announced that Paul Sironen, and not Benny Elias, would be first grade captain for the year. I was getting a bit used to such decisions by now - but I was still disappointed. With Blocker having retired, I was hopeful the job would be mine. I thought I had served the necessary apprenticeship and that my past record and experience would stand me in good stead.

But Alan Jones saw it differently. I congratulated Sirro and pledged my full support, as I had done with Block the previous year.

As it turned out Sirro decided fairly early that the captaincy was not for him, and before long I was back at the helm. Sirro and I talked about it. His view was that I was best cut out for the job and that he wanted to concentrate on his own game. Jonesy came to me on a Thursday night with the news. I was happy to accept the offer; second choice is better than none.

With our stalwarts, Roach, Jack and Brooks, gone we needed a big new signing for '93 - and he arrived in the shape of Mark Geyer, the formidable and explosive ex-Penrith second-rower. Mark arrived at Leichhardt determined to rebuild his football career after the traumas and sadness that had divided his former club in 1992. Geyer had cut his ties with Penrith in the midst of the upheaval which followed the tragic death of Ben Alexander, the club's young utility player.

My own goals were well set - to contribute consistently and outstandingly to a successful Balmain year, to win the NSW State of Origin hooking job ... and to win back the Test no. 9 jersey.

Our premiership kick-off, amid high hopes on March 13, was to set the standard for one of the most frustrating periods of football I have been through in my life. At Leichhardt Oval we were locked 14-all with Canterbury with three minutes to play. At that point Terry Lamb chipped in to kick what will probably remain as the freak field goal of the season, from 42 metres out. We lost 19-14 in the end - a game we had every chance to win.

A week later we ran into a gale in the first half of our match against St George at Kogarah, and held the Saints, the previous season's losing grand finalists, to 6-all. The winning of the match was in our hands. But a discordant and disorganised second half brought us down, and we were beaten again, 12-6. Then at Leichhardt we seemed to have Canberra on the ropes nearly all the way, but they escaped late to defeat us 17-10, with the clinching try coming just three minutes from the end.

Things refused to get better. At Penrith Park we had the

better of the Panthers throughout the first half, but at the 37th-minute mark Sirro was sent from the field, and we succumbed 26-10.

It was immensely frustrating. We had played a month of premiership football and hadn't won a game, yet we could have won all four of them. The pressure was once again building on Alan Jones, and on all of us. The coach stayed strong and positive. "We don't think we're finished," he remarked. "We won't be lying down and building coffins. We're a good side, and we've been very, very unlucky."

Premiers Brisbane beat us 12-6 in a tight one at Leichhardt - in a game in which our young centre Jacin Sinclair confirmed his outstanding promise and the certainty that he was heading for bigger things by outplaying the Broncos' internationals, Chris Johns and Steve Renouf. On April 17 our win/loss ledger clicked over to a horrible 0-6 when Cronulla, who like us had been struggling, suddenly found form and beat us 18-4 at Caltex Field.

In the Cronulla game I suffered a bad muscular spasm in my right shoulder. It was ill-timing with the representative season looming. The selectors selected me for the City Origin side to play Country, but I was in trouble. The League's doctor, Nathan Gibbs, advised me to take a break, and get it right for the Origin matches. I could have played for the City at a pinch, but it would have been a dicey one. So I crossed my fingers and watched guys like Wests' Joey Thomas, St George's Wayne Collins and Robbie McCormack of the Newcastle Knights stake their claims for the state hooking job.

For just about the first time in this testing season, the ball bounced for me and in late April the selectors stuck with me for the first Origin game, to be played at Lang Park on May 3. But almost as soon as I made the team I was in the middle of a media-inspired controversy ...

On the Thursday before State of Origin I, 1993, a story appeared in the *Sydney Morning Herald*, spread spectacularly across the back page, under the seven-column heading: "Elias Casts Doubts On Wally's Role". Written by Daniel Williams, the article read in part:

Senior NSW player Ben Elias questioned yesterday whether Wally Lewis was the ideal person to coach Queensland, in comments that will intensify the build-up to next Monday night's State of Origin opener at Lang Park.

Elias queried Lewis' suitability on two grounds; the brief gap between the Queenslander's role as an Origin player and now coach, and his relatively lax approach to training during his training days ...

"It's a funny situation when you've got a bloke like Wally, who was playing the game only two years ago, now coaching them," Elias said. "It's a big ask."

"... You're either a 'Do as I say' coach or a 'Do as I do' coach. Now, if Wally's 'Do as I do' - I don't know what he used to be in their training sessions. He wasn't renowned for his great fitness or his great (attitude) towards training."

The story, inevitably, became instant headline news in Queensland. Talk about a red rag to a bull! What I had been quoted as saying was akin to going to Rome and parading around with a megaphone, bagging the Pope.

Frankly, I was furious. The quotes that were blown up into such a theme, and in such gigantic proportions, came from a long interview I had given to Williams. I spoke to him for half an hour or so and it was, fair dinkum, all positive stuff. He asked me about Wally and I said: "Well mate, I can't really comment on Wally because I've never been coached by him." I made the observation about the difficulty of switching from player to coach in a short time, briefly expanded on that and we skipped through it and onto the next topic.

Next day, there I was - all over the bloody front page of the Brisbane *Courier-Mail*.

I was really filthy. I rang Daniel Williams and told him not to bother calling me again. I believed what had been done by the paper in the interest of a racy headline was a genuine case of material being presented out of context, with gross and unfair emphasis on what had been a minuscule part of a long interview. I had given my time freely, and they had come up with a cheap headline. Williams perhaps sees it differently; anyhow, I told him straight not to ring me again to get my comments on rugby league.

I could have done without it, although I laughed at the suggestion that my "outburst" was going to be just the motivation the Queensland side needed. "The boys have all seen Benny's comments and we'll respond to them on Monday night," was the quote from an unnamed Queensland player. I smiled at that. I thought to myself - well, if they need extra motivation for a game like this, then they're in trouble.

On the Sunday before the game a huge headline dominated the front page of the *Sunday Telegraph* sporting section. It read: "Benny Carpeted - Action Over Lewis Jibes". The article suggested that I was in official hot water over the *SMH* story. That was wrong again. I had explained the situation to the team management of Geoff Carr and Bob Saunders and they had told me not to worry about it.

The publicity guaranteed that my reception in Brisbane was going to be even warmer than usual. I wasn't bothered - I had been going up there for a while, and was pretty good at switching off.

Telegraph Mirror journalist Lisa Olson wrote a piece about the sort of atmosphere that greeted me in Brisbane. She wrote of the drunken louts standing outside our team hotel, shouting "Benny's a wimp. C'mon out here and let some real men show you how to play." And she wrote of the oaf in a maroon-and-white jersey who grabbed my arm at the ground and spluttered: "We're going to bury you in Lang Park under Wally Lewis' statue."

In 1993 the State of Origin matches were played on a

Monday night, earlier in the week than in previous years. We went to Brisbane late - on the Sunday - happy to spend as little time up there as possible. We traditionally stay at the Parkroyal, and it's become a nice home away from home. The only change in the build-up that I have noticed in the seasons since 1985 is that the atmosphere has become more intense, and the edge of excitement sharper by the year.

This year, in Origin I, the mob really gave it to me. I had never had any trouble switching-off on the way to the ground, and this year was no different. In the bus, perched next to a window, I was in a world of my own, oblivious to everything outside, my thoughts focused on what lay ahead.

But when we finally hit the field that evening, to a tremendous avalanche of booing, I was well aware that I was the villain of the night with the crowd. It was hard not to notice the big sign that read: "Benny's a wanker" ... and *impossible* to miss the chant as it rolled around the ground, again and again.

As always, everything outside the green rectangle of the football field became no more than a blur once the game was underway. It was a breathtaking match - literally - one of the most demanding I have ever played. We hadn't won at Lang Park since 1987 and in the second half, as we defended the generous lead we had set up by halftime (12-2), the Maroons came back at us in great waves of attack. They were relentless. Their second 40 minutes was about as close to perfect as you can get. At times we were hanging on by a finger-nail, but the resolve of the side never wavered. We had come to win, and that's what we were going to do.

Twenty minutes from the end, Queensland winger Michael Hancock went into a threshing-machine act after our defence had nailed him 25 metres out from his own posts. Hancock plays with a barely-controlled fury at all times, with a pent-up determination to break tackles and make ground. But this time he over-reacted and gave me a hefty push as he struggled to his feet, knocking me back to the ground. The penalty that resulted, right in front of the posts, was a key moment. We edged away to 14-6, and held on, despite a late try by the Maroons' other winger, Willie Carne.

The celebrations were very special that night. We didn't do anything too fancy, just stuck together as a team back at the Parkroyal and soaked up the feeling. The mateship and camaraderie in the NSW side has grown to a level that few people ever experience in their lives. It's all to do with supporting each other - to share the thrill of playing sport at that standard, in that sort of atmosphere ... and to win!

It was a wonderful treat to head home the next day and not be confronted with newspapers proclaiming: "Maroons Do It Again!" or "Queensland's Great Night". Funnily enough, this year the opening Origin game didn't even make the Brisbane street-corner posters. I wonder why?

People ask me what I think about Brisbane and Queensland. They probably expect a furious diatribe from me against the place. But that's not how I feel. I like Queensland, it's a good place - and there's every chance I'll holiday there after my footballing days are over.

I appreciate very much the role that Queensland, and Queenslanders have played in making State of Origin football what it is. They're the ones who started the ball rolling, building Origin football into the great event that it is today. They grabbed the idea with great enthusiasm right from the start, and turned the concept into Australia's very own Superbowl. Sydney people were slower to react, though they're thoroughly converted now.

I take my hat off to the Lang Park mob. There is no crowd like them in the world. English crowds make as much noise, but they're nowhere near as threatening. But the Brisbane mob can be a bit of a worry. I mean, you have to be concerned about anyone who'd throw a *full* can of beer ...

My football life was looking better again. I had been happy with my own game at Lang Park, and Balmain had suddenly found winning form too. Long-shot outsiders for the game against in-form Parramatta at Leichhardt on the Sunday after the City-Country game, the Tigers clicked, and won 26-2, with the giant second-row combination of Sironen-Geyer really smashing the Eels. My troublesome shoulder kept me out of the game, but I enjoyed every minute of it from the sidelines as we ran in five tries to nil.

It seemed the season had turned for the better. But what's that line about being a rooster today, a feather duster tomorrow?

In the match against Western Suburbs at Leichhardt on Sunday, May 9, I was sent from the field for the first time in my 12 years of grade football. Many thousands of words have been spoken and written about what occurred that day. Some of them told part of the story, without explaining exactly what went on, while others were just plain wrong. I'll tell you what really happened ...

Late in the first half of a very scratchy Balmain performance, our centre, Jamie Corcoran, was judged to have made some sort of contact with Wests' half Jason Taylor just as, or fractionally after, Taylor had punted a clearing kick away. It was a "nothing" event. Corcoran barely touched Taylor, if at all. Significantly, at the later judiciary hearing, Alan Jones was able to establish that the Corcoran "tackle" was *not* late. The score at the time was 18-8 to Wests. We had played poorly in the game to that point, but they weren't going much better and we believed that if we went anywhere near close to getting our game together we could still beat them.

The Corcoran-Taylor incident brought touch judge Ross Picard scampering onto the field. I had seen what had happened, and I knew it was a non-event, not deserving of a warning, let alone a penalty.

"You've gotta be joking," I said to Picard. "There was

nothing in it." Mark Geyer chipped in and said basically the same thing. Corcoran was called over and the touch judge gave his version, suggesting that the Balmain's centre's action had been illegal. I was standing there, boiling. I argued the case that Corcoran had made no contact with Taylor, but referee Graeme West preferred the opinion of his touch judge and awarded a penalty - a gift two points - to Wests.

At 18-8, right on halftime, and with a kicker like Jason Taylor on the other side, that was the last thing we wanted to happen. I was fuming. I considered the penalty unjust and unwarranted.

Behind the posts, as Taylor lined up the penalty kick, I said to our fullback, Tim Brasher: "What about this fucking linesman - he's going on like a fucking goose!"

Picard heard the comment and said to me: "Shut up Elias - or I'll report you."

I turned around to him and said: "I'm not talking to you - I'm talking about you."

The touch judge said something along the lines of "there's no need for that", then repeated his threat to report me.

"Go for your life," I said.

Taylor kicked the goal and we headed off the field and into the tunnel for the halftime break. I was about halfway up when Joe Thomas, the opposing hooker, called me.

"Benny, the referee wants to see you," he said.

I walked back to where referee West and touch judge Picard were waiting for me.

"I've got a complaint about you," said West, a bloke who has been refereeing me since I was 11 years old.

Picard then asked the referee to ask me if I had called him "a fucking goose".

I repeated that my comment had not been directed at the touch judge, but was made to a team-mate (Tim Brasher subsequently confirmed this in his evidence to the NSWRL Judiciary).

"Did you call it out?" asked the ref.

"Yeah, of course," I replied.

Then - boom!! - West sent me off.

"What for," I asked.

"Get off!"

"What for, 10 minutes?"

"No, you're off."

"You're kidding," I spluttered. I couldn't believe it.

Ten minutes later I stayed in the sheds while 12 Balmain boys came out to resume the battle. Wests faded, as we thought they might, and we fought back. The game evolved into a thriller, but our revival was too late, and we missed out, again, 24-20.

I was devastated. State of Origin selection was only 24 hours away, and I had been sent off for the first time, after more than 200 first grade games. And on a pathetic charge. As I was later quoted as saying, I had heard far worse things said to referees and touch judges many, many times - and no action had been taken.

Before discussing the traumatic period that followed I will freely admit that I did the wrong thing. I was angry at the penalty, and frustrated at the way the match was running. My comment to Tim Brasher was made in that sort of atmosphere. It was a heat-of-the-moment thing, and I regret what I said. However, I don't believe that it warranted what was to happen to me the following night ...

Alan Jones was very angry about the *principle* of what had happened, and he counselled me during that Monday, declaring that he would gladly give up his time to present my defence. He believed that the punishment already meted out (my send-off) was way out of proportion with the crime. Jonesy is a persuasive bloke, and I appreciated his support, which couldn't have been any more genuine, or any stronger.

Alan was bristling and ready when we arrived at League HQ in Phillip Street. The atmosphere was electric - a bit like that at a State of Origin game. And inevitably, the media were there in droves.

I fronted the Judiciary on a triple-decker charge: "Offensive or obscene language; disputing the ruling of a touch judge; and behaving in a way contrary to the spirit of the game."

It was a long hearing, with Alan Jones in full flight as he fought to get me cleared. The *Sydney Morning Herald's* Roy Masters found one rare light moment in an otherwise dour night, and commented: "This was the only humour in an evening that went on as long as Jones' top-rating radio show."

At the end of it all Judiciary Chairman Vince Bruce announced that I had been suspended until May 24 - meaning that I would miss State of Origin II, plus the Tigers' next premiership match, against Easts. After that decision, all I could say was: "I can't believe it."

Alan Jones described the finding as: "An extraordinary decision against a player who has never been sent from the field in 12 seasons of grade football. The Judiciary chose to believe the evidence of two officials against Ben Elias."

He told the gathered press of "a very serious conflict of evidence by the officials" and of "uncorroborated evidence accepted by the judiciary."

I said nothing - to anyone. I was too upset ...

My anger at the sentence I had received intensified when I read that week's edition of *Rugby League Week.*

A story headlined "Cooking His Own Goose - Benny Spurns The Olive Branch" claimed that I had been given every chance by Graeme West to apologise to Ross Picard. The magazine claimed that I had "flatly rejected all offers to defuse the time bomb that had developed", and continued:

When it was established Elias had directed obscenities towards touch judge Ross Picard ... referee Graeme West asked him to apologise.

Elias would not do so, triggering West's decision to send him from the field ...

Elias had no-one to blame for the suspension but himself, given the invitation he received from West.

This, the major story on page seven of that week's *RLW*, usually such a good and reliable magazine, was completely wrong. I was *not* given the option of apologising to the touch judge that day. The conversation that took place between myself and Graeme West on halftime went exactly as I have related above.

I rang the magazine's editor, Norm Tasker, to register the strongest complaint, requesting that they make amends in print for the wrong they had done me.

As often seems to have been the way with me, there was an instant polarisation of opinion on the punishment I had been given. On the same day, two senior league journalists, the *Telegraph Mirror's* Peter Frilingos and Ian Heads of the *Sydney Morning Herald*, disagreed sharply.

Frilingos wrote in strong support of the suspension:

Balmain's Benny Elias should be counting his blessings instead of complaining about the two-match suspension he copped from the Judiciary for abusing a touch judge this week.

From the moment the hearing opened there was never the slightest doubt Elias would be found guilty as charged.

It was just a matter of how seriously the Judiciary viewed the offence, and as the case progressed it became increasingly obvious that panel members thought it was anything but a laughing matter ...

There is no more vilified sporting species than the referees and the Judiciary again made sure the other night they won't be hunted into extinction.

Heads, on the other hand, believed I had been harshly treated. He wrote:

Based on any number of criteria, Balmain's Benny Elias was dealt a bad hand by the NSW Rugby League judiciary this week. The two-week suspension for his outburst at Leichhardt was a tough call.

Heads compared my suspension to penalties that had been given to other players who had found themselves in front of the Judiciary on the eve of representative matches in previous years, and continued:

Rarely, though, has any one of them been dealt with as sternly as was Elias - a man who has captained both his state and his country. With a clean 12-year record (never been sent off) he was entitled to a "send-off sufficient" verdict last Monday night. He had already paid the price of 40 minutes in the sheds as his team crumbled to defeat. That was enough.

The *Sydney Morning Herald* compared my sentence with one given to Canterbury rookie Luke Goodwin earlier in the year. In the World Sevens tournament in February, Goodwin had abused referee Graham Annesley in a very vigorous and aggressive manner. He was fined and suspended for a couple of (pre-season) matches. My punishment, which included banishment from one of rugby league's showpiece events - a State of Origin game - was far, far tougher than what they gave the kid.

I was like a Tiger with a sore head for the rest of the week, bitter and frustrated as Origin night approached. Robbie McCormack won the nod as my replacement. But amid the personal gloom, there was a nice gesture of support and mateship from within the Blues' camp. They invited me to their team dinner, and I popped in, but only for 10 minutes or so. I didn't want to intrude too much. I was no longer part of the team, for that game anyway, but I welcomed the gesture of solidarity at such an unhappy time in my football career.

Team manager Geoff Carr invited me to sit in the NSW bunker for the match, at the Sydney Football Stadium, and I sweated it out with the rest of the non-playing Blues camp as the series was clinched with a 16-12 victory, after a brilliant match.

The following Saturday I was a spectator again, as Balmain beat the Roosters 18-7 at the Stadium. Because of two words directed at a Balmain team-mate, I had missed two winning matches, lost $4000 in win bonuses, and had the chance of playing in a series-clinching Origin game stolen away.

I had no choice but to pick myself up and fight another round. But, oh boy, I was hurtin'.

22

Standing Tall

I HAD NO more than a few days in late May of 1993 to endure the bitterness I felt over what I believed was a cruel and unfair suspension. The NSW selectors provided an instant spirit-raiser when they slotted me straight back into the team for the third Origin match.

With the series already decided, it was always going to be a problem game for NSW. It became increasingly so as the lead-up week unfolded, with selection mix-ups and injuries disrupting the camp. Not until the morning of the match did we finally settle on the football team which was to go into battle against the Maroons. On that final Monday morning we were still doing walk-throughs of our moves to try and get everyone comfortable. It was not the way to prepare for a State of Origin battle.

History now records that my 16th State of Origin match was a loser; the Maroons stormed home in the second half at Lang Park to get us 24-12, thoroughly deserving their win. Our winger and goalkicker, Rod Wishart, missed a not-too-difficult goal just before halftime (it would have put us in front 14-8), and early in the second half Mal Meninga made a freakish tackle on Andrew Ettingshausen as ET drove for the line. A try then might have wrapped it up for us. But it wasn't to be. Fired by the dual inspiration of Allan Langer and Dale Shearer, the Queenslanders charged back as we faded, to win going away.

It was in many ways the most eventful of the three games of the series, and talk afterwards revolved around a first-half brawl in which I reluctantly became involved. I really was roped into that one, by my old "mate", Steve Walters.

The trouble started in a scrum near the NSW line. The ball was in and out in no time, but opposing props Paul Harragon and Martin Bella remained behind the play, hanging onto each other. Bella was really mouthing off and eventually Sirro (Paul Sironen), lurking near the two protagonists, yelled out to Harragon: "Belt him - just belt him!"

Which Harragon did, and it was on between the pair of them.

Meanwhile Trevor Gillmeister, the Queensland second-rower, and I had grabbed onto each other on the fringe of the trouble. We were just standing there, sort of holding each other back and watching the action.

Next thing ... whack! ... Steve Walters came in and belted me. I wasn't going to stand there and cop it, so away we went - the old firm of Walters and Elias, coming to blows again. Referee Greg McCallum's whistle finally called a halt to proceedings, and I was promptly marched to the sin bin. First one off! Walters followed, then Harragon and Bella. All of us received 10 minutes, and the match resumed, 11 against 11.

Later there was talk of us all being cited and punished, but the League chose to let it lie. There are funny standards sometimes. You can go onto the football field and stand toe-to-toe with someone in a blue, and get no more than a mild slap over the wrist. Utter a couple of words *about* a touch judge, though - and you're a chance of getting two weeks!

The handshake between Steve Walters and me after the game was as quick as the blink of an eye. I knew he was bound for the Test team, and that hurt more than a little.

Queensland were hungrier and more settled, and deserved to win that final game. We were intense and ready though, and the match was a tough and exciting finale which I'm sure was value for money for the fans. Our only incentive on the night was the rather tenuous one of clean-sweeping the series, which, admittedly, would have been nice. The Australian team to tour New Zealand had pretty well been picked two weeks before, although there had been, and would be, official denials of such a suggestion. Barring injuries there weren't going to be any changes to that team. But we were disappointed with the way we fell away in the second half, a slide that might have come about because of the constant changes in our line-up. Lock Brad Mackay missed most of the second half after copping a nasty knock, while Harragon was exhausted after playing for the Knights against Parramatta just 24 hours earlier. Things seemed to be changing all the time. It seemed after every second scrum that I had an arm around someone different. At one stage even Sirro packed in the front row!

I believe the NSW and Queensland Leagues need to have a close look at the situation of a team leading 2-nil in an Origin series, and do one of two things:

(1) Not play a third game. In most other "best of" contests, such as the annual international one-day cricket finals and American baseball's World Series, the event is over once a team wins the number of games required to take it. In the cricket a 2-0 lead means there is no third game. In the best-of-seven World Series, once one team has won four games, that's it. The Leagues should consider the same format, but are unlikely to do so in the light of the assured one-million dollar gate that results from each Origin match.

(2) Make the third game as fair dinkum as the first two by standing players down from their club rounds the preceding weekend. There is no doubt that allowing clubs to use their players 24, 48 or 72 hours before an Origin match erodes both the quality of the state side's prepara-

tion, and the match itself.

Our party to celebrate the winning of the series was a little muted early that Monday night. We had to come to terms with the disappointment of defeat, before taking in the wider and more important picture - that we had won the series. But in the end we had a hoot of a night. The mission we had set out on five weeks before had been accomplished. We partied at the Parkroyal and then at the Cafe Neon for a time. The Queenslanders were there too, but they were in their part of the joint, and we were in ours.

Just like in the game.

Next morning Brisbane radio and the newspaper posters crowed of Queensland "triumph" and "revenge". You'd have thought they'd won the bloody series! They're good winners up there - I'll tell you that.

Sore and tired, I came home to Kelly, and to a resumption of my normal busy life. The 12th State of Origin series was over, and Balmain, the football club I had loved and admired for so many years, once again became the total focus of my sporting life. We had a match to play - against Gold Coast - a chance to edge another two points up the ladder. We knew we needed a string of wins to again become contenders, and the desire for that still burned bright in the Tigers.

I had given up hope of winning a Test jumper during the series against New Zealand in 1993. The cards on that one had long since been slotted into place. Steve Walters was the man in favour, and the decision to name his brother Kerrod as the shadow hooker for the third Test confirmed I was out of the picture for the international season. But I looked beyond '93 - to the Kangaroo tour year of 1994. Season 1994 would mark the 31st year of my life, and my 25th in the game of rugby league.

On the flight home from Brisbane after the final Origin match, on the first day of winter 1993, I closed my eyes and conjured up my own field of dreams.

Standing Tall

I saw the black and gold men of Balmain lapping the Sydney Football Stadium as premiers of the Rugby League, and I saw the green-and-gold Kangaroos going into battle on a misty north-of-England day. In both scenes I was there - in the front-line.

Benny Elias, the kid from Tripoli, Lebanon, who was always too small to play the game he loved, still had some unfinished business to take care of ...

POSTSCRIPT

By Ian Heads

MIDWAY THROUGH THE first half of a match against Canterbury, at Belmore Sports Ground on Sunday, July 18, 1993, Benny Elias crouched low to tackle Bulldogs lock forward Jim Dymock. It was just another tackle in another game, but, for reasons that Elias knows he can never explain, this time something went horribly wrong. As he toppled Dymock, Elias felt a searing pain in his left arm.

"It was like a knife being plunged into my arm", he said later. "I heard something snap."

In the crunch of the tackle the major muscle in the arm had torn away at the elbow ... ripping all the way up to the bicep. Benny Elias' 12th year with the Tigers was over. For him the off-season had arrived in the middle of winter.

July '93 was a month the Tigers won't soon forget. Less than 48 hours after the Canterbury match, a story broke that was to be the biggest in town for days. Coach Alan Jones announced he was quitting the club at the end of the season. Jones' resignation, news of which came at a dramatic press conference on July 20, almost certainly short-circuited his sacking as coach by the club's board.

"I'm sure there were people on the board who did not want me there," Jones told the gathered media. His financial proposal for the club's future had been rejected by the board the previous week.

Virtually within a day Balmain had lost their captain for the season and their coach for good. Skipper Elias was circumspect and diplomatic when quizzed by the media on Jones' stunning departure.

"You could never knock Jones' attitude or enthusiasm towards coaching; he always gave it his best," he said. "But now we have to start afresh. I've got to say as captain that the club has made a decision they believe is for the best."

Elias headed within a week to the Ashfield Masonic Hospital for some repair work. An operation planned for an hour or so in fact took four, as doctors worked the muscle back into place, adding a screw at the elbow to hold all intact. Even while the doctors were operating, more news was emanating out of Leichhardt. Elias awoke to find that Wayne "Junior" Pearce had been officially confirmed as the new coach of Balmain.

"I have confidence in what Junior is about," says Elias. "He is successful at everything he takes on. If he coaches the way he played, then we're in good hands."

As he began the long recovery from his operation, and coped with his disappointment and discomfort, Elias was buoyed by thoughts of what lay ahead. "The next couple of years represent a very telling time for Balmain," he explains. "Success on the field and good management off it can set us up for a great long-term future."

In late July, Elias checked the final manuscript of this book as he contemplated the strange twists and turns of a life in football. His arm strapped and in a sling, he faced a lengthy period of convalescence. Through a simple tackle that went wrong he now had that rarest of commodities in a football season - time to contemplate.

Ahead lay the prospect of a north coast holiday with Kelly, and then, on October 1, a return to training . Behind him lay a season of mixed fortunes - of good times (NSW's Origin success) and bad (suspension, injuries). Season '93 represented a pretty fair microcosm of the Elias career - of success, mixed with some controversy and high drama.

"I'll tell you what," Benny told me. "I see 1994 as an entirely fresh start for me. And I feel great about it.

... In fact, I can hardly wait."

My Ben

By Kelly Crawford-Elias

I've been asked to write a tale
On my husband and dearest friend
At this I could not fail
'Cause the stories never end!!

I was 19 when we met
And started going out,
And I certainly don't regret
Meeting this football "lout"

I'd never seen a game of league
'Til the final in '89
I remember the depression and fatigue
For the Winfield Cup did this Tiger pine

He was different from any man I'd met
His confidence did abound
This one, I made myself a bet
Was going to stand his ground

It took some time and lots of talk
But a date we finally had
To my local coffee shop we did walk
To this day I'm forever glad!

Finally we professed our love out loud
Then, alas, my Kangaroo went away
But he was happy, and I felt proud
For the Ashes he would play

Kelly Crawford my name was then
But "Elias" now I've added
'Cause you see I married Ben. Yes!
Down the aisle we padded!!!

We've had our ups and our downs
And been through thick and thin
We've dealt with rumours from all those clowns
And decided love and trust will make us win!

To me, my husband is my friend
He does just what others do
At times he drives me round the bend
The things he puts me through!!

He makes me laugh and sometimes cry
We love movies, books and pasta
I know for me he would gladly die
As a best friend he is the Master!

The aches and pains, the glory and woe
Play only a small part with us
But if football was our only foe
There would certainly be less fuss!

I look forward to our future life
I'm sure league will play a part
Ben will always be in some sort of strife
This Tiger is a devil at heart!!

A critic I'm not and would never judge
A person I've not yet met
Is it right to hold a grudge?
And let your mind be set?

At Ben's reputation people tear
Is success such an evil thing?
Talk can be cheap and often unfair
It's his praises they should sing

As a man he is good, and strong
And plays his life by the rules
Of course, at times he gets things wrong
But so do you - you fools!

I know to most, Benny's a number nine
But I rate him as a 10
I love this man that I call mine
To me, he's just called Ben!

Ben Elias' Career in Rugby League

Compiled by David Middleton

As at June 13, 1993 (end of round 11 of the 1993 NSWRL Premiership)

SCHOOLBOY FOOTBALL

Played for Holy Cross College, Ryde First XIII 1978-1981.
Played in Commonwealth Bank Cup final teams 1979, 1980, 1981, winning in 1981.
Commonwealth Bank Cup Player of the Year 1980, 1981.
Played for Australia 1979-81.
Toured with Australian Schoolboys to England, 1979.

CLUB RECORD

Played with Balmain 1982-1993
First Grade:
Played: 213 (including 14 as a replacement)
Tries: 31
Goals: 2
Field Goals: 32
Total Points: 156
Total Grade Matches: 261 (including 14 as a first grade replacement)

Played in 1988, 1989 losing Grand Final teams.
Played in 15 finals matches (including one as a replace ment)
Played in mid-week Cup final teams in 1985, 1986, 1987 and 1988, winning in 1985 and 1987.
Rugby League Week Player of the Year 1988
Dally M Hooker of the Year 1985, 1988, 1992

REPRESENTATIVE RECORD

Represented City Firsts in 1985, City Origin in 1987, 1988, 1989, 1990, 1992.
Captained City in 1990, 1992.
Represented New South Wales in 16 State of Origin matches 1985-93.
Captained NSW in 1990, 1991.
Represented Australia in five Test matches: 3rd Test v New Zealand, 1985; 2nd and 3rd Tests v Great Britain, 1990; 1st and 2nd Tests in France, 1990.
Represented Australia in 1988 World Cup Final.
Played in 19 tour matches (1986, 1990 Kangaroo tours and 1985 tour of New Zealand).
Vice-captain on 1990 Kangaroo tour; captained Australia in seven tour matches, 1986, and two tour matches, 1990.